The Asaba Massacre

In October 1967, early in the Nigerian Civil War, government troops entered Asaba in pursuit of the retreating Biafran army, slaughtering thousands of civilians and leaving the town in ruins. News of the atrocity was suppressed by the Nigerian government, with the complicity of Britain, and its significance in the subsequent progress of that conflict was misunderstood. Drawing on archival sources on both sides of the Atlantic and interviews with survivors of the killing, pillaging, and rape, as well as with high-ranking Nigerian military and political leaders, S. Elizabeth Bird and Fraser M. Ottanelli offer an interdisciplinary reconstruction of the history of the Asaba Massacre, redefining it as a pivotal point in the history of the war. Through this, they also explore the long afterlife of trauma, the reconstruction of memory and how it intersects with justice, and the task of reconciliation in a nation where a legacy of ethnic suspicion continues to reverberate.

S. ELIZABETH BIRD is Professor of Anthropology at the University of South Florida. She has published over 80 articles and chapters on popular culture, media, heritage, and memory, as well as five books, one of which won an Outstanding Book Award from the Gustavus Myers Center for the Study of Bigotry and Human Rights, while another was awarded the International Communication Association's Outstanding Book Award.

FRASER M. OTTANELLI is Professor of History at the University of South Florida. He has authored and co authored four books and several articles and essays on radical movements, ethnic history, and comparative migration in the twentieth century. He currently serves as Chair of the Board of Governors of the Abraham Lincoln Brigade Archives (ALBA), an educational non-profit dedicated to promoting social activism and the defense of human rights.

The Asaba Massacre

Trauma, Memory, and the Nigerian Civil War

S. ELIZABETH BIRD AND
FRASER M. OTTANELLI
University of South Florida

CAMBRIDGE
UNIVERSITY PRESS

CAMBRIDGE
UNIVERSITY PRESS

University Printing House, Cambridge CB2 8BS, United Kingdom

One Liberty Plaza, 20th Floor, New York, NY 10006, USA

477 Williamstown Road, Port Melbourne, VIC 3207, Australia

4843/24, 2nd Floor, Ansari Road, Daryaganj, Delhi – 110002, India

79 Anson Road, #06–04/06, Singapore 079906

Cambridge University Press is part of the University of Cambridge.

It furthers the University's mission by disseminating knowledge in the pursuit of education, learning, and research at the highest international levels of excellence.

www.cambridge.org
Information on this title: www.cambridge.org/9781107140783
DOI: 10.1017/9781316493168

© S. Elizabeth Bird and Fraser M. Ottanelli 2017

First published 2017

Printed in the United States of America by Sheridan Books, Inc.

A catalogue record for this publication is available from the British Library.

ISBN 978-1-107-14078-3 Hardback
ISBN 978-1-316-50616-5 Paperback

To the people of Asaba

Contents

	List of Figures	*page* viii
	List of Maps	xi
	Acknowledgments	xii
	Prologue	xvi
1	The Road to War and Massacre	1
2	What Happened at Asaba?	21
3	Causes and Consequences	62
4	Surviving the Occupation	114
5	Reclaiming Memory in an Age of New Media	148
6	Trauma, Identity, Memorialization, and Justice	179
	Sources Consulted	218
	Index	232

Figures

1.1   Lt.-Col. Murtala Muhammed (center), along
      with Col. Godwin Ally (left) and Col. Francis
      Aisida, both brigade commanders with the Second
      Division, near Benin City, September 23, 1967.
      Photo courtesy of Associated Press.   *page* 17

2.1   Niger riverbanks, looking toward Asaba,
      Asaba-Onitsha ferry crossing. Photo by
      Simon Ottenberg, c. 1959–1960. Simon Ottenberg
      Collection, EEPA 2000-007-0764, Eliot Elisofon
      Photographic Archives, National Museum
      of African Art, Smithsonian Institution.   22

2.2   Students at Asaba Girls' Grammar School perform
      Shakespeare's *A Midsummer Night's Dream* –
      the "hole in the wall" scene, 1963–1964. Photo
      by Carol Kimmons.   24

2.3   Midwest Premier Dennis Osadebay leads a
      motorcade through the Cable Point area of Asaba
      during the December 1964 general election campaign.
      Photo by Eric Strauss.   25

2.4   Col. Ike Omar Sanda Nwachukwu (center, looking
      through field glasses), and his troops survey the situation
      at the Niger bridge. Photo courtesy of Ahmed Adoke.   34

2.5   The Onitsha end of the Niger River Bridge, after
      it had been blown up by retreating Biafran troops.
      Photo by Ahmed Adoke.   34

2.6   Federal troops progress up a street in Asaba's
      Cable Point District, past houses destroyed by shelling,
      October 1967. Photo by Bill Norris, courtesy of
      The Times.   37

2.7   Members of the extended Isichei family at the
      ordination of Father Patrick Isichei (center, parents
      Flora and Francis Okafor Isichei on either side). Others
      pictured include Osi (first row standing, far right) and
      Emmanuel (next to Flora), both killed at Asaba;
      Celestina (next to Osi); Victor Izegbu (back row,
      far right). Asaba, 1966. Photo courtesy of Victor
      Izegbu.   43
2.8   A home in Cable Point, Asaba, after the arrival
      of federal troops, October 1967. Photo by Bill Norris,
      courtesy of *The Times*.   52
2.9   Col. Ike Omar Sanda Nwachukwu (center), with
      other officers, leaves a ferryboat used for the failed
      attempt to take Onitsha. Photo courtesy of Ahmed
      Adoke.   59
3.1   A typical news image of Biafran starvation, July 1,
      1968. Photo by Kent Gavin, *Daily Mirror*, courtesy
      of Mirrorpix.   63
3.2   A woman combs through abandoned belongings
      looted from homes. Cable Point, Asaba, October 1967.
      Photo by Bill Norris, courtesy of *The Times*.   91
4.1   The Uraih family in Kano in 1962, celebrating
      the admittance of oldest son Ben (sitting far right)
      to medical school in Britain. Sitting: Paul (killed
      at Asaba in 1967), baby Robert, Mrs. Veronica Uraih,
      Victoria, Ben. Standing: Anthony, Ify (on stool),
      Lucy Chineze, Emma (killed in 1967), Ubaka.
      Father Robert Uraih and son Medua not present.
      Photo courtesy of Ify Uraih.   126
4.2   S. Elizabeth Bird interviews Felix Onochie, who
      is showing a photo of his brother Emmanuel,
      killed in the "second operation." Photo by
      Fraser M. Ottanelli.   131

4.3 Refugee camp at St. Patrick's College, Asaba, 1968. Photo by Brad and Jean Abernethy, courtesy of AFSC. 132

4.4 Portions of meat laid out for refugee meals. Two cows were slaughtered each day, yielding portions for more than 2,000 people. Refugee camp, St. Patrick's College, Asaba, 1968. Photo by Brad and Jean Abernethy, courtesy of AFSC. 134

4.5 Families line up outside the Catholic Mission to receive food and other supplies. Asaba, late 1968. Photo by Brad and Jean Abernethy, courtesy of AFSC. 139

5.1 One of several commemorative family plaques in St. Joseph's Catholic Church. Photo by Fraser M. Ottanelli. 149

5.2 Composite photo showing Rose Nduka-Eze, who was killed in Asaba, holding her older son Anthony and with younger son, Chuck, superimposed. Courtesy of Chuck Nduka-Eze. 151

6.1 The October 7 monument at Ogbe-Osowa, Asaba. Photo by S. Elizabeth Bird. 204

6.2 Asaba Commemoration Day Procession, 2012. Survivor Dr. Ify Uraih is center front. Photo by Fraser M. Ottanelli. 205

6.3 Detail from an outdoor mural at the home of Dr. and Mrs. E.A.C. Nwanze, depicting the Oct. 7 massacre. Created by Tony Nwalupue. 207

6.4 Community members view "The Most Vulnerable Nigerians" exhibit. Asaba, 2012. Photo by Fraser M. Ottanelli. 208

6.5 The Mungo Park House Museum, Asaba. Photo by S. Elizabeth Bird. 211

Maps

1.1 The four regions of Nigeria, 1963–1967.
     Cartography by Bill Nelson.   6
1.2 The advance of Biafran troops into the Midwest Region.
     Cartography by Bill Nelson.   13
2.1 Location of Asaba along the Niger River. Troops
     approached via Okpanam-Asaba Road, heading
     to Cable Point, and then to the recently constructed
     Niger Bridge. The exact route from Cable Point
     to the bridge is unclear, since roads have changed
     significantly since then. Cartography by Bill Nelson.   33
2.2 Asaba, 1967. Townspeople came out from the five
     quarters to parade along Nnebisi Road, ending in the
     massacre at Ogbe-Osowa. Other massacre sites – the
     High Court, police station, and football field – are
     also marked, as are the locations of the Isichei
     and Uraih family houses. Cartography by Bill
     Nelson.   45
6.1 Current state boundaries within the area that
     was once part of the former Midwest and Eastern
     Regions, showing the approximate boundaries
     of Anioma. Cartography by Bill Nelson.   187

Acknowledgments

During our seven years of research, including eight visits to Nigeria, we have depended on the support and assistance of many entities and individuals, all of whom made this work possible.

First, we gratefully acknowledge the support of several grants from the University of South Florida (USF), notably from the Office of Research, the College of Arts and Sciences, and the Humanities Institute, as well as our home departments of anthropology and history. In particular, we thank former Vice President for Research Karen Holbrook, who believed in the value of our work and provided some funding at a crucial time. We acknowledge the hard work of Maryann Cairns, who as a doctoral student in anthropology at USF spent many hours transcribing interviews, often making valuable suggestions for our work. Cartographer Bill Nelson created the maps with great patience and attention to detail. We acknowledge our colleague Erin Kimmerle, whose forensic work in Nigeria led to the connections that began this research. Most recently, we were fortunate to receive a Collaborative Research Fellowship from the American Council of Learned Societies (ACLS), which has funded research expenses and release time for writing; we deeply appreciate this support, which has allowed us to complete our work. We also thank Dirk Moses and Daniel Jordan Smith, who both wrote letters of support to the ACLS.

This book builds and expands on several previously published pieces:

S. Elizabeth Bird, "Reclaiming Asaba: Old Media, New Media and the Construction of Memory," in M. Neiger, O. Meyers, and E. Zandberg, eds., *On Media Memory: Collective Memory in a New Media Age*, London: McMillan Palgrave, 2011, 88–103.

S. Elizabeth Bird and Fraser M. Ottanelli, "The History and Legacy of the Asaba, Nigeria, Massacres," *African Studies Review*, 54: 3, 2011, 1–26.

S. Elizabeth Bird and Fraser M. Ottanelli, "The Asaba Massacre and the Nigerian Civil War: Reclaiming Hidden History," *Journal of Genocide Research*, 16, 2–3, 2014, 379–399.

S. Elizabeth Bird and Fraser M. Ottanelli, "Breaking Four Decades of Silence: The Challenges of Reconstructing Collective Memory in Post-Civil War Nigeria," In Bird and Ottanelli, *The Performance Of Memory as Transitional Justice*, Cambridge, UK/Mortsel, Belgium: Intersentia, 2015, 135–152.

S. Elizabeth Bird, "Rebuilding Memory in an Age of New Media: The Case of the Asaba Massacre," in A.H. Hansen, O. Hemer, and T. Tufte, *Memory on Trial: Media, Citizenship and Social Justice*, Zurich: Lit-Verlag, 2015, 85–99.

In Nigeria, we thank the members of our Community Advisory Board and many more people who have assisted our work in myriad (non-financial) ways. Emma Okocha introduced us to Asaba and its sad history; his work underlined the need for a well-documented and reliable account of that history. Chuck Nduka-Eze has been a good friend and occasional critic, whose observations and insight have kept us on track. Chief Dr. Louis Odogwu, former president of the Asaba Development Union, and his wife Marcella have welcomed us to their homes in Benin City and Asaba, and introduced us to many key people in Asaba. Chief Philip C. Asiodu has graciously hosted us several times, facilitated meetings with key individuals, especially former federal military officers, and has committed support to the Mungo Park House Museum initiative. Prof. E.A.C. Nwanze and his wife Victoria have also welcomed us to their home, and assisted with our work, as has Mrs. Martina Osaji. Celestina Isichei-Isamah and her brother Rev. Father Patrick Isichei shared the story of her letter and gave us much useful background informàtion. Victor Izegbu and Juliana Edewor have hosted us, offered advice in several areas, and given their support to the Mungo Park House project. Renny Nwosa has become a dear friend, guiding us around Asaba, and sharing his knowledge of Asaba culture and tradition. Richie Omo, with his unfailing enthusiasm and love of Asaba, has been an inspiration, as has Emeka Okelum Okonta. We appreciate the support of HRM Prof. Dr. Joseph Chike Edozien, CFR, the Asagba of Asaba, who received us at his palace in Asaba several times and gave his official approval for us to conduct interviews in Asaba.

Most of all, we thank Dr. Ify Uraih, who has been a steadfast friend and ally throughout the work. He has provided endless logistical support, arranged meetings with survivors, and offered advice whenever needed. Like everyone else we met and worked with in Nigeria, he always provided encouragement, but never tried to influence the direction our work should take. Ify, we are deeply grateful.

We each have those we wish to thank:

S. Elizabeth Bird: The Nigerian Civil War was the first major international conflict to make an impact on me while I was growing up in Britain in the 1960s. Like most in my generation, my memory of the war is dominated by the searing images of starving Biafran children; I knew little about the larger context of the war. I am grateful for the opportunity to learn more and to tell a story that has long been neglected. During this work, archivists and librarians at all the collections visited were generous with their time and expertise; all are listed in our sources. In particular, I thank Don Davis at the American Friends Services Committee Archives; he went out of his way to locate hard-to-find documents for me, and provided copies of photos at no charge. As the research progressed, I developed an active presence on social media, through which I was able not only to keep in touch with Nigerian friends, but also to learn much new information. In particular, I thank Ed Keazor, Chika Omeje, Max Siollun, Joseph Anene Okafor, and Emmanuel Mordi for sharing their knowledge and experiences. Members of the Nigeria Nostalgia Project Facebook group thoughtfully responded to our work on several occasions, as did members of the groups Proudly Asaba, Ahaba Forum, and Asaba Development Association.

On a more personal note, I thank my husband, Graham Tobin, for his love and patience throughout this research. When the project began, I did not expect it to become such a meaningful part of my life; he has supported and encouraged me throughout. I thank our sons Thomas and Daniel Tobin, who have both grown into wonderful young men; Dan also provided the narration for our video. And I remember my parents, Tom and Eileen Bird. My father enjoyed following my work in Nigeria, and he would have liked to see it completed.

Fraser M. Ottanelli: I am grateful to a special group of friends for their camaraderie and support as I embarked on this new journey, especially Vasco Lionel Bonini, Peter N. Carroll, Tami Davis, Phil Levy, Theresa Lewis, and Mary Anne Trasciatti. Some of my debts of gratitude are not for the first time. One is to my parents, Ann Fraser Ottanelli and Vittorio Ottanelli, who never wavered in their interest in the new directions of my research even when, as in this case, it caused them some apprehension. The other is to my sons, Carlo and Vittorio Benadusi Ottanelli, who as they make their own way in the world continue to be a great source of pride and happiness.

Together, we appreciate the work done by Cambridge University Press to bring this book to fruition. Lew Bateman encouraged us to bring the proposal to Cambridge and worked with us until his retirement in 2016. Maria Marsh, Claudia Bona-Cohen, Victoria Parrin, Jeevitha Baskaran, and James Gregory have provided support and assistance whenever needed. We also thank the anonymous reviewers who read the proposal and made many useful suggestions. As always, any errors that remain are ours.

Finally, and most important, we both thank the many people of Asaba who agreed to tell their often painful stories. All our interviewees are listed at the end of the book; many others also spoke with us informally and shared their memories. These stories form the backbone of this book, and it is dedicated to them.

Prologue

In the summer of 1967, Celestina Isichei was preparing for her final college exams, looking forward to a career as a teacher and to marrying Peter Isamah, her long-time sweetheart. Soon she would be home in Asaba, a peaceful town on the banks of the Niger River. Celestina knew about the ominous events that were worrying her friends and family – that war had broken out in Nigeria that July, and people were on the move across the country. But surely it wouldn't last, nor should it affect her family of educators and professionals, who considered themselves to be loyal Nigerians.

Yet that October, Celestina sent an anguished letter to her older brother Patrick, a Catholic priest and student at Oxford University. She described the catastrophe that had descended on Asaba, which now lay in ruins, its male population decimated and its women and girls terrorized. She described how their 16-year-old brother Osi had been shot in front of her, and how their brother Emmanuel, a young married father, had been slaughtered along with hundreds of others in a sustained killing spree. She listed all the family members and neighbors who were now dead, many hastily buried in common graves. It seemed incomprehensible that soldiers of her own government had done this, and she desperately wanted Patrick to make it known in the wider world. Celestina's letter reached her brother, who tried to get someone to pay attention. But Asaba's fate caused barely a ripple. Even with the end of the war, through years of military rule and then the country's return to democracy, the tragic events of Asaba remained officially unacknowledged. For decades, the memory of the massacre was preserved in the recollections of the survivors, while Celestina's letter, the only account of the Asaba Massacre written in the immediate aftermath of the disaster, remained ignored in an Oxford archive.

In the pages that follow, we tell the story of that massacre, as seen through the eyes of survivors and supported by available archival sources. We describe the sustained horror that befell Asaba during the Civil War, and we examine the immediate and long-term consequences, exploring the lingering impact of such a traumatic event, even decades afterwards. And we show how a full understanding of Asaba changes the accepted narrative of the progress and history of the war. The Asaba massacre was, unfortunately, just one of the atrocities that marked that conflict, but we argue that it was actually a pivotal event that contributed to prolonging a war that claimed well over a million lives. We examine how and why the massacre happened, and how the Nigerian Federal Military Government, supported by Britain, worked to keep the world from learning about it.

Finally, we explore the process of memory formation, as new media offer opportunities to reclaim the story of Asaba. And we suggest that while the bitter burden of memory can serve to divide and to feed resentment and continuing ethnic tension, an active academic/community collaboration that helps "recalibrate" memory may offer opportunities to reach a more complete understanding of a nation's troubled history, and even open the door to reconciliation.

I   The Road to War and Massacre

To understand how so many Asaba families, like Celestina's, came to be devastated in 1967, we must briefly review the long chain of events that culminated in war. It was a conflict that eventually claimed up to two million lives, before ending in 1970 with the collapse of secessionist Biafra.[1]

THE ROOTS OF NIGERIA

The origins of the Nigerian Civil War lie in the country's colonial past.[2] Starting at the end of the nineteenth century and over a period of 40 years, the British took control of previously independent territories with distinct languages, religions, and customs that represented over 200 ethno-linguistic groups from the Bight of Benin on the Atlantic coast to the fringes of the Sahara desert to the north. Both topography and culture had created historical divisions between the northern and the southern parts of what would later become Nigeria. Trade routes crossing the Sahara Desert linked Northern Nigeria to Muslim North Africa, the Middle East, and Southern Europe, eventually leading to the spread of Islam among the majority Hausa population between the eleventh and fourteenth centuries. Fulani pastoral nomads began to enter the north at about the same time; by the beginning of the

---

[1]   The most comprehensive history of the war, written soon after its end, is John de St. Jorre, *The Brothers' War: Biafra and Nigeria*, Boston: Houghton Mifflin, 1972. The most recent account is Michael Gould, *The Biafran War: The Struggle for Modern Nigeria*, New York: I.B. Tauris, 2012. Other accounts, written from various points of view, are listed in the Sources Consulted.

[2]   The name by which the war is known is contentious. Depending on point of view, it may be known as the Nigeria-Biafra War (which suggests a conflict between two sovereign entities), the Biafran War (which places the emphasis on the struggle for Biafra), or the War of Nigerian Unity (which underlines the purpose of keeping Nigeria as one). We chose to use the term Nigerian Civil War because it is the most common and arguably the most neutral.

nineteenth century, they had asserted their dominance over multiple Hausa kingdoms and established the powerful Sokoto Caliphate, which exerted control over the vast area that comprises present-day Northern Nigeria. In contrast to the southern part of the country, dominated by the Yoruba to the west and Igbo-speaking groups to the east, the environment allowed for the development of cattle-herding and agriculture, and a more decentralized power structure in which local chieftains exerted control over discrete areas.[3]

The divisions between the two parts of what would become Nigeria were exacerbated by interaction with Europeans. Starting in the sixteenth century, the arrival of European merchants redirected economic and trade routes away from the Mediterranean area to the Atlantic coast. Slave trading was a central component of this relation-ship. After it was abolished by Britain in 1807, it was gradually replaced by palm oil, the main cash crop of the colonial era, and other forms of "legitimate" commerce. The expansion of trade, with the Niger River providing the locus of contact with European mer-chants, in turn led to an influx of missionaries. Christianity was first introduced with the arrival of the Portuguese in the fifteenth century, but it truly began to gather momentum in the first half of the nine-teenth century, when evangelical fervor led to an increase in mission-ary activities that were channeled through churches and mission schools offering Western-style education.[4]

During the second half of the nineteenth century, competition increased between British, French, and German trading companies in the area. In order to protect and develop its commercial interests from the expansionist aims of other European powers, Britain annexed Lagos as a Crown colony in 1861, and starting in 1886, the newly formed Royal Niger Company was granted a monopoly over trade in the Niger River basin. Between the end of the nineteenth century and the early years of the twentieth, Britain's colonial ambitions led to

[3]   Toyin Falola and Matthew M. Heaton, *A History of Nigeria*, Cambridge: Cambridge University Press, 2008, 21–37; Michael Gould, *The Biafran War*, Chapter 2.
[4]   Falola and Heaton, *A History of Nigeria*, Chapters 2 and 3.

a series of successful and often punitive military campaigns to expand its sphere of influence and commercial opportunities throughout Yorubaland in the west, the kingdom of Benin in the center, Igboland in the east, and the Sokoto Caliphate in the north. In 1900 the British government revoked the charter of the Royal Niger Company, dividing its territory into the newly formed Protectorate of Northern Nigeria and the Niger Coast Protectorate. In 1906, with the addition of the Lagos colony, the latter was renamed the Protectorate of Southern Nigeria.

NIGERIA UNDER COLONIAL RULE

In 1914 the Colonial Office amalgamated this complex ethnic mosaic into a single entity called "Nigeria" by joining these separate jurisdictions into a single colony. Existing economic, political, and social differences between the various sections of Nigeria were exacerbated as a result of British policies. In order to limit expenditure, foster political stability and protect trade, Britain followed a policy of "indirect rule." Outlined by Frederick Lugard when he served as first High Commissioner of the Protectorate of Northern Nigeria between 1900 and 1906, indirect rule enabled British authorities to govern by relying on existing local power structures. Operating under firm British supervision, traditional rulers oversaw day-to-day administration; in exchange for prestige, security, and limited colonial interference into local political, social, and even legal matters, they would agree to submit to British authorities and relinquish control over matters of trade, taxation, and finance. In 1914, with Lugard as the newly appointed Governor General of a united Nigeria, indirect rule was extended to the southern part of the new colony.[5]

While protecting British commercial interest and preserving the power of a small oligarchy, indirect rule fostered localism based on religion and ethnicity which, in turn, shaped a representative system

[5]   See Frederick John Dealtry Lugard, *The Dual Mandate in British Tropical Africa*, London: William Blackwood, 1922; Penelope Hetherington, *British Paternalism and Africa, 1920–1940*, London: F. Cass, 1978.

that increased internal political tensions and led to uneven economic and social development between Northern and Southern Nigeria. Colonial emphasis on regionalism and ethnicity was challenged by nationalist leaders such as Herbert Macaulay and Nnamdi Azikiwe, who sought to create a party based on a pan-Nigerian identity. However, these efforts were undermined by colonial policies and successive constitutional changes that favored a representative system that combined a national legislature with regional assemblies representing different ethnic groups. By the time of independence, this blended representative system had led to the formation of political parties each representing a separate region and its dominant ethnic group. The Action Group Party was led by Yorubas from the Western Region; the National Council of Nigerians and Cameroons, initially established by Macaulay and Azikiwe as a national political party, had evolved into an organization supported mainly by Igbos[6] of the east. The Northern People's Congress drew on a core of support from the Hausa-Fulani, led by the Sardauna of Sokoto, although some Hausa also supported other parties, such as the Northern Elements Progressive Union.[7]

Another major consequence of indirect rule was Britain's policy toward access to formal Western education and, in turn, its role in encouraging regional prejudice. In the north, in order to avoid estranging the local feudal Islamic hierarchy comprised of Emirs, colonial authorities curtailed Christian evangelizing and the establishment of Western-style missionary schools in that area. Consequently, there were never enough Western-educated Northerners to fill expanding colonial government jobs, or to take advantage of entrepreneurial opportunities and professional advancements that required familiarity with colonial bureaucratic and commercial structures. The result was that the area remained economically, socially, and educationally less developed. In contrast, Southerners, particularly the Igbo because

---

[6]   The spelling "Ibo" was predominant until recent years; we use the current preferred spelling (Igbo) unless quoting directly from older sources.

[7]   Falola and Heaton, *A History of Nigeria*, 148–154.

of their presence along the main trade routes, such as the eastern portions of the Niger, and their relatively non-hierarchical political structures, had been exposed early to European-style entrepreneurial practices and education. As the country approached independence, British authorities turned to South-Easterners with the necessary education and skills to take over administrative and commercial responsibilities. In addition Igbos became increasingly represented in business activities and professions throughout the country, including in the north. Here, in spite of their crucial role, and even though many had lived in the area for generations, Igbo were required to live in segregated *Sabon Gari* or "strangers' quarters."[8] Thus British "indirect rule" had fostered a lopsided situation that fed Northern fears of Southern intrusion, with the relatively wealthy Igbo being especially suspect. By the mid-1960s, across Nigeria,

> Ibos filled urban jobs at every level far out of proportion to their numbers, as laborers and domestic servants, as bureaucrats, corporate managers, and technicians. Two-thirds of the senior jobs in the Nigerian Railway Corporation were held by Ibos. Three-quarters of Nigeria's diplomats came from the Eastern Region. So did almost half of the 4,500 students graduating from Nigerian universities in 1966. The Ibos became known as the "Jews of Africa," despised – and envied – for their achievements and acquisitiveness.[9]

INDEPENDENCE

Nigeria gained independence from Britain in 1960, and in the immediate post-independence years, it was a three-region Federal state. While the Hausa/Fulani dominated the Northern Region, the south had been divided into the Yoruba-dominated Western Region separated by the Niger River from the Igbo-dominated Eastern Region. A fourth, smallest, and most ethnically diverse region, the Midwest, was carved out

[8]   Douglas Anthony, *Poison and Medicine: Ethnicity, Power and Violence in a Nigerian City, 1966–1986*, Oxford: James Currey, 2003.
[9]   Pauline Baker, "Lurching toward Unity," *The Wilson Quarterly*, 4, 1980, 70–80, 76.

MAP I.I The four regions of Nigeria, 1963–1967. Cartography by Bill
Nelson.

of the Western Region in 1963. Its capital, Benin City, was ethnically
Edo; the state also included a substantial Igbo-speaking population,
along with many other smaller groups, and was governed by an NCNC
(National Council of Nigerians and Cameroons) majority.[10]

Each region – and by extension its dominant party – was allo-
cated seats in the Federal House of Representative based on its total
population. The North, with approximately 50 percent of the population, enjoyed the largest parliamentary representation, setting up

[10]   Nowamagbe A. Omoigui, "Benin and the Midwest Referendum of 1963," http://www
.waado.org/nigerdelta/ethnichistories/egharevbalectures/Fifth-Omoigui.htm

a highly competitive environment that led to major conflicts around national censuses. In particular, the census count of 1962–1963 was tainted with extensive charges of fraud.

Immediately after independence, the Federal Government was controlled by a coalition of the predominantly Hausa-Fulani Northern People's Congress (NPC) and the largely Igbo-supported National Council of Nigerians and Cameroons (NCNC), with the predominantly Yoruba and socialist-leaning Action Group (AG), led by Chief Obafemi Awolowo, in opposition. Ideological differences and exclusion from national power led to dissention within the AG, which climaxed in the formation of a new political organization, the Nigerian National Democratic Party, led by former AG premier of the Western Region, Samuel Akintola. The new party not only unseated the Action Group from power in the Western Region but also formed an alliance with the Northern People's Congress in the elections of 1964, excluding the Eastern NCNC. The campaign was fraught with violence and intimidation, and when the vote was announced, the NCNC and what was left of the Action Group unsuccessfully tried to boycott the election. A similarly contested election in the Western Region led to renewed chaos and violence in October 1965, claiming many lives. Growing unrest within the country was the product of fear that one region, through its dominant party, would prevail over the others, gain control over federal assemblies, and divert allocation of development resources, while fostering patronage, corruption, and nepotism.[11]

THE COUPS

This volatile combination of regional tensions, claims of electoral fraud, and widespread corruption provided motivation for the overthrow of civil rule on January 15, 1966, by a group of military officers, prominent among them Major Patrick Chukwuma Nzeogwu, a Midwesterner from the area around Asaba. The coup failed, and

[11]   Falola and Heaton, *A History of Nigeria*, 164–172.

most of its leaders were arrested, but not until several prominent Northern leaders had been brutally killed, among them the Federal Prime Minister, Abubakar Tafawa Balewa; the Northern Region Premier, Sir Ahmadu Bello (the Sardauna of Sokoto); and the Western Region Premier, Samuel Akintola. The fact that the instigators were mostly Igbo convinced many Northerners that the coup was an attempt to impose Igbo domination over the country. This perception was reinforced by the facts that the coup leaders spared several prominent Igbos, including the premiers of the Eastern and Midwestern Regions, and the commanding officer of the Nigerian army, Maj.-Gen. Johnson Aguiyi-Ironsi, who was then appointed as the new head of state. Federal President Nnamdi Azikiwe was out of the country at the time and, thus avoided being caught up in the coup events. Once in power, in spite of having played a central role in putting down the coup in the south, Ironsi resisted pressure to swiftly prosecute its ringleaders.

Northern suspicions grew when Ironsi, in an attempt to undermine regionalism and corruption, and to foster a stronger unified rule, then adopted several measures similar to those originally advocated by coup leaders. Specifically, he abolished the federal system, creating a centralized structure in which regions were replaced by provinces, and their civil services amalgamated and placed under the direct control of the government in Lagos. In addition, in order to undermine the power of ethnically based parties, all political activities were banned for two years, and military governors were appointed to run each region. Among this group of new appointees was the Igbo governor of the Eastern Region, Lt.-Col. Chukwuemeka Odumegwu Ojukwu.[12]

The failed coup, along with Ironsi's actions, provided the opportunity for many to act on a long-festering animosity against the Igbo.

---

[12]   Falola and Heaton, *A History of Nigeria*, 172–174; John de St. Jorre, *The Brothers' War*, 29–58; Mohibi Amoda, "Background to the Conflict," in Joseph Okpaku, ed., *Nigeria, Dilemma of Nationhood. An African Analysis of the Biafran Conflict*, 1972, Westport, CT: Greenwood, 14–75.

A series of mob riots directed against the Igbo broke out in Northern and Western Nigeria in May 1966. This outburst of bloody violence set the stage for a second coup, this one led by Northern officers, which in turn led to the revenge killing of scores of Igbo soldiers, including Ironsi. On July 29, 1966, Lt.-Col. Yakubu Gowon emerged as Supreme Commander of the Nigerian Armed Forces and new head of the Federal Military Government. One of his first decisions was to reestablish the federal system based on Regions. Gowon was a Christian Northerner from the small Angas ethnic group, and thus represented a compromise choice acceptable to most military leaders from the North and the West. However, this choice was challenged by other officers who felt senior to him and questioned his fitness to lead. Chief among them were Lt.-Col. Murtala Muhammed, backed by Northern leaders, and Eastern Governor Ojukwu.[13]

Far from decreasing ethnic tensions, the second coup led to an escalation of violence, again mostly directed against Igbos. Killing, looting, and burning of property escalated into systematic massacres of several thousands of Igbo living in the Muslim north. These blood-baths (which the Igbo commonly referred to as "pogroms"[14]) lasted through October. In at least some cases, soldiers actively joined civilian mobs; on October 2, 1966, the *New York Times* reported that soldiers, defying the orders of their officers to keep the peace, opened fire on a large group of Igbos trying to board an airplane at Kano.[15] These Igbos were attempting to join the many thousands who, in fear for their lives, were fleeing to their ancestral homes in the east, which included both the region east of the Niger and portions of the Midwest, such as Asaba. Later in October, the same reporter wrote that Nigeria "had reached the brink of dissolution and despair" as the massive population movements continued – not only were Igbo fleeing east,

[13] Gould, *The Biafran War*, 40–48; de St. Jorre, *The Brothers' War*, 58–81.
[14] The term "pogrom" was first used by the Ministry of Information in Enugu, Eastern Nigeria, in 1966. A book, *Pogrom* (Ministry of Information, Enugu 1966), includes graphic photographs and firsthand accounts of attacks and killing.
[15] Lloyd Garrison, "300 Ibo Tribesmen Killed by Troops and Nigerian Mob," *New York Times*, Oct. 2, 1966, 1; 17.

but non-Igbos living in the east were rushing home.[16] Garrison pointed to the "lonely task" of Gowon: "to reinstall discipline among his northern troops who not only joined civilian mobs in the anti-Igbo massacres, but defied their own officers to the point of mutiny."[17] This "breakdown of the army as a responsive cohesive force,"[18] along with the apparent unwillingness or inability of the military government to protect the Igbo, provide support for those forced to relocate, or more generally to ensure Igbo of their rights as Nigerians, was to have further bloody ramifications in the year to come.[19]

The combination of the widespread killing of Igbos and the erosion of military discipline led to the decision to order soldiers to return to their region of origin and to the establishment of a military structure that corresponded to the country's regions at the time: the Northern, the Western, the Midwestern, and the Eastern Regions.

SECESSION AND WAR

In early January 1967, at a two-day summit in Aburi, Ghana, between federal authorities and the country's regional governors, Gowon and Ojukwu were unable to reach a compromise over whether Nigeria should become a loose confederation of semi-independent states or remain a federation. The failure of the Aburi summit accelerated the Eastern Region's movement toward secession. Faced with this possibility, Gowon declared a state of emergency on May 27, 1967, and proclaimed that the country would be divided into 12 states. Under this new system the East would be broken up into three separate states, only one of which was Igbo-dominated, which could effectively cut off the Igbos from the oil-producing areas of the region and dilute the influence of an administratively unified East.[20] In the end, the combination of the persecution of Easterners in the North, failure to

16   Lloyd Garrison, "Nigeria Totters on the Brink," *New York Times*, Oct. 9, 1966, E3.
17   Ibid. E3.
18   Ibid., E3.
19   de St. Jorre, *The Brothers' War*, 84–88.
20   Gould, *The Biafran War*, 48–53.

reach a settlement at Aburi and, finally, the administrative reorganization, provided Ojukwu justifications for the decision to secede from the rest of the country and establish the sovereign state of Biafra on May 30, 1967.[21] The "state" was not initially framed as Igbo, but as a multi-ethnic entity – the Eastern Region had been majority-Igbo, but it also included significant numbers of other ethnic groups, such as the Ibibio, Ijaw, Efik, and Ogoni. Leaders of those groups met and offered support to Ojukwu, but the level of commitment varied considerably.[22] Interviewed in 1999, Ojukwu stated that secession was "not so much a declaration of independence. It was more a demarcation of a line – this far, no further."[23] Nevertheless, the path to war had now been laid.

Contending sides provided different justifications for the conflict. Ojukwu and the other leaders of Biafra, responding to the pogroms in the North and West, argued that Igbos were not safe within Nigeria, and secession was therefore a matter of survival. In contrast, Federal authorities were insistent that the integrity of the country must be preserved, as must the rich resources, such as oil, that were located in the newly named Biafra. They believed that secessionists could be subdued easily and quickly through a "police action," combined with an economic blockade that soon extended to oil.

Hostilities began on July 6, 1967, when the newly formed Federal First Infantry Division advanced into the northeastern corner of Biafra, led by Col. Mohammed Shuwa. Proceeding in two separate columns, federal troops quickly overran the university town of Nsukka and made strong advances toward the Biafran capital of Enugu before they were stopped. Further to the south, the Nigerian 3rd Marine

---

[21]   Gould, *The Biafran War*, 45–48; Falola and Heaton, *A History of Nigeria*, 174–176; de St. Jorre, *The Brothers' War*, 91–122.

[22]   Roy. S. Doron, "Forging a Nation while Losing a Country: Igbo Nationalism, Ethnicity and Propaganda in the Nigerian Civil War 1968–1970," Doctoral dissertation, University of Texas at Austin, August 2011.

[23]   "My Century," audiotaped interview with Ojukwu, 1999, archived in Imperial War Museum, London, Reference 20541.

Commando Division launched a successful seaborne assault, which led to the occupation of Bonny Island in the Niger Delta.

THE MIDWEST INVASION

Thus within three weeks of the onset of hostilities, federal troops had scored major victories and put Biafran forces on the defensive. In an attempt to thwart further federal advances on Enugu and, more generally, to turn the tide of war, Biafra's leaders conceived an ambitious plan that targeted the Midwest Region. The small, ethnically diverse Midwest was seen by some as a successful microcosm of what the Federation could have been. Nevertheless, this very diversity and strategic location led local authorities to legitimately fear that it would become a battlefield between the warring parties. This concern spurred the region's governor, Brig. David Ejoor, to attempt to mediate between Lagos and Enugu. This produced an uneasy policy: on the one hand, the Midwest did not embrace secession but, on the other, it declared opposition to federal troops advancing through its territory to attack Biafra from the west. The Midwest also continued close trade ties with the Eastern Region in defiance of the federal trade embargo. Finally, in hope of avoiding being drawn into the conflict, Ejoor kept the total number of Midwestern troops down to two battalions, totaling a few hundred mostly unarmed soldiers scattered across the region. This precarious balance depended on the willingness of both Biafran and federal authorities to respect the neutrality of the Midwest.

However, in the early hours of August 9, the region's tenuous neutrality came to an abrupt end. Under cover of darkness, commanded by Brig. Victor Banjo, up to 3,000 militiamen and soldiers of the 101 Biafran Division, traveling in a convoy of assorted cars and trucks, crossed over the recently constructed Niger Bridge from the important Eastern market town of Onitsha into Asaba. It was apparent that Igbo officers of the Midwest Army, which was garrisoned in Asaba, had colluded with the Biafrans to allow unhampered crossing of the bridge and offer little resistance; several defected to Biafra

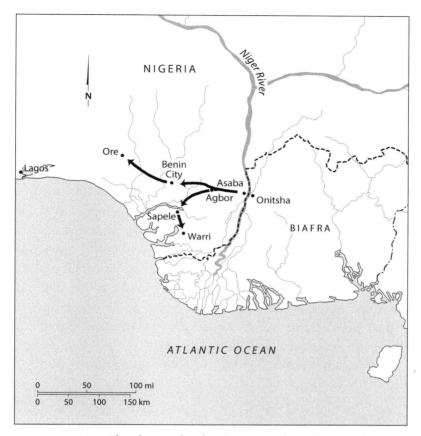

MAP 1.2 The advance of Biafran troops into the Midwest Region.
Cartography by Bill Nelson.

almost immediately. According to Godwin Alabi-Isama, the Asaba
garrison commander and one of the few Midwest soldiers to put up
a fight, the Biafran invaders paused to kill several civilians in the
Hausa area of Asaba, possibly in revenge for the 1966 Northern
"pogroms."[24] Having met little opposition, Biafran troops continued
on unchallenged, fanning out southwest toward the Delta towns of
Warri and Sapele, and west about 70 miles through Agbor and on to

[24]   Godwin Alabi-Isama, *The Tragedy of Victory: On the Spot Account of the Nigeria-
Biafra War in the Atlantic Theatre*, Ibadan: Spectrum Books, 2013.

Benin City, capital of the Midwest region, which they secured by mid-morning. From there the Biafrans continued west for several weeks toward the strategic crossroads town of Ore in the Western state, about 100 miles from Lagos. Only then were they stopped by federal troops, who blew up key bridges in the Biafrans' path.[25]

For Biafran troops, the brief occupation of Ore marked the high point of the entire war effort. Six weeks after the invasion, federal forces regained the initiative. A Second Infantry Division had been hastily raised by combining soldiers initially scheduled to be deployed with other units, former soldiers pressed back into service, support personnel, and a significant number of untrained volunteers. Ibrahim B. Haruna, at the time commanding the Lagos garrison, described these volunteers as "riff-raff, the unemployed, embittered people, who had seen an opportunity."[26] Paul Ogbebor, who as a young officer was with the Second Division from the beginning of the Nigerian Civil War, confirmed the haphazard way the division was thrown together. Given command of 11 trained soldiers, he was ordered to form a battalion usually composed of 700 to 800 men. Since "we had no troops on the ground," Ogbebor adopted a course followed by other officers in his situation:

> I went to Abule Ado Garage in Lagos, where they have these area boys.[27] I just arrested all of them, commandeered them. I went to Ikoyi prison and removed many prisoners, I went to Kirikiri Prison ... brought them to Ikeja and started training. That was how I formed my battalion.

---

[25]   Stanley E. Orobator, "The Biafran Crisis and the Midwest," *African Affairs*, 86: 344, 1987, 367–383; Nowamagbe A. Omoigui, "The Midwest Invasion of 1967: Lessons for Today's Geopolitics," http://www.dawodu.net/midwest.htm, 1–7; "2 Division Operations," in H.B. Momoh, *The Nigerian Civil War, 1967–1970: History and Reminiscences*, Ibadan: Sam Bookman Publishers, 2000, 83–84; authors' interviews with retired Gens. Ibrahim B. Haruna, April 11, 2016, Abuja, and Paul Osa Ogbebor, Oct. 12, 2016, Benin City.

[26]   Authors' interview with retired Gen. Ibrahim Haruna, April 11, 2016, Abuja.

[27]   "Area boys" also known as *Agberos* are loosely organized gangs of young men who survive through various forms of informal and non-legal strategies.

These new recruits, many of whom were happy to be free and employed, received a few days of physical training in "shorts, singlets ... carved wood for guns" before they were moved out on commandeered trucks. Only as they approached the front lines did they receive uniforms and weapons. Unsurprisingly, when they first experienced combat, many of the new recruits "threw down their guns and started running." Ogbebor had the deserters rounded up and, to give them what he referred to as "battle inoculation," subjected them to a mock execution, after which "they became good soldiers."[28]

The new division was placed under the command of Col. Murtala Muhammed, a strong-willed officer often at odds with Gowon.[29] As federal troops advanced east toward Benin, the fragile peace among Midwest ethnic groups was breaking down, for several reasons. Many among the non-Igbo-speaking peoples of the region were resentful of the several prominent Igbo-speaking Midwesterners, including the majority of the region's military leaders, who had either not opposed or had even openly supported the invasion.[30] Furthermore, many resented the Biafrans' overbearing policies during their six-week occupation of the Midwest, when they had declared the "independent and sovereign republic of Benin." This declaration had apparently been part of an attempt to win over Midwesterners that began as soon as Banjo and his soldiers crossed into the Midwest; on August 9, he had broadcast over Benin Radio that the invasion was "designed to insulate the people of the Midwest from the coercive threats of Northern military presence ... "[31] However, placing mainly Igbo in positions of power, this new "republic" only served to stoke ethnic resentment further, building on anger

---

28   Authors' interview with retired Col. Paul Osa Ogbebor, Oct. 12, 2016, Benin City.
29   De St. Jorre deemed him "a strong willed but rather unstable Hausa," *The Brothers' War*, 69.
30   Authors' interview with retired Gen. Philip Onyekweli, April 16, 2016, Lagos.
31   For full text of Banjo's broadcast, see Anthony H. M. Kirk-Greene, *Crisis and Conflict in Nigeria: A Documentary Sourcebook, 1966–1970*, Vol. 2, London: Oxford University Press, 7.

created by the actions of Biafran troops as they moved through the area. According to Fola Oyewole, a Yoruba serving with the Biafrans,

> Troops of the Liberation [Biafran] Army did not behave in a manner likely to improve their relationship with the people ... The worst hit towns were Warri, Benin, and Sapele. Men of the 18th Battalion based in Warri were notorious, looting anything they could turn into cash.[32]

In addition, reports were accusing the Biafran forces of rape, theft, extortion, and other violence, including the killing of non-Igbo civilians in Abudu, Boji-Boji, Agbor, Ibusa, and Asaba.[33] There is some disagreement about the extent of Biafran violence against civilians, but it is clear that the occupation was heavy-handed, and non-Igbo Midwesterners were eager to be rid of the occupiers.[34]

As the federal troops advanced, they were generally received well by local people, who had not welcomed the Biafran incursion.[35] However, fear of retaliation spread among Igbo-speakers in Benin and other Midwest towns. Many decided to leave, and began joining the Igbos who had fled after the pogroms in the North, heading for ancestral homes in the Igbo-dominated Midwest around Asaba, or across the Niger into Biafra. This fear was felt not only by civilians but also by Igbo-speaking soldiers in the Nigerian army. Philip Onyekeli, a junior Midwestern officer, was aide de camp to Gov. Ejoor in Benin when the Biafrans took over. Ejoor escaped to Lagos, while Onyekeli and other soldiers remained, unharmed by the Biafrans but unsure how to proceed. As news came about the impending recapture of Benin by Murtala Muhammed, they were anxiously discussing what to do. According to Onyekeli, he supported the government – "no question about that" – and he planned to rejoin the federal troops when they

---

[32]   Fola Oyewole, *Reluctant Rebel*, London: Rex Collings, 1975, 48.

[33]   Orobator, "The Biafran Crisis and the Midwest," 379; Omoigui, "The Midwest Invasion of 1967," 10–12, 18–19.

[34]   Egodi Uchendu, *Women and Conflict in the Nigerian Civil War*, Trenton, NJ: Africa World Press, 2007.

[35]   Authors' interview with retired Gen. Ike Omar Sanda Nwachukwu, Oct. 11, 2016, Lagos.

THE MIDWEST INVASION 17

FIGURE 1.1 Lt.-Col. Murtala Muhammed (center), along with Col. Godwin Ally (left) and Col. Francis Aisida, both brigade commanders with the Second Division, near Benin City, September 23, 1967. Photo courtesy of Associated Press.

returned. However, an old classmate convinced him that when the troops arrived, Igbo-speakers would become targets of soldiers from Benin. Although born a Midwesterner, Onyekeli was raised in Onitsha (now in Biafra). His friend asked: "are you going to stay in Benin and be firing across to your parents?" Although conflicted, Onyekeli agreed to leave with his friend and join Biafra: "it wasn't an easy thing."[36]

Fears were realized once Muhammed's forces retook Benin City on September 21, only a day after the Biafrans had officially announced the creation of the new Benin republic.[37]

The Biafrans' incursion, followed by their heavy-handed policies, had aroused dormant resentment as angry civilians turned on

[36] Authors' interview with retired Gen. Philip Onyekeli, April 16, 2016, Lagos
[37] Orobator, "The Biafran Crisis and the Midwest," 380.

their Igbo neighbors.[38] Murtala Muhammed did little to dampen this resentment. On September 21, he made a radio broadcast, announcing the appointment of Lt.-Col. Samuel Ogbemudia as the temporary administrator of the Midwest State and warning,

> I would like to advise all innocent citizens . . . to keep out of the way of the federal troops . . . anybody that stands in the way of the federal troops will be regarded and treated as a rebel . . . I would like to appeal to all my brothers and sisters in the Midwestern State of Nigeria to assist the federal troops in locating, and in the eventual destruction of the rebels that may be hiding around the Midwest.[39]

Whether he intended it or not, this call was consistent with an approach that characterized events from then on – that any Igbo-speaker was assumed to be a sympathizer or saboteur, and could be legitimately targeted. Drawing from witness accounts, Egodi Uchendu described how civilians reacted to the establishment of federal control in Benin City:

> Operating under the protection of the army, unruly crowds visited hospitals in Benin City, where the majority of the senior medical personnel were of Anioma [Igbo-speaking] origin. They also gained entrance into the Benin City prison and other government establishments . . . and killed any Igbo found in those places . . . Victims . . . had their property, market stall, shops, workshops, and residences looted.[40]

Events in Benin were repeated as troops advanced: non-Igbo civilians attacked Igbos who had stayed behind, often those with the fewest resources. Furthermore, the attackers were tacitly and actively supported by troops, pointing to the problems of discipline that were becoming increasingly acute.[41] *New York Times* writer Alfred

---

[38]   Ibid., 367–383.
[39]   For text of the speech, see Kirk-Greene, *Crisis and Conflict*, 162.
[40]   Uchendu, *Women and Conflict*, 67.
[41]   De St. Jorre, *The Brothers' War*, 164; Omoigui, "The Midwest Invasion," 18–19.

Friendly reported that in Warri, 400–500 Igbos were killed by "civilian mobs," with a similar number slaughtered in Sapele.[42]

Having contained and then rolled back the Biafran offensive, the Federal Government escalated its conduct of the conflict from "police action" to all-out war. As the Second Division moved through the Midwest, its ranks were steadily increased by an influx of untrained Midwestern recruits, some of whom were likely motivated by resentment against their Igbo-speaking former neighbors, while others may simply have welcomed a regular paycheck. According to Haruna, "people just turned up, followed the wagon, and were given uniforms, given weapons ... "[43] These troops, added to the many others who also lacked serious training, formed a volatile force that rolled through several small towns on their way to the Niger. Knowing what had been happening, many community leaders organized collections of money and goods to be offered in formal welcomes to federal commanders as troops arrived. Although this did seem to appease the troops at times, there were still many reports of indiscriminate killing of civilians, assumed to be sympathizers or saboteurs.[44] By early October, the federal troops had pushed the Biafrans all the way to Asaba. After some fighting on the western outskirts of the town, the Biafrans crossed the Niger Bridge to Onitsha before blowing up the eastern spans behind them and preventing the federal forces from pursuing them, a situation that had disastrous consequences for Asaba.

Indeed, the invasion of the Midwest was a disaster for all the Midwest Igbos who, once the Biafrans had retreated were, in the words of John de St. Jorre, left "to face the red-eyed wrath of the civilians and Federal troops."[45] While the exact death toll is unknown, a senior editor at *Look* magazine estimated in 1968 that "perhaps 8,000 Ibo civilians died when the Midwest was 'liberated' by troops under Col.

---

[42] Alfred Friendly Jr., "City Shows Scars of the Nigerian War," *New York Times*, Sept. 26, 1967, 1, 3.
[43] Authors' interview with retired Gen. Ibrahim Haruna, April 11, 2016, Abuja.
[44] Uchendu, *Women and Conflict*.
[45] De St. Jorre, *The Brothers' War*, 173.

Murtala Muhammed."[46] Wole Soyinka, who had once tried in vain to broker a peace between the warring sides, dubbed the Midwest Igbos "the most vulnerable Nigerians,"[47] while Uchendu noted, "the clash in the Midwest, which was to be between the Nigerian and Biafran armies, evolved into a contest between the Nigerian army and Anioma civilians."[48] And of all the communities who were involuntarily caught up in the violence, none suffered more at the hands of troops than Asaba.

[46]   Jack Shepherd, "Memo from Nigeria: Old Headaches for our New President," *Look*, Nov. 26, 1968, 74.

[47]   Wole Soyinka, *The Man Died: Prison Notes*. London: Rex Collings, 1972, 75.

[48]   Uchendu, *Women and Conflict*, 70.

2   What Happened at Asaba?

When Celestina Isichei began her 50-mile journey from college to Asaba, she was one among the thousands of Easterners and Midwesterners who had decided to flee home. The Northern pogroms in 1966 had taken the lives of thousands, and the declaration of secession had left others feeling fearful so far from home. At her once harmonious college, Celestina and others of Igbo ethnicity had found herself taunted and insulted by fellow students, and she was happy to be leaving, even with her hopes of graduation dashed. When she arrived, her family was relieved to see her; they believed the sleepy town of Asaba would be a safe haven until a short war was over.

ASABA BEFORE THE WAR

Compared to the bustling and much larger (Biafran) market center of Onitsha, one mile across the Niger River Bridge, Asaba was a quiet town of about 10,000 people. Until 1965, when the bridge was completed, ferryboats were the only way for people to travel between the two towns, which emphasized the sense of difference between them (Figure 2.1). Asaba is made up of five distinct "quarters" (or *ebos*) – Umuezei, Ugbomanta, Umuagu, Umuaji, and Umuonaje – the originators of which were descended patrilineally from Asaba's legendary founder, Nnebisi. These in turn include about 30 villages (or *ogbes*), clustered around small open squares. Before the war, the majority of Asaba residents were "indigenes," claiming direct descent from Nnebisi. The highest ranking traditional position, the *Asagba*, is not a hereditary chiefdom; the role rotates among the five quarters. When the *Asagba* dies, the quarter that is next in line elects his successor from among its high-ranking

FIGURE 2.1 Niger riverbanks, looking toward Asaba, Asaba-Onitsha ferry crossing. Photo by Simon Ottenberg, c. 1959–1960. Simon Ottenberg Collection, EEPA 2000–007-0764, Eliot Elisofon Photographic Archives, National Museum of African Art, Smithsonian Institution.

leaders.[1] Each quarter had extensive agricultural lands; like other Nigerian communities, many of its people made a living through traditional farming and lived a peaceful, simple life:

> Well, life before the war was just kind of a normal life . . . It was, like, we are living in a communal environment . . . You can go to any house, you know? Take your food, no problem . . . In the night we, the little ones, would gather around our parents for moonlight stories . . . and moonlight play . . . At that time . . . seven to eight, every place is very dark. And then the moon comes out and we go to the village square, where we play and then, at night retire to our various homes.[2]

[1] For a detailed discussion of Asaba's history and traditional social structure, see Augustine N. Ndili, *Guide to the Customs, Traditions and Beliefs of Asaba People*, Asaba: His Bride Publications, 2010.

[2] Interview with Onyeogali Okolie, Dec. 13, 2009, Asaba.

However, Asaba also had a history that made it distinctive among other similar communities. Strategically located on bluffs overlooking the Niger, it had become an important river port during colonial expansion. In 1896, it was chosen as the administrative headquarters of the Royal Niger Company, making it briefly the de facto capital of what became Nigeria.[3] Missionaries settled early in Asaba; the subsequent embracing of Western-style education produced an educated middle class whose influence spread widely.[4] Writing in 1934, colonial administrator H. Vaux noted that Asaba, with a total population of around 5,500, had "one Government School, one Catholic School, one Convent, two C.M.S. Schools, one Salvation Army School, and a Catholic Seminary."[5] Indeed, Vaux described Asaba as "the cradle of Nigerian education ... for many years the only source from which a local supply of suitable men could be counted upon to oust Native Foreigners from higher Secretariat Posts in Government and Commerce."[6]

Before the war, many of these schools were well respected and thriving, staffed by local and missionary teachers, often with the support of foreign volunteers from organizations like the US Peace Corps and the UK Voluntary Service Overseas. One well-known school was (and still is) St. Patrick's College (SPC), a prestigious, Catholic-mission-run boys' high school, many of whose graduates go on to top universities in Nigeria and abroad. A girls' school, Anglican Girls Grammar School (AGGS), was run by the long-established Church Missionary Society (Figure 2.2). Carol Kimmons, a Peace Corps volunteer, remembered the school as "quiet ... the younger students used grass machetes to cut the grass in the school yard every day. On Sundays, the girls braided each other's hair."[7]

---

3   H. Vaux, "Intelligence Report on the Asaba Clan, Asaba Division," File No. 30927, Class Mark CSO 2614, Nigerian National Archive, Ibadan.

4   For details about the early history of Asaba, see Elizabeth Isichei, "Historical Change in an Ibo Polity: Asaba to 1885," *Journal of African History*, 10, 1969, 421–438.

5   Vaux, "Intelligence Report," 2.

6   Ibid., 1.

7   Carol Kimmons, e-mail to Elizabeth Bird, March 24, 2016.

FIGURE 2.2 Students at Asaba Girls' Grammar School perform
Shakespeare's *A Midsummer Night's Dream* – the "hole in the wall"
scene, 1963–1964. Photo by Carol Kimmons.

The girls followed British-style curriculum, including science and
performances of classic plays. In 1968, a letter to CMS from the
principal, Jane Backhouse (who Kimmons remembered as "a terrifying
and tough Anglican missionary)," noted the diversity of ethnicities in
the school: "These girls had learned to live together and to gain trust
and respect for others ... only the federal schools in Nigeria had such
a tribal mixture as Midwest schools."[8] Respected schools like these
took boarders from outside Asaba, emphasizing the recognition of the
town as an educational hub.

Asaba still prides itself on its history of producing professionals –
doctors, lawyers, teachers, and many high-ranking members of the
Civil Service – and a common claim is that the community has
produced more university professors than any comparable town.
The first premier of the Midwest Region, Dennis Osadebay, a poet
and intellectual, was an Asaba indigene and much-esteemed leader

[8]   No Author, "Letter from Diocese of Benin," *CMS Historical Record*, 1968, 1.

FIGURE 2.3 Midwest Premier Dennis Osadebay leads a motorcade
through the Cable Point area of Asaba during the December 1964 general
election campaign. Photo by Eric Strauss.

(Figure 2.3). Before the war, middle-class Asaba people were working
all over the country; many served in regional government offices in
Benin City and elsewhere, while others were professionals and entre-
preneurs in Northern towns like Kano and Kaduna, as well in the
Western Region. However far afield they might go, Asaba indigenes
keep a home in Asaba, where they expect to retire, die, and be buried.[9]
Indeed, Asaba indigenes include many who were actually born elsewhere, while retaining deep roots in their ancestral home.

As the war loomed, Asaba people had found themselves in an
increasingly difficult and complicated situation. Asaba was part of the
small, multi-ethnic Midwest Region; while ethnic tensions were
never far under the surface in Nigeria, people in the Midwest had
learned to get along, as students had at Celestina's college. Asaba

[9]   Daniel J. Smith, "Burials and Belonging in Nigeria: Rural-Urban Relations and Social
       Inequality in a Contemporary African Ritual," *American Anthropologist*, 106, 2004,
       569–579.

had never been part of Ojukwu's Biafra; indeed, leaders of the region officially favored the government's ideal of "One Nigeria."

At the same time, the people of Asaba were linguistically and culturally Igbo, and recognized an affinity with their cousins in the Eastern Region. They and other related communities had been known by colonial administration as the Western Igbos, although in more recent years, many had come to prefer the designation "Anioma;" we will return to a discussion of this identity in our final chapter.[10] Opinions about secession and the war ran the gamut in Asaba; many remained staunchly pro-unity and regarded Ojukwu as a traitor, while some firmly supported the Biafran cause. Others did not fully trust the government, believing it had condoned the previous atrocities against the Igbo in the North, yet preferred the idea of continued unity. Indeed, Asaba people took prominent roles on both sides of the conflict; Joseph Achuzia (known popularly as "Hannibal") became one of the most well-known commanders of the Biafran army, while Philip Asiodu, who was deeply committed to the principle of a united Nigeria, rose to become a permanent secretary serving in Gowon's war cabinet. But most people simply wanted to avoid trouble from either side. As Patience Chukura, a young mother in Asaba at the time, put it, "we're not politicians, we're not soldiers, we are just minding our business."[11]

Yet among many, there was a perception that neither side accepted them. The complicated nature of Asaba's identity was summed up by Asaba indigene Gertrude Ogunkeye, who before the war had been attending school in Enugu, the capital of the new Biafra:

> Those of us who were not core Igbos, who came from the Midwest, were singled out and ostracized ... and there was all this talk: "go back to where we are from, to the Midwest." ... As well, we were

[10]   Don C. Ohadike, *Anioma: A Social History of the Western Igbo People*, Athens: Ohio University Press, 1994.

[11]   Interview with Patience Chukura, Dec. 10, 2009, Lagos. See Egodi Uchendu, *Women and Conflict in the Nigerian Civil War*, Trenton, NJ: Africa World Press, 2007, for discussion of Anioma sympathy for Biafra.

hearing about the horrible things happening to Igbos in the West ...
I felt I really didn't belong anywhere because we are not core Igbo,
and yet the Nigerians thought we were Igbo anyway ... we felt safe
in Asaba ... You're neutral ... We really didn't have any sympathies
for the Biafrans ... We didn't have sympathies for Federal Troops
either.[12]

Celestina Isichei expressed similar sentiments: "we were like bats,
being neither mammals nor birds. The Biafrans called us Hausa Ibos,
and the Nigerian troops called us Ibos ... "[13]

Nevertheless, even before the arrival of troops from either side,
the war had already had its effect on Asaba. Its population had been
swollen by the arrival of refugees fleeing the killing in the North and
West, as well as those, like Gertrude's family, returning from the East
as war loomed. Coming home was the natural response to danger, and
families returned from all over the country. Joseph Nwajei was 15 and
living with his parents in Ibadan when the war began. In June 1967 his
father sent his mother and school-age brothers back to Asaba, where
they lived in a family compound with his grandfather, his two uncles,
and their families:

> My father's older brother, George, was a public service
> commissioner of the then-Midwestern Region ... he came back
> home with his wife, his younger children ... The compound was
> filled with kids ... Because there was nothing we could do, we just
> played all day long.[14]

THE WAR REACHES ASABA

The calm of everyday life was shattered early in the morning
of August 9, when Biafran troops crossed the Niger Bridge at Asaba.
While sudden, the arrival of the Biafrans was fairly uneventful. For

[12]   Interview with Gertrude Ogunkeye, Dec. 11, 2009, Lagos
[13]   Celestina Isichei-Isamah, *They Died in Vain*, London: CreateSpace Independent
        Publishing Platform, 2011, 30.
[14]   Interview with Joseph Nwajei, Oct. 10, 2009, Tampa, FL.

students at St. Patrick's College, on the outskirts of the town, it was a briefly exciting moment:

> There was a long column of troops in various vehicles ... enough time passed for us all to rush to the main gates, and we saw the troops ... I can remember some of them hanging on trucks wearing bedroom slippers. And some of us really wondered ... Much later, I knew there was a word for that – ragtag army.[15]

Further into town, Joseph Nwajei and his brothers watched the troops go by:

> It was very early in the morning. We just heard rumblings, so we knew something was up in the road. So, we all came out ... we saw soldiers. We saw troops and tanks, singing joyously and advancing, going towards Benin. That was all. And after they passed, we continued with school. Nothing happened.[16]

However, things soon changed. Following the Biafrans' occupation of the Midwest and their advance to the Western town of Ore, by late September reports were reaching Asaba that the federal troops had regained the initiative and were swiftly retaking the lost territory. Celestina Isichei recalled hearing on the radio the voice of Murtala Muhammed, announcing the recapture of Benin City on September 21, and stressing the need for civilians to help clear the "rebels" from the Midwest: "The mention of Asaba would have sent shivers down the spine of many indigenes," and at this point, many decided to leave, heading across the Niger or elsewhere.[17] By early October, the Biafrans were retreating in some disarray. Emmanuel Odiachi, then a young boy living in Agbor, between Benin City and Asaba, recalls the sight of the Biafrans fleeing through the town:

---

[15]   Interview with John Esenwa, Oct. 10, 2009, Tampa, FL.
[16]   Interview with Joseph Nwajei.
[17]   Celestina Isichei-Isamah, *They Died in Vain*, 31.

> I remember playing outside one day near the main road, and hearing
> lots of music coming, and there was a military lorry ... and all
> I could see was legs sticking out ... My mum rushed out and took
> me back to the house ... they were all talking ... these are the boys
> that were killed in Benin.[18]

By early October, the sound of fighting was heard on the outskirts of
Asaba, and by October 5, the Biafrans were retreating across the Niger
Bridge.

By now, fear was rising. As federal troops advanced, the town
was rife with accounts of what happened during the "liberation" of the
Midwest, where local mobs had gone on a bloody rampage against Igbo
communities. Asaba indigene Emmanuel Nwanze, then an 18-year-
old living with his aunt in Benin City, described the chaos that followed the arrival of Nigerian troops. Nwanze joined a crowd that
assembled to welcome the soldiers, but the mood against Igbos turned
ugly, and he ran home:

> I went into the back of the compound knowing that the house was
> no longer safe because everything had been vandalized ... the
> windows torn open, our foodstuff and the stove brought out and
> spread all over the ground. And then you could hear from around the
> corners – youths with soldiers ... hounding and hunting people out
> and you could see the people being dragged, even on the streets.
> Nude. They'd take them out for, uh, slaughter, we'll call it now.[19]

Many Igbos fled Benin, or went into hiding, as did Nwanze, who was
protected by a Yoruba neighbor who claimed to soldiers that he was his
son. Eventually, having spent time in prison camps, he made his way
back to Asaba several months later. Stanley Okafor, then a second-year
student at the University of Ibadan, was ordered home by his father, the
State Minister of Education in Benin; when Benin fell, his father escaped
home to Asaba. The mutual tolerance in the Midwest was collapsing.

[18]   Interview with Emmanuel Odiachi, Oct. 10, 2014, London.
[19]   Interview with Emmanuel Nwanze, Dec. 16, 2009, Benin City, Nigeria.

All this news was too much for some in Asaba, and many more began to flee, including the *Asagba, Obi* (Chief) Umejei Onyetenu.[20] According to Emmanel Chukwara:

> The tension was so much. Every place you see people gathering, discussing what was happening ... there is no security, there is danger. My mother-in-law ... was then at Onitsha, and I decided I should take my wife and my children [there] ... I was with my most senior brother, Christian Chukwara and my senior brother Edwin Chukwara, we were drinking along the road here when I took that decision.[21]

The decision to leave saved Chukwara's life, as we shall see.

Nevertheless, most of Asaba's population, whose leaders now included many current and retired high-ranking civil servants, maintained their allegiance to a united Nigeria. Many hoped that a July statement issued by a group of their leaders in support of "One Nigeria" and condemning secession would shield them from retaliation by returning federal forces.[22] In addition some must have also believed in the professionalism of the country's armed forces and may have been aware of General Gowon's Operational Code of Conduct, issued in July 1967. This laid out the principles that troops were fighting for national unity, observing the Geneva Conventions, and not conducting a jihad or religious war. It listed prohibitions on harming women and children, and treating all civilians humanely, even if they were hostile to the federal forces.[23] Gertrude Ogunkeye noted a sentiment shared by several community leaders:

---

[20] According to tradition, once installed the *Asagba* should never leave Asaba, so his departure was cause for concern, even anger.

[21] Interview with Emmanuel Chukwara, Dec. 16, 2009, Asaba. Emmanuel spelled the family name Chukwara, while his sister-in-law Patience spelled it Chukura; such variations are not uncommon.

[22] See *Daily Times* (no byline), "Asaba and Ika People Accept New Identity," July 24, 1967, 3.

[23] For text of the Code of Conduct, see Anthony H. M. Kirk-Greene, *Crisis and Conflict in Nigeria: A Documentary Sourcebook, 1966–1970, Vol. 1*, London: Oxford University Press, 1971, 455–457.

The Sunday before the horrible events of October, at mass the Reverend Father had said people were to stay calm and remain in their houses and just stock food and water because if there's going to be a war, it might take a while for things to calm down ... wait for the war to pass through Asaba and then your life can continue as normal.[24]

Even many who had witnessed firsthand the slaughter of Igbos by civilians in Benin City and elsewhere had faith that non-combatants would not be at risk from soldiers. According to Christopher Mkpayah, whose father had been killed in Jos during the 1966 pogroms,

> We weren't afraid because most of our fathers and our grandfathers, they fought the World Wars and everything, so they thought that we shouldn't run. That soldiers don't shoot somebody that is not carrying arms. They cannot just shoot civilians.[25]

The remaining Mkpayah family, like Celestina's father and many others, decided to stay put.

VIOLENCE COMES TO ASABA

The progress of federal troops toward Asaba could be measured by the approaching sound of heavy guns and the rattling of machine gun fire. A published eyewitness account describes 24 hours of "ferocious" shelling, during which Asaba suffered its first casualties.[26] According to Emmanuel Chukwara, his mother, Mgboke, whom he had left behind while taking his wife and children to safety, was the first person killed, when shells hit the family home. He discovered her death when he returned to Asaba to check on the rest of his family on October 5. Other accounts name the first casualties as two elderly pensioners,

[24]   Interview with Gertrude Ogunkeye, Dec. 11, 2009, Lagos.
[25]   Interview with Christopher Mkpayah, Dec. 10, 2009, Lagos.
[26]   Stanley I. Okafor, "The Nigerian Army and the 'Liberation' of Asaba: A Personal Narrative," in *The Nigerian Civil War and Its Aftermath*, ed. E. Eghosa, E. Osaghae, R. Onwudiwe, and R. Suberu, Ibadan, Nigeria: John Archers, 2002, 295.

Chief Ezeoba Njoteah and Eunice Chukwumah.[27] Approaching Asaba from along the Okpanam-Asaba Road, federal troops reached the outskirts of town on October 4, where they overcame some Biafran resistance before occupying the grounds of St. Patrick's College later that day (Map 2.1). Emmanuel Obi, whose family had recently returned from Benin City, saw some of the action firsthand:

> We were locked in. Why? Because right behind our house, the
> Biafran soldiers lay ambush, and were shooting the Nigerian
> soldiers on the other side. The Nigerian soldiers, on the other hand,
> were shelling right across our house to try to kill those guys.[28]

People in Asaba recall seeing fleeing Biafrans run through the streets, headed for the bridge, some discarding their uniforms as they ran. Muhammed's eventual goal was to take the strategically important town of Onitsha, but at this point in the operation, his instruction from Commander-in-Chief Gowon was that "under no circumstances were they to cross over through the bridge because we need the bridge ... if you try, they are going to blow it."[29] Troops under Col. Ike Omar Sanda Nwachukwu passed quickly down the main road of the town, and reached the bridge on Thursday, October 5, where they established mortar positions and assessed the situation (Figure 2.4). Retreating Biafran troops under Col. Joseph Achuzia had indeed placed explosives at the Onitsha end of the bridge, ready to thwart any federal advance (Figure 2.5).[30] Nwachukwu remembers that "common sense"

---

[27] Affidavit of Anyibuofu Onya-Onlanwah; affidavit of John Kanayo Hudson Oddittah. Both included in *Investigators' Report on a Complaint Laid Before the Directorate of The International Commission for the Study of the Crime of Genocide*, 1969, accessed at University of Oxford, Rhodes House, Mss Afr.s 2399. This report included sworn affidavits by three survivors of Asaba, given in Magistrates Court, Jan. 20, 1969. These testimonies were later included in *The Violations of Human and Civil Rights of Ndi Igbo in the Federation of Nigeria* (1966–1999), October 1999. Ohanaeze Ndigbo, a pan-Igbo rights group, presented this "Ohanaeze petition" to the Human Rights Violations Investigation Commission (known as the Oputa Panel). For more details of the Oputa Panel, see Chapter 5.

[28] Interview with Emmanuel Obi, Oct. 10, 2009, Tampa, FL.

[29] Interview with Gen. Yakubu Gowon, Oct. 10, 2016, Abuja.

[30] Joe O.G. Achuzia, *Requiem Biafra*, Asaba: Alcel Concerns, 2002 (2nd ed.), 86.

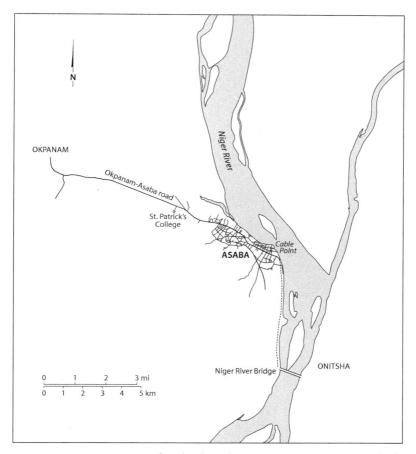

MAP 2.1 Location of Asaba along the Niger River. Troops approached via Okpanam-Asaba Road, heading to Cable Point, and then to the recently constructed Niger Bridge. The exact route from Cable Point to the bridge is unclear, since roads have changed significantly since then. Cartography by Bill Nelson.

would dictate that attempting to take troops across the bridge would be foolish: "When you capture a place, you consolidate."[31] However, Murtala Muhammed, who was "in a hurry to get the job done," was convinced that the Biafrans did not have enough explosives to blow up

[31]   Interview with retired Gen. Ike Omar Sanda Nwachukwu, Oct. 11, 2016, Lagos.

FIGURE 2.4 Col. Ike Omar Sanda Nwachukwu (center, looking through field glasses), and his troops survey the situation at the Niger bridge. Photo courtesy of Ahmed Adoke.

FIGURE 2.5 The Onitsha end of the Niger River Bridge, after it had been blown up by retreating Biafran troops. Photo by Ahmed Adoke.

the bridge and, in spite of arguments from his officers, he led a group of them onto to the bridge in a show of bravado. According to Nwachukwu, Muhammed had been advised by his army imam, Major Ndayawo, that the omens were in his favor: "I remember clearly on that day when we got to the crest of the bridge, he gave some kind of incantation and threw things into the water." Almost immediately afterwards, "there was this flash across the horizon, and then came this bang, and then dust, and I said I'd never seen a more beautiful sight ... that was the bridge gone, and we came under a hail of fire."[32] According to another observer, "the whole bridge shook;"[33] the Biafrans had destroyed several spans, leaving it impassable. As quickly became apparent, Muhammed's defiance of clear orders was only one of many disastrous decisions he made as commander of the Second Division.

Federal troops entered Asaba proper the same afternoon. As witness Gertrude Ogunkeye recalled,

> the village was very quiet, streets were empty, there was nothing
> there ... [then] I heard the sound of heavy traffic noise along the
> road ... We started hearing people speaking Hausa, Yoruba. And
> then looking out from the window, I saw people in helmets. They
> were not like walking normally; they were walking stealthily,
> hiding and coming.[34]

According to Paul Ogbebor, whose Eighth Brigade troops were among the first to enter Asaba, they were cautious, but all was calm at first. He stationed troops at St. Patrick's College, where had been a student just a few years before, and proceeded into town: "The natives were very friendly. They brought us yam, goat, everything they had, they were dancing, very elated."[35] Ogbebor reported that at the beginning of the occupation, there was a plan to evacuate civilians from the

---

[32]   Ibid.
[33]   Griot, "Roundabout, the View from the Bridge, Asaba," *West Africa*, Oct. 21, 1967, no. 2629, 1355.
[34]   Interview with Gertrude Ogunkeye.
[35]   Interview with retired Col. Paul Osa Ogbebor, Oct. 12, 2016, Benin City.

town, as a prelude to an organized attempt to clear out any remaining Biafran soldiers. Survivor Ify Uraih described how soon after troops arrived, soldiers ordered his family out of their home:

> So we came out with our hands raised in surrender . . . my parents and eight of us. They took us to the main road. There was a cattle truck there. They were putting other families in there, saying they would transport them to safety about 45 kilometers away from Asaba . . . When we got there the truck was full, so they said we should wait for the next truck. But no truck came, so they took us from that place and we walked to St. Patrick's College. The soldiers were there and there were many civilians. They camped us there for the night of the fourth, the fifth of October, and they were very nice. They gave us food, and they said to us, "Look, the federal troops don't harm people like that. If they wanted to kill us, they would have killed us." So, we were all totally relaxed.[36]

However, it is clear that not all the occupying troops were of the same mind, and if evacuation was the plan, it soon fell apart. Ogbebor himself must have seen the ominous signs of violence; on October 6, he posted soldiers to protect the family home of Frank Obi Ogosi, where he had stayed while a student at SPC. These soldiers remained there for some time, and no one in the family was harmed.[37] Meanwhile, groups of soldiers began going from house to house looting, demanding money, and rounding up boys and men accused of being Biafran sympathizers or, if they showed signs of having worn boots, of actually being Biafran soldiers (Figure 2.6).[38] Victoria Uraih, then a young teenager, recalls the troops barging into the family house and singling out her 18-year-old brother, Medua:

> As soon as he came out, they said he was a Biafran soldier . . . He didn't know what was happening. They asked him, Attention! He

---

[36]   Interview with Ify Uraih, Oct. 9, 2009, Tampa, FL.
[37]   Interview with Frank Obi Ogosi, Dec. 15, 2009, Asaba.
[38]   Affidavit of Francis Dike Okwudiafor, *Investigators' Report*, 1969.

FIGURE 2.6 Federal troops progress up a street in Asaba's Cable Point District, past houses destroyed by shelling. Photo by Bill Norris, October 1967, courtesy of *The Times*.

did attention. He said, "Hey, look at this, he's a soldier." Then my mother intervened, because my mother was a very vibrant woman, so she stood in the middle and said, "No, he's a student on holidays."[39]

Medua was spared, but many others were not so lucky, being shot on the spot or herded in groups to be killed elsewhere.

In some cases, it was apparent that soldiers were seeking specific individuals, many of whom were executed. Stanley Okafor, then a 19-year-old student, reported being taken to the local police station on Nnebisi Road (Asaba's main street), where a large crowd was forcibly assembled outside:

At the police station they would come around and they would say, do you know Mr. X, Mr. B, do you know Dr. this, or Dr. that, and do you know his house? If you take us to his house, you'll be free. You

[39]   Interview with Victoria Nwanze (née Uraih), Dec. 16, 2009, Benin City.

know, they had names they wanted to kill ... and once in a while they pick someone from the crowd and they go to the back of the house and you hear gunshots, and the crowd would wail ... [40]

Like Okafor, several others reported that those who had held Midwest government appointments in Benin City were specifically targeted. Thus Akunwata S.O. (Sylvester) Okocha, a senior civil servant in Benin City who had fled home to Asaba, reported in a self-published book (and in an interview with us)[41] that officers from Benin City arrived in Asaba with "a sheet filled with the names of senior prominent Asaba civil servants."[42] Lt. Igbinosun came to his door; Okocha speculated that his mission was "to clean out Asaba elites who dominated the civil service."[43] Okocha recognized the lieutenant, who "did not know I saw my name on the prepared list."[44] Lt. Igbinosum asked for directions to another home; Okocha sent him in the wrong direction, and fled into the bush. Later he learned that his brother Benedict Okocha had been singled out and killed, possibly mistaken for him. Others provided similar accounts; Joseph Nwajei, for example, said troops were looking for his uncle George Nwajei, a prominent civil servant, even though there were other uncles present in the family compound. Indeed, they removed George and summarily executed him.[45]

Others report indiscriminate group killings,[46] and a horrific episode when youths were lined up at the soccer field, ordered to dig

[40] Interview with Stanley Okafor, Oct. 12, 2011, Ibadan; Interview with Medua Uraih, Dec. 13, 2009, Asaba.
[41] Interview with Akunwata S.O. (Sylvester) Okocha, Dec. 13, 2009, Asaba.
[42] Akunwata S.O. Okocha, *The Making of Asaba: A Compendium of over Sixty-Five Years of Patient Research within and without Africa*, Asaba: Rupee-Com Publishers, 2013, 193. Okocha kept records of the events in Asaba, eventually turning them over to his nephew, Emma Okocha, who used them as the basis of his book, *Blood on the Niger*. The records are now lost.
[43] Akunwata S.O. Okocha, *The Making of Asaba*, 193.
[44] Ibid.
[45] Interview with Joseph Nwajei. See also, interview with Victor Izegbu, described in Chapter 3, which also mentions the list of targeted names.
[46] Interview with Patience Chukura.

a grave, stand in it, and then shot. Nicholas Azeh, then 17 years old, almost died in that incident, recalling the helplessness of the victims:

> Run away? The whole town was filled; there were soldiers. Where are you running to? We're just like zombies, like robots. We've lost our willpower ... The whole town was littered with soldiers, these horrible-looking people. Some were screaming, some were crying. It was a hopeless situation. It was a hopeless situation.[47]

Several hundred people were executed in groups all over town. Males who had been singled out were either shot on the spot or taken to the police station, the High Court on Okpanam road, the soccer field, or the riverbank, where they were executed. Witnesses remembered seeing the streets littered with corpses. Many families fled, while others hid in the ceilings of their houses. Patrick Okonkwo recalled that his compound was crowded with extended family members who had fled home, when soldiers entered and shot his two brothers, a cousin, and two other relatives. His father buried them in shallow graves in the compound.[48]

Fabian Oweazim, then 12 years old, describes being at the home of Michael Chukwudebe Ugoh, Secretary of the Senior Age Grade Council, when troops arrived, looking for another community leader, *Ogbueshi* (Chief) Leo Okogwu. The troops proceeded to harass and humiliate the family:

> "You have money, Okogwu. Bring me money." Mrs. Ugoh went somewhere where she had kept some money ... and brought a can of Ovaltine beverage that she had stuffed money in ... and gave it to the guy. The guy stuffed them in his bag. One of the soldiers with him – he had two – was literally crying. He said, "Boss, it's okay. Let's go. Let's go. Let's go." He curled his whip on the face of the guy and told him to shut up. At this point, he told Mr. Ugoh ... to roll on

47 Interview with Nicholas Azeh, Oct. 5, 2011, Asaba.
48 Interview with Patrick Okonkwo, June 27, 2010, Asaba.

the ground . . . The man rolled on the ground . . . When he stood up, he must have been dizzy. He fell.[49]

After meeting up briefly with two of his brothers, Edwin and Christian, Emmanuel Chukwara fled to join his family. His sister-in-law Patience, 27, married to Edwin (Eddie), and pregnant with their fourth child, described what happened on October 6:

> Somebody came looking for my brother-in-law and said that the Federal troops have come into Asaba, and they were burning houses . . . you open the door and tell them that no Biafran troop was there – then the house would be burnt, everything would be burnt.[50]

People who went into the streets were stopped, and soldiers gathered men together:

> My husband and brother, and all those, about 400 people who were following them, they were shot in front of the police station at Asaba. That made me hysterical . . . I held onto the person I saw, the soldier, I said, "Why did you kill my husband?" . . . The man with the butt of the gun hit me on the chest and said, "Woman, if you're not careful, you'll get killed as well." . . . Papa – that's my father-in-law – when he heard that his two sons were killed, he went out . . . They shot him. They killed him . . . We were in fear that they were going to wipe out everybody in Asaba, especially male children.[51]

When Emmanuel eventually returned to Asaba, he had lost both parents and four brothers (Eddie, Christian, Dennis, and Samson). Many survivors gave vivid accounts of acts of brutality carried out against individuals and groups:

> On the main road, I just heard one young boy, a secondary school student, he was . . . begging. He was saying things like, "Please,

---

49   Interview with Fabian Oweazim, Oct. 10, 2009, Tampa, FL.
50   Interview with Patience Chukura.
51   Ibid.

come and tell them I'm not a soldier, come and tell them I'm not
a soldier" ... Then I heard this shot, pop, and the boy screamed ...
and said in our language, "They've shot me, they've shot me" ...
and they were kicking him, lying on the ground ... with a gunshot
wound. The next thing I heard was, uh, something like
(*indescribable noise*). And I looked again, and the lorry had gone
over him.[52]

On the evening of October 6, in an attempt to end the violence, the
Asagba-in-Council,[53] a group comprising members of the most senior
age grades (approximately 50–70 years old), along with the town's
chiefs and other senior leaders, met to discuss the best ways to impress
on the troops that Asaba had played no role in the Biafran incursion
and welcomed the return of federal forces. *Obi* Okwuarue, as well as
Mr. F.O. Isichei, Celestina's father, addressed the meeting. Adopting
a strategy that had been used in other Midwest towns,[54] they decided
that each of the town's five quarters would raise a levy of £50 for the
troops, while the *Omu* of Asaba, the most important women's leader,
would present a traditional woven cloth to their commander.[55]
Immediately a first donation of £50 to pay for drinks was delivered
to a federal officer, who expressed regret for the number of civilians
killed by what he called "stray bullets."[56] Early the next morning four
men from another quarter were dispatched to deliver their contribution, and when they failed to return another group of four was sent to
find out what had happened. They also vanished.[57] On the 6th, community leaders ordered town criers with gongs to summon everyone
to assemble the next day to welcome federal troops and offer a pledge
to "One Nigeria." People were encouraged to wear *akwa ocha*, the

[52]   Interview with Gertrude Ogunkeye.
[53]   For details of traditional Asaba governance, see Akunwata S.O. Okocha, *The Making
of Asaba*.
[54]   E. Uchendu, *Women and Conflict*, p. 76, notes that several Midwest communities had
staged formal shows of support for "One Nigeria," hoping to avoid reprisals.
[55]   Affidavit of John Kanayo Hudson Oddittah, *Investigators' Report*, 1969.
[56]   Affidavit of Francis Dike Okwudiafor, *Investigators' Report*, 1969
[57]   Affidavit of Anyibuofu Onya-Onianwah, *Investigators' Report*, 1969.

ceremonial white, woven clothing that signifies peace, and to make banners declaring loyalty to Nigeria. Some also chalked "One Nigeria" on the outside of their homes.[58] Traditionally, Asaba people performed this kind of processional dance for all important events and festivals; residents would begin from each of their home villages, before gradually joining the main parade until the entire town was participating. Fabian Oweazim recalls that he was ordered to bring a typewriter to Mr. Oguh, who typed the welcome address to the troops and had it sent to a leader in another quarter. Thus the word went out. Another witness recalled that criers informed him that the announcement was made at the order of occupying troops;[59] many believed this would be "the last painful sacrifice that we would be called upon to make,"[60] and some of those who had fled into the bush returned to town.[61] The Uraih family, and others camped at St. Patrick's College, came back home.

THE OCTOBER 7 MASSACRE

Although there was much trepidation and some refused to participate, hundreds of men, women, and children – including some who had originally fled to the bush – assembled for a parade. Witnesses report both traditional criers with gongs and vans with loudspeakers, calling everyone to participate. Luke Enenmoh recalls that the "chief information officer" from Benin City, an Asaba man named Frederick Konwea, was on one of these vans, which helped assuage some people's anxieties.[62]

[58]   Interview with Catherine Odiwe, Oct. 7, 2011, Asaba.
[59]   Affidavit of John Kanayo Hudson Oddittah, *Investigators' Report*, 1969.
[60]   Affidavit of Francis Dike Okwudiafor, *Investigators' Report*, 1969. None of the survivors we interviewed were able to give specifics about the negotiations and planning for the march, although many knew such meetings took place. Most were children, teenagers or adults in their 20s or 30s at the time, and thus would not have been part of the planning process; they were simply summoned to participate in the march. The affidavits written in 1969 are thus important in reconstructing these details, since men who were mature leaders in 1967 are almost all now dead.
[61]   Ibid.
[62]   Interview with Luke Enenmoh, Oct. 10, 2014, London. He noted that in hindsight, he believed Konwea was coerced into participating.

FIGURE 2.7   Members of the extended Isichei family at the ordination of Father Patrick Isichei (center, parents Flora and Francis Okafor Isichei on either side). Others pictured include Osi (first row standing, far right; Emmanuel (next to Flora), both killed at Asaba; Celestina (next to Osi); Victor Izegbu (back row, far right). Asaba, 1966. Photo courtesy of Victor Izegbu.

Others were dragged out from their home by soldiers and ordered to participate. Celestina Isichei's father lived in one of the grandest homes in Asaba, a compound that included a main brick-built house and several outbuildings. The family – which included her parents, older brother Emma with his wife and small child, younger brother Osi, and sisters – had felt relatively safe (Figure 2.7). Her father was an influential man, and only a year before, the family had celebrated the ordination of her brother Patrick as a Catholic priest. Now they were cowering as bullets began to hit their home. Osi and his friend Callistus, then 16-year-old students at St. Patrick's College, hid under beds:

> We were besieged ... then they rushed into the house. Panic made my brother and his friend rush out ... They said they were Biafran soldiers ... we pleaded that they were not. I don't know if they were drunk, or under the influence of drugs ... [63]

[63]   Interview with Celestina Isichei-Isamah, Oct. 10, 2014, London.

The soldiers ordered the family to leave, and they obeyed. Seeing a group of women had gathered for the forced dance outside the gates of the compound, they tried to join them:

> Callistus and Osi were running in front; first of all Callistus was dragged out and shot ... Osi tried to mingle among the women ... they pulled him out ... and he was shot down. I fell on him, thinking he would wake up. I shook him ... [64]

Celestina had no choice but to continue on the road with the women. With community elders in front, up to 4,000 townspeople participated. Many gathered by a large tree across from the High Court on Nnebisi Road, where they were joined by groups coming out from houses throughout the five quarters of Asaba (Map 2.2). Christopher Mkpayah, a St. Patrick's College student, was anxiously waiting in his home, having already witnessed the death of a school friend:

> After some time we started hearing a dancing group ... One Nigeria, One Nigeria, One Nigeria, One Nigeria ... and some people, relations, were running into the house, coming from another village ... they now told us, they have started killing people, and this dancing group that are coming, you should go and join them. That the soldiers said we must come down to welcome ... I said, let us go, myself and my cousin ... So as we are coming out towards the Nnebisi Road ... the dancing group ... soldiers surrounded them, were guiding them, that is Nigerian soldiers, carrying guns ... Then we all raised up our hands and were shouting, One Nigeria, One Nigeria, and we continued. [65]

The crowd advanced along the main Nnebisi Road past St. Joseph's Catholic Church. Any expectation that these gestures of goodwill would appease the troops was quickly dashed. As Mkpayah noted, marchers were flanked by federal soldiers to prevent them from fleeing, and witnesses report that they would also randomly select

[64]   Ibid.
[65]   Interview with Christopher Mkpayah.

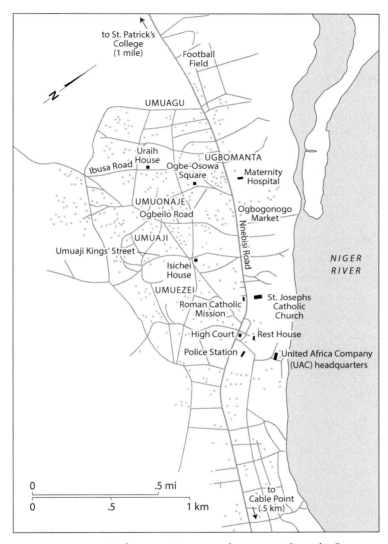

MAP 2.2 Asaba, 1967. Townspeople came out from the five quarters, to parade along Nnebisi Road, ending in the massacre at Ogbe-Osowa. Other massacre sites – the High Court, Police Station, and football field – are also marked, as are the locations of the Isichei and Uraih family houses. Cartography by Bill Nelson.

males and execute them in full view of participants, as they did with Osi Isichei. Survivors recalled seeing dozens of bodies, including that of one of the town criers, along with the mangled bodies of the four who had been sent earlier to deliver money.[66] Once the crowd reached the corner of Ogbogonogo and Ogbeke markets, troops separated out women and small children, many of whom were corralled into the maternity hospital on Nnebisi road, while the men and boys of around 12 and above were channeled between two rows of soldiers down the side road that led to the square at Ogbe-Osowa, a village in the Asaba quarter of Ugbomanta. As the violence escalated, some federal officers, like Paul Ogbebor, tried to intervene:

> I was coming on my jeep, and I saw a boy being taken away to be shot and the mother held him by the waist and then I came out and asked for this nonsense to be stopped. And when they refused, I cocked my gun, said don't do it or I'll kill you. I managed to save some lives there ... we contacted our headquarters at Umenede, saying what should we do?[67]

However, things were now out of control. Ogbebor reported that he left the scene to join his own troops, who were camped on the outskirts of town. At this point, witnesses describe mothers attempting to protect young sons:

> Women who came with their sons were removing their skirts and gloves to disguise, so that their male children ... they are no longer men, but women. So when I saw this scenario going on and I felt something is wrong. If these women can disguise their children, and my mother is not here, what do I do? And I looked at the whole place, there is nowhere for escape.[68]

The men and boys were kept moving into the open area:

---

[66]   Affidavit of John Kanayo Hudson Oddittah; affidavit of Anyibuofu Onya-Onianwah, *Investigators' Report*, 1969.

[67]   Interview with retired Col. Paul Osa Ogbebor, Oct. 12, 2016, Benin City.

[68]   Interview with Peter Okonjo, Dec. 14, 2009, Asaba.

When we got there, they said we should now stop ... As we stopped
there, they now surrounded us, sat us all down, they start whipping
us ... The next thing we saw, the officer ... spoke in Hausa. I was
born in the North, so I heard what he said ... He said they should
take us 10 by 10 and start firing us. I said, we are finished. Some
people said they are just trying to threaten us ... That officer now
picked out somebody from the midst, shot him, picked out another
person, shot him ... then people were praying, Father, forgive them,
they don't know what they did.[69]

According to another witness,

Twenty of our men were selected and lined up in front of us and told
as follows, "Today, I be your God. Me first, God second. God give
you life, me I go takem. Two minute time you go die." ... Two
minutes afterwards these 20 men were shot. Another 20 were
picked up and the same ritual followed.[70]

Apparently tiring of killing individuals with rifles, the soldiers then
readied machine guns, both mounted on trucks and freestanding, and
mass shooting began. Fifteen-year-old Ify Uraih had joined the parade
with his father and three older brothers, Paul, Emmanuel (Emma), and
Medua; he described what happened:

Some people broke loose and tried to run away. My brother was
holding me by the hand; he released me and pushed me further into
the crowd ... They shot my brother in the back, he fell down, and
I saw blood coming out of his body. And then the rest of us ... just
fell down on top of each other. And they continued shooting, and
shooting, and shooting ... I lost count of time, I don't know how
long it took ... After some time there was silence. I stood up ... my
body was covered in blood, but I knew that I was safe. My father was
lying not far away; his eyes were open but he was dead.[71]

---

[69]   Interview with Christopher Mkpayah.
[70]   Affidavit of Anyibuofu Onya-Onianwah, *Investigators' Report*, 1969.
[71]   Interview with Ify Uraih.

Exactly how many died in this single incident is unclear; around 700–800 seems likely,[72] in addition to many who had died in the previous days. Sporadic shooting continued for hours until darkness caused the soldiers to disperse. Survivors, including Ify Uraih, lay still under the heap of bodies for a long time before feeling it was safe to wriggle out and run into the nearby bush.

> My cousin said we should wait till it was dark so that we could go together, and I agreed. You could hear the sound of the injured crying. One man, who heard us talking, he was as old as my father. He had his hand almost severed from the rest of his body. And he told me that he had a knife, that I should please help him amputate the hand ... I told him I could not do it. He died later. I knew his children.[73]

Ify Uraih and his cousin ran to their grandmother's house, where they found his sisters and three younger brothers. He told them their father and three older brothers were dead; later he learned that Medua had survived, gravely wounded, and had been carried to the bush by his friend. Community elders Michael Ugoh and Leo Okogwu were among large numbers of the leading age grades to die. With all the men in hiding, it was left to women and children to attempt to retrieve the bodies of their fathers, brothers, husbands, and other relatives and then drag them back to their compounds for burial.[74] Joseph Nwajei, the boy who had returned with family from Ibadan, had escaped into the bush from the family compound after watching the earlier

---

[72]   No precise number of casualties has been established. In 1981, the Asaba Development Council compiled a list of names of 373 confirmed dead, but acknowledged that many more were not included (a point our interviews have supported). Eyewitness estimates range from a minimum of 500 to well over 1,000. Mensah's *Investigators' Report* (1969) estimated 2,000, although this probably included the killings over several days. In October 1968, David Scanlon of Quaker Relief Services reported that 759 men and boys had been massacred in Asaba after "the recapture of the city" the previous year, although no source is cited. (Relief report to American Friends Service Committee, Philadelphia, Oct. 3, 1968, AFSC Archives, Philadelphia.)

[73]   Interview with Ify Uraih.

[74]   Traditionally, the family compound is the appropriate place for burial, rather than a cemetery.

execution of his uncle George, a prominent civil servant. When he returned a few days later, he learned of the death of his two brothers, aged 12 and 17, in the mass shooting:

> Mum told me that in the evening hours of the 7th, she had to go and look for their corpses at the mass place where they were shot ... Mum, in the evening, was able to identify their corpses, took them in a wheelbarrow, pushed them to the family house, where they were buried. So, I never saw their corpses, I never saw their bodies.[75]

Most victims, however, were dumped in mass graves or thrown into the Niger. Few people had any opportunity to conduct requisite burial practices – an affront that is deeply resented to this day. When it was safe to move about, Frank Ijeh, a local Red Cross worker, enlisted surviving men to dig hurried, shallow graves wherever they found bodies around the town: "There are so many, I cannot remember. So many, so many, so many."[76] In spite of these efforts, many lay unburied for several days. Interviewed in 1977, a Mrs. Mordi reported that "for nearly two days ... the soldiers wouldn't let us come near ... without opening fire. It was only when the stench of decaying corpses was all over the place that the soldiers relented ... "[77] She retrieved her husband's body, but not that of a Catholic lay brother, Ignatius Barmah, who had died beside him. She was able to put *tinyele'a*, a white cloth, over him – an important ceremonial act usually done by close relatives. Esther Nwanze recalled how wives went searching for their husbands, dragging them home if they could find them: "Some dragged two days before they reached home."[78]

As more people began to trickle back into town, it became urgent to dig mass graves for the many unclaimed bodies. Patrick Obelue, then 13 years old, recalled,

[75] Interview with Joseph Nwajei.
[76] Interview with Frank Ijeh, Dec. 13, 2009, Asaba.
[77] Patrick A.C. Isichei, "Ex-Seminarian Ignatius Bamah in Asaba (c. 1900–67)," in *Varieties of Christian Experience in Nigeria*, ed. Elizabeth Isichei, London: MacMillan, 1982, 183.
[78] Interview with Esther Nwanze, Oct. 7, 2011, Asaba.

Some were already decomposing, where you can poke somebody, and their head would roll off. And we just put them into one grave, there was no coffin, nothing, nothing ... We were the youths of the village. Just dug shallow graves, and then put them there ... Everywhere was stinking ... We knew it was our duty at that time to bury the dead.[79]

Emeka Okonkwo was a small child in 1967, but recalls that his father also helped bury the dead: "He left the house with shovel, and he took this scented leaf and put it in his nostrils. That would enable them to stand the stench."[80]

In a chilling account of the massacre's aftermath, Felix Obi described his first ever encounter with death, as he tried to return home from hiding, and his path was blocked by a heap of dead bodies:

I could recognize some of them, including one of my uncles. Part of his face was removed by a bullet, but I could recognize him because he was a tall, huge man.

Felix could hear bullets flying not far away, and in panic, he began to climb over the heap. "In the process, even some brain matter stained my leg. I remember trying to use sand to rub off blood and – you know." As Felix continued toward home,

So as I moved on, two people [soldiers] were just sitting and drinking palm [wine]. They said, "Who are you?" I said, "Please, I am going home" ... When I looked at them, they were sitting on a corpse. The corpse had been drained by rain, it was swollen, and they used that as their seat. They were drinking palm. I was looking at them, I didn't know whether I was dreaming or I was still in this world.[81]

---

79   Interview with Patrick Obelue, Dec. 12, 2009, Asaba.
80   Interview with Emeka Okonkwo, June 28, 2010, Asaba.
81   Interview with Felix Obi, Dec. 15, 2009, Asaba.

Celestina Isichei also witnessed the "heaps of bodies" at Ogbe-Osowa, among them her older brother Emma. Eventually she made her way back to her home, and with the help of a soldier, she buried Osi in a shallow grave inside the compound.

THE IMMEDIATE AFTERMATH

The first week of October 1967 was a time of chaos and fear for the people of Asaba. Over the course of several days, it is likely that considerably more than 1,000 people were killed, although the exact number will never be known. By far the majority of those who died were male, but there are many accounts of women also being killed. For instance, Egodi Uchendu described the death of an elderly woman who, after grabbing the soldier who had just shot her husband at Ogbe-Osowa, was immediately killed herself. She also notes the killing of an 80-year-old woman who was burned to death in her home, and a six-year-old girl shot in her house with her brother.[82] Rose Eziunor Mordi was a 27-year-old staff nurse trained in the UK who had returned to Asaba with her husband – the well-known labor leader, socialist, and nationalist politician, Nduka Eze – and two small children.[83] Rose was the first child and daughter of *Obi* Okechukwu Mordi, a red cap chief. Chuck Nduka-Eze, a young child at the time, describes what he was told about the death of his mother:

> ... She had been near Ogbe-Osowa and observed the soldiers brutalizing and harassing people along the road and felt unable to ignore them and walk on ... She intervened, pointing out that their conduct was unacceptable; the soldiers reacted violently and shot her on the spot.[84]

---

[82] Uchendu, *Women and Conflict.*

[83] For more information about the life and contributions of Nduka Eze, see Kingsley Azuh, "Nduka Eze: A Life Dedicated to Selfless Public Service," *ThisDay*, Oct. 2, 2016: www.thisdaylive.com/index.php/2016/10/02/nduka-eze-a-life-dedicated-to-selfless-public-service/

[84] Chuck Nduka-Eze, personal communication, July 3, 2016.

FIGURE 2.8 A home in Cable Point, Asaba, after the arrival of federal troops. Photo by Bill Norris, October 1967, courtesy of *The Times*.

Akunwata (Sylvester) Okocha also noted that women were killed when they refused soldiers' sexual advances, a point also confirmed by several interviewees.[85]

Witnesses paint a picture of soldiers who were out of control, intent on looting, and often behaving in a randomly sadistic way (Figure 2.8). Joseph Nwajei, who had run away from his family compound after witnessing the execution of his uncle, found himself near a stream with his cousin, where from the cover of bush he saw soldiers who had rounded up men and boys:

> Soldiers just shoot you, you know, line you up, and they were defecating themselves because of the extreme fear. Some would pee on themselves. The soldiers just thought it was fun. They just kept on shooting at them.[86]

[85]   Akunwata S.O. Okocha, *The Making of Asaba*, 192. Interviews with Felicia Nwandu, June 28, 2010, Asaba; Nkandelin Maduemezia, June 23, 2010, Asaba; Esther Nwanze.
[86]   Interview with Joseph Nwajei.

Gertrude Ogunkeye described how her cousin was stopped by soldiers as he returned to his family compound:

> they questioned him, told him he was an escaping Biafran soldier, that he had met his Waterloo, and told him to dig his grave ... As he was digging, my female cousin was begging them to spare him, telling them that he was a student at a secondary school ... he was digging this grave with bits and pieces of items he saw in the compound. So when he had dug a grave they felt was okay, they asked him to lie in it, and they shot him inside of the grave. And having shot him, they now told my female cousin to cover it.[87]

Soldiers seemed especially intent on stealing cars and other valuable items. Stanley Okafor, who escaped injury by hiding in the ceiling of his home for two weeks, saw soldiers carrying away "radiograms, electric cookers, refrigerators ... they stole cars, they stole dismantled car engines ... beds, mattresses ... "[88] His father Benedict, a high-ranking education official, had advised the family to "be polite and nice to the soldiers ... entertain them if you need to ... he wasn't going to go into hiding. He thought that soldiers were human beings." Indeed, when soldiers arrived, Benedict tried to make peace:

> My dad had come home with an officer, he brought a Hausa with him ... one of his students at the teacher's college from earlier in his career ... we had some whisky – White Horse – the guy took the rest of what was left in the bottle.[89]

Benedict then offered the officer a lift, and they left in his car. Not long after, the family found his body, shot through the chest. Three of Benedict's brothers were also killed during the occupation. Stanley Okafor recalled that long after the war, the car was recovered in Lagos, identified by the fact that his young brother had proudly carved his father's initials on the fender of the brand new Peugeot.

[87]   Interview with Gertrude Ogunkeye.
[88]   Interview with Stanley Okafor.
[89]   Ibid.

Many survivors remember the federal soldiers as rapacious and terrifying, conforming to popular stereotypical images of Northern, Hausa people as tall, very dark, and often bearing distinctive facial scars. Along with the recruits from the West and Midwest, the federal army also had contingents of soldiers from the border areas with Chad, known for their fearsome appearance.[90] They were (and still often are) referred to as *gwodogwo*, a derogatory term that suggests the soldiers were large, hulking, and almost ape-like in their movement:[91]

> Their eyes were so bloody red that you dared not look at their eyes. Whether they were all on some kind of drugs or whatever, I have no idea, but they didn't look human.[92]

But although the *gwodogwo* soldiers are perhaps remembered most vividly, most of the occupying troops were actually recruited from other areas of the country.

SOLDIERS AS UPSTANDERS: CAPTAIN MATTHIAS

Even amid the violence, it is clear that not all federal troops took part in or supported the killings, and that Paul Ogbebor's intervention to save the life of a young boy was not unique. Several survivors recalled seeing troops arguing about whether or not to kill people, along with other instances of individual officers and common soldiers intervening directly to save and protect civilians. For instance, Francis Dike Okwudiafor recounted how he was part of a group that was marched to be executed in a field next to the High Court on the Okpanam road, when at the last moment a federal major intervened and had them escorted back to their homes to ensure their safety.[93] Sometimes, these specific acts of mercy happened only because of past relationships. Charles Ugboko described meeting an old classmate from Benin

---

[90]   John Oyinbo, *Nigeria, Crisis and Beyond*, London: Charles Knight, 1971, 86.
[91]   E.g. Fabian Oweazim recalled them as "like giants;" Christopher Mkpayah and Ify Uraih describe the facial scars and the Hausa language.
[92]   Interview with Emmanuel Obi.
[93]   Affidavit of Francis Dike Okwudiafor.

City, Patrick Idahosa, then a major in the federal forces, who was rounding up men:

> I called his name. He was shocked . . . he said, "Charles! What are you doing here?" I told him, "Your men are holding me." He said, "Come out of the line."[94]

Ugboko protested that he needed to find his younger brother, but Idahosa dragged him out of the line and had him taken to a place of safety. According to Ugboko, Idahosa was clearly among those gathering people to be killed, and he never saw his 15-year-old brother again. Patience Chukura reported that when ordered to shoot her husband and brother-in-law, a soldier refused, telling his colleague that he knew the men. He paid dearly for this admission; the other man responded by executing the soldier before killing the Chukuras.[95]

However, some soldiers, perhaps motivated by professionalism, or revulsion at what was going on, acted with genuine kindness and compassion. Patrick Okonkwo spoke gratefully of a soldier named Joseph, who intervened when others threatened to shoot his father, who was attempting to bury five relatives shot earlier:

> Joseph was the one who challenged the other one: "If you shoot, me, I will shoot you. Look at that man today – he lost five of his children, and you want to kill him . . . Let that man be today." So he spared our father.[96]

Later, Joseph returned to the compound and protected the family from further harm. Nicholas Azeh, who reported the incident where dozens of youths dug their own graves, had just covered the body of a boy shot before him. He lived to tell the tale because of an officer he described as his "messiah," who had just arrived on the scene:

---

[94] Interview with Charles Ugboko, Dec. 12, 2009, Lagos.
[95] Interview with Patience Chukura.
[96] Interview with Patrick Okonkwo.

> He spoke English. Not Hausa. When he saw us he was amazed . . .
> I remember him saying "What have these young boys done? Leave
> them alone!" . . . He was an officer, a decent young man . . . He said
> leave them alone. They obeyed.[97]

While the identity of that officer is unknown, one name is well
remembered in Asaba. We heard numerous accounts of a Captain
Matthias, who seems to have singlehandedly prevented many
deaths. Witnesses did not know his full name, but he has since
been identified as Capt. Matthias Ogbude.[98] Red Cross worker
Frank Ijeh reported how after the massacre, when he had boldly
sought help from an army platoon, Matthias stepped in to prevent
him from being shot.[99] Luke Enenmoh described how in the chaos
right after the soldiers arrived, as youths were being dragged out and
accused of being Biafrans, Matthias arrived and ordered the violence
to stop. Later, as people assembled from all over for the dance to
Ogbe-Osowa, he diverted a large number to a family compound that
was in the area he was commanding, telling them not to continue on
to Ogbe-Osowa. Luke Enenmoh was in this group, which he estimated at several hundred.[100] From the compound, they heard the
sound of machine guns; eventually Matthias returned and told them
they could go back to their homes; none were hurt in the October 7
massacre.[101] Ironically, this compound belonged to the family of
Robert Uraih, who had already left for the dance. Robert and two of
his sons died at Ogbe-Osowa, but the surviving family members
reported that Matthias protected them when they returned home,
with one seriously wounded. He was perhaps an unlikely hero: "he
had deep tribal marks down his cheeks, probably from the same tribe
as Gen Gowon. He looked very, very scary, but his actions didn't

[97]   Interview with Nicholas Azeh.
[98]   Personal online communication to Elizabeth Bird from writer Igbonekwu
        Ogazimorah, July 2, 2016. We have no other confirmation of Matthias's identity, so
        we cannot be completely certain.
[99]   Interview with Frank Ijeh.
[100]   Interview with Luke Enenmoh.
[101]   Interview with Medua Uraih; also interview with Catherine Odiwe.

support his appearance."[102] By all accounts, Matthias was a professional soldier and around 30 years old, a little older than many of the other men (and officers).

Captain Matthias's influence apparently extended to those who served under him. Michael Ogbogu reports meeting a group of soldiers as he headed to his village in Asaba:

> One said, where are you coming from? And I said ... I'm going back to my village. And they said well, are you a soldier? I said, no, I was never a soldier and I would never be a soldier. They said you're lying, you should undress. They stripped me nude, looked at my legs. And someone wanted to shoot me. One man said no, don't shoot. Let's interrogate him. So they said how old are you? I said I'm a student. They said you're lying. They said I should lie down on the road. So I lay down on the road. Nude ...

The soldiers stole money from him, and he assumed he would die. Then an officer he described as the "second of Matthias" arrived. "He asked, 'Who is this young man? Is this a gun of the army we captured?' I said that I was never a soldier, and I've never been a soldier." The officer then ordered the troops to return his clothing and he explained what he was doing. "So the man said, 'okay, if I find out that you are not a true person of this Asaba, I will kill you.' I said, fair and good.'"

While some interviewees had overwhelmingly negative memories of the federal troops, others wanted to make sure that examples of restraint and professional conduct were noted and remembered.

THE OCCUPATION BEGINS

In the weeks following October 7, the worst killing stopped. However, federal soldiers remained in Asaba as a series of attempts were made to cross the Niger into Onitsha. On October 12, Murtala Muhammed decided to cross by boat, against the advice of his brigade

[102]   Interview with Luke Enenmoh.

commanders. According to Patrick Idahosa, one of his officers, he was furious, declaring, "I will not sit here in Asaba and see those bastards over there."[103] Some of his officers refused to participate, and Muhammed pressed on. There are many reports of his continuing reliance on soothsayers for guidance: "They would just sit down without any plan for war but would be praying and chanting that today is a good/bad day for attack."[104] Soldiers of the Eighth Brigade, under Col. Francis Aisida, commandeered an abandoned ferry and other crafts, and were sent across the river to secure the bridgehead to Onitsha, with the plan that the Sixth Brigade would come behind and take Onitsha.[105] However, the Eighth failed to establish the bridgehead, and the crossing was a disaster:

> The soldiers . . . had been left behind without any clear directives. Instead of holding the bridgehead they spread out in the town and commenced vandalizing . . . these troops ran out of ammunition and were unable to receive reinforcements in time . . . then
> a detachment of Biafran troops led by the rebel Colonel Joe Achuzia began to ambush them at will. The success of these tactics was aided by the fact that the majority of the Federal troops had become drunk on looted liquor and were bereft of leadership.[106]

In his memoirs, Achuzia described the attempted crossing as a "colossal success" for Biafra, claiming that the arms and ammunition captured from the federal forces "was sufficient to equip two brigades for six months."[107] He also reported capturing "a boatload of civilian personal clothing and possessions which I suspected were

---

[103]   Patrick E. Idahosa, *Truth and Tragedy: A Fighting Man's Memoir of the Nigerian Civil War*, Ibadan, Nigeria: Heinemann Educational Books, 1989, 80.

[104]   Interview with retired Gen. J.J. Oluleye, in H.B. Momoh, *The Nigerian Civil War, 1967–1970: History and Reminiscences*, Ibadan, Nigeria: Sam Bookman Publishers, 775. In the same volume, Ibrahim Haruna mentions the influence of "para-psychists" (p. 583), while others, e.g. E.O. Abisoye, Gen. J.J. Oluleye, and Ishola Williams report the arguments between officers about the risky plan.

[105]   Interview with retired Gen. Ike Omar Sanda Nwachukwu, Oct. 11, 2016, Lagos.

[106]   Idahosa, *Truth and Tragedy*, 87.

[107]   Achuzia, *Requiem Biafra*, 127.

FIGURE 2.9 Col. Ike Omar Sanda Nwachukwu (center), with other officers, leaves a ferryboat used for the failed attempt to take Onitsha. Photo courtesy of Ahmed Adoke.

looted from homes in Asaba as it comprised a lot of Asaba hand-woven white ceremonial clothing."[108] For Paul Ogbebor, with the Eighth Brigade, this was a terrible moment: "All those troops I took from the prison, from the garage and everything – 90 percent of them died." He himself was shot, but he jumped into the river, eventually reaching a barge, from which he was rescued and taken to Benin City for treatment.[109]

Muhammed made several more failed attempts to capture Onitsha by direct river assault over the next few weeks, resulting in high federal casualties and no doubt contributing to the level of anger among the troops (Figure 2.9). Meanwhile, Muhammed faced increasing dissatisfaction with his leadership,[110] especially in contrast to the

[108]   Ibid., 127.
[109]   Interview with retired Col. Paul Osa Ogbebor, Oct. 12, 2016, Benin City.
[110]   British authorities monitoring the action reported "criticism amongst officers in 2 Division of planning and conduct of recent operation to take Onitsha ... aimed directly at Col. Muhammed," FCO Sitrep 83, Oct. 18, UK National Archive, FCO 38/285, file 207. As troops were massing for another crossing several days later, they

success of First Division Commander, Col. Mohammed Shuwa, who had successfully taken Enugu, the capital of Biafra, on October 4.

THE OCCUPATION: THE WAR DRAGS ON

As the Second Division failed to advance, more troops joined those already in the town, often occupying abandoned homes or being billeted in the houses of families whose menfolk they had executed.[111] In mid-October, Celestina Isichei's fiancé, Peter Isamah, braved the occupying soldiers to come to Asaba and take her to nearby Ogwashi-Ukwu, where he worked as a postmaster. She was desperate to get word out, but soldiers were censoring all correspondence. Finally, Peter managed to have a soldier friend take a letter to Lagos, where it was mailed to her brother in Oxford. "I asked him to pass on the sad news to my other brothers and sisters in Austria, London, and Germany." Her letter concluded,

> More than four battalions of soldiers are now at Asaba. All that we have at Asaba have been looted. Doors and windows broken. Houses burnt down ... Nobody can be seen outside ... Please write soon ... Nothing like life in Asaba. Pray for us.[112]

Under occupation, the remaining residents settled into an uneasy and often frightening coexistence with the troops. While the area under Captain Matthias's command reportedly remained quite free of violence and destruction, elsewhere individual acts of violence and rape continued.

By October, with the fall of Enugu, many believed that the war was about to end with a decisive federal victory and the collapse of Biafra. *Time* magazine was reporting that Biafra was doomed,[113] a sentiment echoed by *Newsweek*, which declared that "the sun was

noted "open dissatisfaction amongst many officers of Col. Muhammed's handling of the original operation," FCO Sitrep 88, Oct. 24, UK National Archive, FCO 38/285, file 212.

[111]   Interview with Medua Uraih
[112]   Celestina Isichei-Isamah, *They Died in Vain*, 131.
[113]   *Time*, "Drums of Defeat," 90:14, Oct. 6, 1967, 70.

setting" on Biafra.[114] However, Muhammed's lack of progress and heavy losses in the repeated attempts to take Onitsha created a stalemate, and the beginning of "the war of attrition,"[115] that would continue for another two years, condemning over a million Biafrans to starvation and death. And as we shall see, the horrific events at Asaba, while largely ignored at the time, were pivotal in helping ensure that Biafra would fight to the end.

[114]   *Newsweek*, "Nigeria: Setting Sun," Oct. 9, 1967, 41–42.
[115]   John de St. Jorre, *The Brothers' War: Biafra and Nigeria*, Boston: Houghton Mifflin, 1972, 173.

3   Causes and Consequences

In October 1967, the people of Asaba had just experienced the worst civilian atrocity of the war to date, leaving their town in ruins and families devastated. Today, in an era of "citizen journalists" and instantaneous flows of images and information, it can be hard to understand both how this atrocity could have been allowed to happen and how it apparently remained mostly unnoticed outside of Asaba. Indeed, it was not until well into 1968 that the world would start taking serious notice of the Nigerian Civil War, after the Federal Military Government (FMG) tightened its all-out blockade on Biafra and media began bringing images of starving children into living rooms across Europe and North America. In fact, these grim images defined (and continue to represent) the international memory of Biafra and the civil war.[1] However, in spite of the mounting international global awareness of the impact of the use of starvation as a weapon of war, the conflict dragged on for another 18 months, with Biafra effectively starved into submission by early 1970 (Figure 3.1).[2]

This lack of early international attention to the tragic events taking place in Nigeria was an important factor in allowing federal forces to act with impunity. The neglect was well established as early as 1966, when the pogroms in the northern parts of the country led to the massive movement of the Igbo population eastward. Irish writer Conor Cruise O'Brien commented in December 1967, "If the movement had taken place across an international frontier, it would be already classified among the great refugee problems of the twentieth century . . . [Instead, it was] from one region to another in what was still

---

[1]   Paul Bartrop, "The Relationship Between War and Genocide in the Twentieth Century: A Consideration," *Journal of Genocide Research*, 4, 2002, 519–532.

[2]   See Chapter 4 for a summary of the progress of the war after the occupation of Asaba.

FIGURE 3.1 A typical news image of Biafran starvation. Photo by Kent Gavin, *Daily Mirror*, July 1, 1968, courtesy of Mirrorpix.

nominally one country."[3] A key reason for this indifference, O'Brien argued, was that this was a case of black Africans killing each other, which failed to arouse the "humanitarian rhetoric" that would stir action. The same could be said about the events in the Midwest in the early months of the war. In 1966 and 1967, the eyes of the world were not focused on Nigeria but on other conflicts, such as those in the Middle East and Southeast Asia. This indifference not only made it easier for atrocities such as those committed in Asaba to take place, but also ensured that international public reaction to the war remained muted. Here we trace the broad strategic context that created the conditions for the Asaba massacres to happen, with special attention to the British role; we then explain how both the event and efforts to keep it under wraps significantly affected the subsequent progress of the war.

Undoubtedly, the chain of events that led to the massacres at Asaba began with the Biafran decision to invade the Midwest. This

[3]   Conor Cruise O'Brien, "A Condemned People," *New York Review of Books*, Dec. 21, 1967, 14.

brought the war to a region that had attempted to remain neutral, stoked resentment among the region's non-Igbo population, and left the Midwest Igbo exposed to retaliation. As we shall show, the hasty mobilization of undisciplined federal troops under a volatile and insubordinate leader effectively allowed existing anti-Igbo sentiments to escalate as they moved east, culminating in the slaughter at Asaba.

From the beginning of the conflict, Gen. Yakubu Gowon's Federal Military Government had maintained the position that the war was not directed at Igbos, per se, but was motivated by the desire to preserve the unity of Nigeria, including, of course, the oil-rich areas of the Eastern Region. It is a position he has maintained to this day: "It's not a war that we wanted at all ... I did it to keep the country together."[4] Gowon was acutely aware that civilian casualties could potentially erode support for the war both domestically and (more important) internationally. In July 1967, Gowon issued his Operational Code of Conduct for the Nigerian Army, as described in Chapter 2, and he repeatedly voiced the importance of minimizing harm to civilians, while working for a quick and decisive victory that would bring Biafra back into the fold.

However, Gowon's proclamations and policy statements came up against the reality that many in the military were resentful against the Igbos in general, and in particular for their perceived role in the first 1966 coup – sentiments that led some of his subordinates to have fewer scruples about how to achieve victory. Gowon also had to deal with the internal tensions and hostilities that plagued the military leadership of the Nigerian armed forces, with some senior officers questioning his qualifications to be head of state. Prominent among them was Lt. Col. Murtala Muhammed, described by *New York Times* journalist Alfred Friendly as "a fire-breathing 28-year-old Northerner whose dislike of Ibos has never been disguised."[5] And so throughout the war, Gowon, a 32-year-old Christian and member of a minority

---

[4]   Interview with Gen. Yakubu Gowon, Oct. 10, 2016, Abuja.

[5]   Alfred Friendly Jr., "City Shows Scars of the Nigerian War," *New York Times*, Sept. 26, 1967, 1.

ethnic group, was attempting to ensure international support for his government, while simultaneously holding his own army together.

THE KEY ROLE OF BRITAIN

Only seven years after the end of colonial rule, Nigeria and Britain continued to have strong political, cultural, and economic ties. Many of the country's institutions, such as the educational system, mirrored those of Britain, and many of Nigeria's elites had gone through education or military training in the UK. For their part, British authorities maintained a somewhat paternalistic attitude toward their former subjects. As the conflict progressed, Britain's actions not only helped shape the war in general, but also helped create the conditions that produced the massacres at Asaba and other areas of the Nigerian Midwest.

At the outset of the hostilities, the British government, under Prime Minister Harold Wilson, was ostensibly neutral in the conflict. A July 27 confidential memo from Sir David Hunt at the new British High Commission in Lagos noted that "in principle the progress of hostilities does not directly concern British interests though we have an interest in preserving the unity of Nigeria and, consequently, in as early an end as possible to the civil war which shall leave as little bitterness as possible."[6] While part of Britain's public stance was the importance of maintaining the integrity of its former colony, now declassified documents show that London's first priority was to ensure continued access to the oilfields of the petroleum-rich Niger Delta.[7]

---

[6]   Foreign and Commonwealth Office (FCO), Summary of Lagos Dispatch No. 9, "War and Oil in Nigeria," July 27, 1967, UK National Archive, FCO 38/284, file 62, 1.

[7]   As Roy Doron noted ("Forging a Nation while Losing a Country: Igbo Nationalism, Ethnicity and Propaganda in the Nigerian Civil War 1968–1970," Doctoral dissertation, University of Texas at Austin, August 2011), there is a serious lack of Nigerian archival records on the civil war. The confidential records of the British Foreign and Commonwealth Office began to be declassified in 1997; they have been used by several scholars and allow the development of a clear picture of UK/Nigerian relations during the conflict.

In his memo, Hunt went on to point out that major oil companies were in the Eastern Region, and this had important consequences
on the relationship between Nigeria and Britain, "and even, thanks to
the Middle East war, on the British motorist contemplating a summer
holiday."[8] A few days later George Thomas, Minister of State for
Commonwealth Affairs, mirrored Hunt's assessment when he wrote
that "the sole immediate British interest in Nigeria is that the
Nigerian economy should be brought back to a condition in which
our substantial trade and investment in the country can be further
developed, and particularly so we can regain access to important oil
installations."[9] The most important oil installation to which he
referred was the Shell/BP refinery in Port Harcourt, which had begun
production in 1965.[10]

This concern over oil quickly became the key reason why
Britain's position moved from one of somewhat pro-unity neutrality
to one of active support for the FMG.[11] British authorities supported
the Federal Government because, in their view, small independent
states would not extend the same favorable economic conditions as
had been granted by "a unified Nigeria." Specifically, Thomas stated
that there was no guarantee that the Shell/BP oil concession could be
renegotiated "on the same terms as in the past if the East and the mid-
West assume full control of their own economies."[12]

Ironically, focus on oil also meant that some officials were
ready to consider jettisoning support for the Federal Government if
conditions on the battlefield turned against it. On August 3,
a confidential review of the military situation had noted that the
British government was trying to maintain good relations with
both Gowon and Ojukwu, especially since "the Ibos have fought

8   "War and Oil in Nigeria," July 27, 1967, 2.
9   Quoted in Mark Curtis, *Unpeople: Britain's Secret Human Rights Abuses*, London:
     Vintage, 2004, 170.
10   Gary Blank, "Britain, Biafra and the Balance of Payments: The Formation of London's
     'One Nigeria' Policy," *Revue Francais de Civilisation Britannique*, 2013, 18:2, 66–86.
11   See also Chibuike Uche, "Oil, British Interests and the Nigerian Civil War," *Journal of
     African History*, 49, 2008, 111–135.
12   Quoted in Curtis, *Unpeople*, 170.

much better than expected."[13] This was followed by the Biafran invasion of the Midwest on August 9. Their early successes as they sped west toward Lagos briefly led to some discussion of how to deal with the possibility of a federal defeat; an August 21 telegram from James Parker, High Commissioner in Enugu, speculated that Biafra might actually win. He quoted the Biafran Chief of Staff, N.U. Akpan, arguing that "the war could be over in about three weeks with Biafran forces in Lagos and West." Parker suggested that Shell/BP should now reopen negotiations "in order to restore British influence before the war ends and it is too late."[14] In 1998, Michael Leapman described this moment as "a rethink in Whitehall":

> The Commonwealth Office set out five choices. A and B involved maintaining or increasing arms to Nigeria, C was to stop all supplies, D to promote a peace initiative and E a combination of the last two. Thomas wrote to Wilson, holidaying in the Scillies, recommending Option E.[15]

However, David Hunt flew to Britain, intent on asserting the federal cause, and the more conciliatory options were rejected. And once it became apparent that the FMG again had the upper hand, Britain settled into what became unwavering support of the Gowon regime, with the influence of Hunt, who was widely seen as anti-Igbo, becoming increasingly important.[16] As noted by Gary Blank, Gowon's "One Nigeria" goal

> was fully accepted by both the British government and Shell-BP once it became clear that only the abject defeat of the Biafrans

---

[13] Report of talks with Sir David Hunt, Aug. 3, 1967, UK National Archive, FCO 38/284, file 78 and file 114.

[14] James Parker, Telegram, Aug. 21, 1967, UK National Archive, FCO 38/284, file 113.

[15] Michael Leapman, "British Interests, Nigerian Tragedy," *The Independent*, Jan. 3, 1998, accessed online at: www.independent.co.uk/voices/british-interests-nigerian-tragedy-1136684.html. Leapman was using the FCO records, which at that time had just been declassified.

[16] Gary Blank, "Britain, Biafra and the Balance of Payments," 82.

would ensure the maintenance of Shell-BP's investments, and – crucially for Britain – a resumption of Nigerian oil flow.[17]

In his reports Hunt noted that the Biafrans were fighting well, supported by Czech-supplied automatic weapons and mercenary airmen, and he advocated for selling more arms to the FMG to help ensure its victory.[18] Hunt's hardline stance was facilitated by the lack of attention and interest among media, politicians, and the public:

> If the British media and backbenchers had really wanted to shape policy on Nigeria, they should have developed a clear view in the first six months ... when the official line was flexible. Instead, they were largely indifferent ... and so allowed policy to become clearly pro-federal.[19]

Nevertheless, as its involvement in the war deepened, the Wilson government was aware of the potential for growing international and domestic criticism. Specifically, as fighting intensified, ministers quickly realized that full-fledged support for a united Nigeria could also create a serious risk for Britain's national and international reputation if things went badly. In particular, it was crucial that the war was seen to be clean and non-punitive. In the same July memo that laid out the importance of oil, Hunt had addressed a concern that would only grow in the months ahead. Noting that the federal forces were progressing rather slowly, he wrote, "Probably it is just as well; more sweeping, rapid movements might result in the soldiers getting out of hand, committing atrocities and losing all discipline."[20] Consequently, in an attempt to preempt accusations of direct interference in the conflict and in the hope of limiting civilian deaths, the

[17]   Ibid., 82.
[18]   Michael Gould, *The Biafran War: The Struggle for Modern Nigeria*, New York: I.B. Tauris, 2012; Mark Curtis, *Unpeople: Britain's Secret Human Rights Abuses*, London: Vintage, 2004.
[19]   John W. Young, *The Labour Governments 1964–70, Volume 2: International Policy*, Manchester: Manchester University Press, 2004, 204.
[20]   "War and Oil in Nigeria," July 27, 1967, 5.

Wilson administration refused to furnish the FMG with jet fighters, bomber aircrafts, and heavy tanks. At the same time, it provided what it defined "defensive" infantry weapons, items such as small arms, light artillery, anti-aircraft guns, armored cars, and fast patrol boats:

> It was agreed that we should take our customary stand of refusing to comment on arms contracts ... however ... we are justified in claiming that we could not reasonably withhold normal replacements. In the last resort, if the supply of the anti-aircraft guns becomes public knowledge, we would, of course, say that they are defensive weapons.[21]

In the end, however, in spite of all efforts to minimize the scope of its involvement, Britain became the recognized main source of military supplies to federal forces, with quantities escalating as the war progressed. It is therefore within this context of intensifying participation that the British government played a key role in both the conduct and the narrative of the war, helping create the conditions that made Asaba possible and subsequently helping to ensure that the story was buried.

A pattern soon began to emerge, as the British used arms sales in an attempt to pressure Gowon into keeping control of his forces. On his side, it appears that Gowon did hope to conduct the war honorably, avoiding military excesses. However, it quickly became clear that the federal troops, especially in Murtala Muhammed's Second Division, were not to be easily controlled and that there were serious issues of discipline. Before the war, the Nigerian army was 10,000 strong; by the end it had ballooned to 250,000, with many of the new troops lacking the most basic training.[22] In addition, the army's leadership had been severely weakened by the events of 1966, which had precipitated the return of many Igbo officers to their natal

[21]   Report of talks with Sir David Hunt, Aug. 3, 1967, UK National Archive, FCO 38/284, file 78 and file 114
[22]   Jimi Peters, *The Nigerian Military and the State*, New York: Tauris Academic Studies, 1997.

regions. It was thus "seriously under-officered,"[23] a point emphasized at the time in reports to London from the field.[24] Muhammed's Second Division, raised quickly in response to the Midwest invasion, was especially lacking in essential military training, and raw recruits, motivated by anything from patriotism to anti-Igbo resentment to the desire for a paycheck, were rapidly added as the troops moved east, as we note in Chapter 1. Furthermore, throughout the war (and especially during the first few months), communication among central headquarters and field commanders was extremely poor, allowing these commanders a remarkable degree of autonomy.[25] Murtala Muhammed had resented Gowon's rise to power from the beginning and was one of the most independent of these "war lords," distrusted even by many of his fellow commanders.[26]

At the same time, the government's fear was increasing about the possible public relations consequences of punitive action against civilians on the part of federal troops. On August 14, during the Biafran surge westward, Hunt had reported to the Ministry of Defence in London that Biafrans had raided the town of Okene, on the way toward Ore:

> Gowon had ordered troops to move there 10 August. Apparently they went to Idah instead. Communication of orders is not Federal forces' strong-point. Some civilians were killed and shops looted and burnt ... "[27]

Shortly afterwards, on August 28, a British situation report (known as "sitreps") from Hunt in Lagos noted that Murtala Muhammed was

---

[23]   Ibid., 109.

[24]   British High Commission (Kaduna), Memo from G.D. Anderson, "as we have known all along, the Nigerian Army is very short of officers," Aug. 21, 1967, UK National Archive, FCO 38/284, file 145.

[25]   Peters, *The Nigerian Military and the State*.

[26]   H.B. Momoh, ed., *The Nigerian Civil War, 1967–1970: History and Reminiscences*, Ibadan, Nigeria: Sam Bookman, 2000. In an interview included in the book, Col. E.O. Abisoye described Muhammed as "fiery," and even "stupid," stressing the lack of a strong central communication system (p. 230), while Gen. J.J. Oluleye commented that Muhammed "had no respect for battle procedure" (p. 774).

[27]   Sir David Hunt, Telegram 1913, Aug. 14, 1967, UK National Archive, FCO 38/284, file 99.

refusing to file his own sitreps from the field.[28] The same report noted that Ore had not yet been taken back by the FMG and that there had been "indiscriminate shooting of suspected Ibos" around the town.[29] Hunt reported every few days that Muhammed was still refusing to submit sitreps. This was "obviously a dangerous form of implied insubordination," and since the daily British sitreps depended on accurate information from the field, this was increasing British anxiety about the conduct of the war.[30] The reports of poor communication, coupled with Muhammed's insubordination, continued throughout the next few months.

As the Second Division moved back through the Midwest, information was sparse. Movements of civilians were noted, including a September 25 air-reconnaissance report of large numbers of civilians moving across from Asaba to Onitsha. This was at the time that Muhammed had retaken Benin City, and news of massacres of Igbos by non-Igbos was filtering back to Asaba.[31] Although no reports describe it at the time, London clearly became aware of the killings by civilians and federal troops in Benin City and was anxious that more would follow as the First Division, under Mohammed Shuwa, advanced toward Enugu. On September 29, a confidential memo from the West and General Africa Department (WGAD) expressed concern about the dangers for "strong political as well as humanitarian reasons," continuing,

> I realise that Gowon is concerned to avoid the killing and harrying of civilians and I fully accept his sincerity ... but I do not see how he can control the situation as it threatens to develop ... There is no doubt that a further round of Ibo-hunting will make it very difficult indeed for HMG to refrain from condemning the FMG ... and denying them the full support they seem to expect.[32]

28 FCO Daily Sitrep 43, Aug. 28, 1967, UK National Archive, FCO 38/284, file 103.
29 Ibid.
30 FCO Daily Sitrep 48, Sept. 2, 1967, UK National Archive, FCO38/284, file 138.
31 FCO Daily Sitrep 64, Sept. 25, 1967, UK National Archive, FCO 38/285, file 183.
32 Confidential Memo, Commonwealth Office to Lagos, Sept. 29, 1967, UK National Archive, FCO 38/268, file 296.

As this memo suggest, this was another point at which the British government could have made a policy change, acted upon its fears, and taken the position that arms sales and active support would end in the event of further actions against civilians. However, Hunt's adamantly pro-FMG position, fueled by the threat to oil, prevailed. Britain continued down the path it was on, expressing hope that the troops would behave, even as officials knew that Murtala Muhammed should be reined in. In an October 5 sitrep, Hunt noted that Shuwa "has assured Gowon that he will do his utmost to control his troops in Enugu to ensure no repetition of the recent massacres in Benin ... The troops under Shuwa's command are largely regular and there has been no evidence of indiscipline in his command."[33] That month, the British Cabinet was told that "Britain was trying to persuade the federals 'on the basis of their victories, to negotiate from strength and in the hope of avoiding massacres.'"[34] Meanwhile, Murtala Muhammed had been ordered to move to Asaba and take the Niger Bridge intact.

Enugu was occupied on October 4, just as Muhammed's forces approached Asaba. A confidential memo to the Commonwealth Office once again notes the reputation of Shuwa as a "noted disciplinarian" who guaranteed "proper soldierly behavior." The memo concludes, "Thank God it was he not Muhammed who captured Enugu.[35]

HOW DID THE MASSACRE HAPPEN?

Unfortunately for the people of Asaba, it was Muhammed who took their town, and "proper soldierly behavior" was in short supply, as we have seen. Indeed, the extent of killing and destruction by soldiers (rather than civilians) was unlike anything that had happened to this point, and the systematic October 7 massacre remained unique. Many factors seem to have contributed to the total death toll. Killings of

[33]   FCO Daily Sitrep 72, Oct. 5, 1967, UK National Archive, 38/285, file 191.

[34]   Young, *The Labour Governments*, 207, quoting from CAB 128/42 (Cabinet Minutes), Oct. 11, 1967, UK National Archive.

[35]   Confidential Memo, Lagos to Commonwealth Office, Oct. 5, 1967, telegram 2477, UK National Archive, FCO 38/269, file 299.

civilians began shortly after troops entered the town; they seem to have been the result of both targeted retaliation, stemming from a range of motivations and opportunistic actions on the part of undisciplined troops. The most common justification for killing (if any was given) was that Asaba men and boys were Biafran soldiers or collaborators, and many were killed simply on that accusation. Any males from the teens upwards, like Celestina's young brother Osi, were targets, and many died, singly or in groups.

In addition, federal troops sought out specific individuals for execution. One reason was supposed association with leaders of the January 1966 coup. The natal village of Major Patrick Chukwuma Nzeogwu, regarded as one of the key coup leaders, was Okpanam, a few miles north of Asaba (although he was born and raised in the Northern town of Kaduna), and several other officers were indigenes of neighboring communities in what had once been the colonial Asaba Division. As Asaba-born Philip Asiodu, then the Permanent Secretary to the Nigerian Federal Ministry of Industries, later commented, "It's not difficult to imagine that they must have said, 'When we reach Asaba, we shall wreak punishment.'"[36]

The connection between the role of officers from Asaba in the 1966 coup and the massacres of October 1967 has become part of the communal memory of Asaba, with several interviewees citing it as a probable cause.[37] However, only one witness specifically recalls soldiers mentioning the coup leaders:

> They started asking "Where's Nzeogwu's house? Where's
> Okwechime's [Colonel Mike Okwechime] house?" We say, "No,
> they are not from here" ... And that was when they started feeling
> remorse about it, say they thought that they are from Asaba.[38]

---

[36] Interview with Philip C. Asiodu, Dec. 8, 2009, Tampa.
[37] E.g. Emmanuel Obi (Oct. 12, 2009); Ify Uraih (Oct. 9, 2009); Medua Uraih (Dec. 13, 2009); Joseph Nwajei (Oct. 10, 2009); Fabian Oweazim (Oct. 10, 2009); Peter Okonjo (Dec. 14, 2009); Emmanuel Nwanze (Dec. 16, 2009).
[38] Interview with Medua Uraih.

Thus it is unclear how important this specific motivation was at the time. However, aside from the issue of coup leaders, as noted in Chapter 2, it is clear that Asabans who had been prominent civil servants or government officials were targeted, continuing the consequences of the festering resentment triggered among the non-Igbo majority in Benin City. Many men from Asaba had held key positions in the Midwest government; the home of Dennis Osadebay, the first premier of the Region, was gutted and destroyed with the first wave of occupying troops.[39] Many of the more well-to-do families had escaped Benin City, only to find themselves targets once again in Asaba.

The experience of the Izegbu family, as recalled by then 14-year-old Victor Izegbu, captures the somewhat chaotic motivations and behavior of the occupying troops.[40] Victor's father, B.R.O. Izegbu, had been a deputy permanent secretary in Benin City, at one time representing the Midwest in Britain. His mother, Beatrice, was the older sister of Celestina Isichei. As the troops moved into Benin City, the parents and their eight children piled into two cars and drove to Asaba, where they took refuge in the paternal family home. On September 25, the youngest child was born in Asaba, and a few days later the federal troops arrived. The family stayed in the home, afraid to venture out, until two soldiers came banging on the door. Victor recalls the soldiers as "sweaty, smelly, red eyed, smelling of alcohol, carrying a bottle of gin." His grandmother, declaring "we are not criminals," answered and the men came in. Immediately, they targeted Victor's father: "You're definitely an officer in Ojukwu's army – we must kill you." Crying in fear, the family protested that the father was actually a civil servant in Benin City. At this point, the newborn baby, hidden under a bed, started crying, and the soldiers demanded he be brought out. The soldiers asked the baby's name, and on being told he had not yet been named, they decided to conduct an impromptu and rather bizarre "naming ceremony," pouring gin on the

[39]   "Griot," "Roundabout: The View from the Bridge, Asaba," *West Africa*, Oct. 21, 1967, 1357.
[40]   Interview with Victor Izegbu, April 15, 2016, Lagos.

floor and "naming" the child as the family looked on in terror. Having finished, they asserted again that Mr. Izegbu was a Biafran soldier, and they challenged him to prove he was a civil servant by telling them his name. When he did so, one of the men "brought out a wet, horrible-looking list of hand-written names" on lined paper torn from a notebook. Quickly they found his name; the family were excited because they believed this proved his identity as a non-combatant. Their hopes were dashed when the soldiers told them that this was a list of people who should be killed. However, the incident with the baby seemed to have calmed the two, and instead of killing anyone, they warned the family to be careful, fired a few shots, "to prove that this bullet was supposed to be for you," and left.

Not long after, the family fled to the home of Francis Okafor Isichei – Victor's maternal grandfather and Celestina's father – thinking they might be safer there. They arrived to find the house abandoned and looted, and they saw the body of young Osi, Victor's uncle, lying near the door. The rest of the family had been rounded up for the parade to Ogbe-Osowa, where Osi's older brother Emma was to die. Terrified, the Izegbus escaped into the bush, where they camped out for the next three months.

Victor Izegbu's story captures the unfocused mayhem that characterized many of the federal soldiers' behavior. There was clearly some rationale that involved tracking down "collaborators" and taking revenge on Midwest leaders, but eyewitness accounts more generally paint a picture of a chaotic, opportunistic lawlessness that prevailed in the town immediately prior to and alongside the more organized event on October 7. Whether actively condoned by their commander or not, this speaks to the culture of indiscipline that Muhammed had facilitated, and about which both the British authorities and Gowon were so concerned. As we describe in Chapter 2, indiscriminate killing, looting, and rape ran rampant across many parts of the town, often simply because the undefended civilians were easy targets and because they were perceived as Igbo. Many in Asaba were relatively well-off, with cars, consumer goods, and other possessions, and many lost everything they owned as soldiers hauled off furniture, appliances, and anything moveable, including "gold trinkets, coral beads, elephant tusks, artifacts, currency notes and the white native cloth."[41]

However, the October 7 Ogbe-Osowa massacre was different. Some of the same sentiments – general dislike of Igbos, resentment of Igbo education and success, anger about the actions of Midwest collaborators – undoubtedly drove the motivation for the organized killing. However, exactly why this unprecedented event was carried out, or who ordered it, remains a mystery. One witness attributed a key role to a Lt. Usman, who berated and beat a large group of men, saying that Igbos "believe in book knowledge, that they were going to destroy that book knowledge."[42] Several interviewees reported that soldiers made comments about hating Igbo people and wanting to kill them; many people in Asaba who had fled there from the north spoke Hausa and were able to understand the soldiers' conversations, or they understood the "pidgin English" that was used across the country to communicate among the multiplicity of languages. Ify Uraih, for example, described being among those gathered for the welcome on October 7, when an officer, Ibrahim Taiwo (Murtala Muhammed's second in command), addressed the group, accusing them of harboring Biafran sympathizers. Leaders asserted their support of "One Nigeria," and initially, the officer appeared to accept that. Later another officer spoke to the group, saying he was from Adamawa State, a northeast state bordering Chad: "He said he was a second lieutenant, and (I'm going to speak the way he spoke), he said ... 'But den born me for Adamawa. I hate all Igbos, and you be Igbo. Therefore, you must die.'"[43] Shortly after that, Uraih heard an order in Hausa to begin

[41]   Akunwata S.O. Okocha, The *Making of Asaba: A Compendium of over Sixty-Five Years of Patient Research within and without Africa*, Asaba: Rupee-Com Publishers, 2013, 192.

[42]   Affidavit of John Kanayo Hudson Odittah, included in *Investigators' Report on a Complaint Laid Before the Directorate of The International Commission for the Study of the Crime of Genocide*, 1969, accessed at University of Oxford, Rhodes House, Mss Afr.s 2399.

[43]   Interview with Ify Uraih, Oct. 9, 2009, Tampa.

killing. Several witnesses point to Taiwo[44] as the instigator, with at least one naming him as the officer who gave the order to start firing, while others name Usman. Some reported that Taiwo later intervened, saying enough people had died, and sending some civilians home.[45]

A PLANNED MASSACRE?

Eyewitnesses provide some evidence that a plan to conduct a mass killing was in place ahead of time. Those who took part in the parade describe how soldiers lined the main Nnebisi Road on the route, keeping the hundreds of participants moving before reaching the point where the women and young children were separated out, and the men were herded into an open area. This certainly points to a coordinated effort. At the same time, the troops were not apparently in agreement about what was to happen. As noted in Chapter 2, federal officer Paul Ogbebor believed the people were being gathered for an evacuation. We heard reports of arguments between federal officers about what was going on: "Some didn't want it to happen, but some were insisting that they had to shoot ... and continued."[46] One witness recalled heated words between Usman and the well-remembered "guardian angel," Captain Matthias.[47] Matthias prevented a large group of people in the neighborhood he was controlling from joining the welcome parade; this would suggest that he knew there were plans among fellow officers to commit the atrocity. Our interviewee Nwaka Obaze, a Fulani woman married to an Asaba man, recounted how her family received warning from a relation serving in the federal army that they should flee. Similarly, Asaba elder Onianwa Omezi told an interviewer in 1992 that he fled Asaba before the parade, having been told by a federal soldier of Midwest Igbo ethnicity that there was a plan to kill those who came to the

[44] Taiwo was named in interviews with Christopher Mkpayah, Dec. 10, 2009, Lagos; Henry Onyia, Dec. 15, 2009, Asaba; Ify Uraih; Medua Uraih, Dec. 13, 2010, Asaba.
[45] Interview with Luke Enenmoh, Oct. 10, 2014, London.
[46] Interview with Igwemma Osakwe, Dec. 12, 2009, Asaba.
[47] Interview with Luke Enenmoh.

welcome ceremony.[48] Egodi Uchendu interviewed another Asaba chief in 2000 who stated that a soldier informed him of a plan to kill everyone in Asaba,[49] while our interviewee Stanley Okafor described his interaction with a soldier who told him they were under orders to kill all males.[50] While none of this offers incontrovertible proof, it certainly suggests far more than a spur-of-the-moment decision, while also suggesting that many of the troops were not privy to the plan.

Those who served in the military have provided few answers, at least publically. Neither Muhammed nor his second-in-command Ibrahim Taiwo is known to have spoken about Asaba, and both are long dead. Not unexpectedly, the military has never officially acknowledged the massacre. A few former military officers have touched on it in their memoirs, but none have accepted any direct responsibility or suggested it was in any way planned. For instance, Olusegun Obasanjo, who served in the Second Division and years later became president of Nigeria, wrote about "an unfortunate incident" in Asaba in which troops of the Eighth Brigade executed about 50 civilians "whom they suspected to be spying on them on behalf of the rebels after the federal troops had suffered heavy casualties from a surprise attack by the rebels."[51] Obasanjo asserted that this happened "without the knowledge or approval of senior or superior officers."[52] While this could describe one of the many smaller killings that happened, it certainly does not come close to matching what we know of the October 7 massacre. Patrick Idahosa, originally from the Benin City area (and now deceased), was a Major with the Second Division in Asaba, and wrote in his 1989 memoir:

---

[48]   Egodi Uchendu, *Women and Conflict in the Nigerian Civil War*, Trenton, NJ: Africa World Press, 2007, 91.

[49]   Ibid., 93.

[50]   Interview with Stanley Okafor, Oct. 12, 2011, Ibadan.

[51]   Olusegun Obasanjo, *My Command: An Account of the Nigerian Civil War, 1967–1970*, London: Heinemann, 1980, 41.

[52]   Ibid., 39.

As we approached the town center ... we met a crowd of Asaba citizens ... bearing branches of trees to signify that they came in peace, and singing songs of welcome. Sadly, the soldiers who had just come out of the heat of battle were not appreciative of this show of welcome and they opened fire on the innocent citizens killing several ... Even though myself and several other officers tried hard to stop the carnage it was an uphill task ... For some days, looting, irrational killing of innocent civilians, and all kinds if carnage became rampant in the town and it took all our ingenuity to bring it under control.[53]

Idahosa's account of the general mayhem gibes with Asaba witnesses, but it is a self-serving narrative, minimizing both the numbers killed at the Ogbe-Osowa massacre and Idahosa's role. As we note in Chapter 2, our interviewee Charles Ugboko identified Idahosa as among those officers rounding people up; he only spared Ugboko because they were former schoolmates in Benin City.

A collection of interviews with civil-war-era officers, published in 2000, occasionally touches on Asaba, although the interviewer never presses the issue. Baba Usman, by then a retired general, was asked directly whether there had been killings in Asaba and other towns; he simply ignored the question.[54] Retired General Ishola Williams served in Asaba as a young lieutenant, although he was wounded in the first attempt to cross the Niger and evacuated to the rear. In the interview collection, Williams was one of the few former officers to acknowledge "general shooting" in Asaba, as well as extensive looting and orders by Muhammed to kill Biafran prisoners, but he did not speak of any organized massacre. He noted that his own battalion consisted mostly of regular troops, and "we did manage to control our troops but then other battalions just couldn't."[55] In a 2016

---

[53] Patrick E. Idahosa, *Truth and Tragedy: A Fighting Man's Memoir of the Nigerian Civil War*, Ibadan: Heinemann Educational Books (Nigeria), 1989, 78–79.

[54] Momoh, *The Nigerian Civil War, 1967–1970*, 869. It is not clear whether he is the Lt. Usman mentioned by several witnesses; Usman is a common Northern Nigeria name.

[55] Quoted in Momoh, *The Nigerian Civil War, 1967–1970*, 880.

interview, Williams plausibly denied firsthand knowledge of any planned killing, but confirmed the poor state of the Second Division: "most of the officers were not combat officers ... they had no control over their soldiers. Very few of the soldiers were well-trained – the rest were rabble-rousers."[56] Ike Omar Sanda Nwachukwu said in 2016 that his Sixth Brigade was not involved in any way, and that he did not hear anything about killings until "much later."[57]

Williams' assessment of the troops was shared by Ibrahim B. Haruna, who replaced Murtala Muhammed as Second Division Commander in June 1968. In a 2016 interview he acknowledged that in war, soldiers can do unthinkable things: "you become like a war dog, doesn't seem human."[58] Nevertheless, he denied the possibility of an organized killing: "Eminent writers have been saying there were unwonted killing at Asaba ... I never heard of it, it never happened in my regiment."[59] Some years earlier, a 2001 news account quoted Haruna's testimony to the Nigerian Human Rights Violations Investigations Commission (HRVIC, the "Oputa Panel," which was formed in 2000[60]):

> As the commanding officer and leader of the troops that massacred 500 men in Asaba, I have no apology ... I acted as a soldier maintaining the peace and unity of Nigeria.[61]

This quote has been widely circulated online, and Haruna has often been named as the perpetrator of the massacre. However, Haruna was nowhere near Asaba at the time and could not have been involved. In 2016, Haruna wrote to us that his words were taken out of context and used to bolster the Igbo case for genocide. Furthermore, in spite of all evidence to the contrary, he maintained his position that there never

---

[56]   Interview with retired Gen. Ishola Williams, April 14, 2016, Lagos
[57]   Interview with retired Gen. Ike Omar Sanda Nwachukwu, Oct. 11, 2016, Lagos.
[58]   Interview with retired Gen. Ibraham B. Haruna, April 11, 2016, Abuja.
[59]   Ibid.
[60]   We discuss the role of the HRVIC in Chapter 4.
[61]   For an account of Haruna's testimony at HRVIC, see Sufuyan Ojeifo and Lemmy Ughegbe, *The Vanguard*, Oct. 10, 2001, www.nigeriamasterweb.com/nmwpg1HarunaIgboMassacre.html.

was a massacre: "The so-called Asaba massacre is a figment of propaganda!"[62] Essentially, Haruna's statements on Asaba are contradictory and self-serving, and are not useful in establishing what happened.

As we noted in Chapter 2, retired Colonel Paul Ogbebor does acknowledge the massacre, while denying that his Eighth Brigade had anything to do with it – indeed his troops were camped some distance away near Cable Point. He was not able or willing to attribute blame to any other contingent of the troops, explaining that he left the scene once it was clear that things were out of control. Unlike other former officers, who claimed to have heard nothing at the time, he reported that he learned about the massacre "within 30 minutes," when he returned to the scene. He recalled: "I particularly felt very bad because there were two of my teachers that died there ... and my friends, classmates, people I knew ... They just dug a mass grave and put them in." Ogbebor estimated that about 1,000 people were killed. Reflecting upon the events years later, he commented that the river-crossing disaster, in which he estimated 5,000 troops were lost, was a kind of "nemesis" for the Second Division: "We paid dearly for what we did in Asaba ... "[63]

Other than Ogbebor, the only former military officer to have fully acknowledged what happened is retired General Chris Alli. He joined the Second Division straight from officer training in late October 1967 and thus could not have been involved. However, he described how discussions about what happened were widespread:

> There were stories of how the natives were lined up in football fields and along the river Niger and shot without provocation ... It was bewildering and I found the tales repulsive and revolting. I could not reconcile these actions to the avowed aims of the Civil War ...
> The Biafran accusations against the genocidal motives of the Federal forces seemed so real and substantiated ... How was I to

---

[62]   E-mail to Elizabeth Bird, July 27, 2016.
[63]   Interview with retired Col. Paul Osa Ogbebor, Oct. 12, 2016, Benin City.

explain to my family back home that ... we were just slaughtering Igbos on the pretext that we were fighting to keep Nigeria one.[64]

Alli was so anguished that he considered deserting, but as things calmed down in Asaba, and relationships between civilians and soldiers improved, he set about tasks that "included the battle for the hearts and minds of the population as well as their physical security."[65] Although Alli's and Ogbebor's accounts certainly suggest that the massacre was no secret among federal troops, none has ever stepped forward with a first-person account.

Thus definitive answers or acknowledgment remain elusive – hardly surprising, since the massacre would constitute a war crime. Ultimately of course, Murtala Muhammed, as Commander of the Second Division, was responsible for its conduct. Headquartered at nearby Umunude, he was in Asaba at the time, as documented in the Nigerian *Daily Sketch* on October 9;[66] two witnesses also report with great certainty that they saw him in the town.[67] Whether he gave direct orders to target civilians is unknowable; that his leadership style fostered a culture of indiscipline is inarguable. According to Gen. Williams, Gowon's Code of Conduct was well known: "he told every damn officer, from Second Lieutenant to General." Of Muhammed, Williams said, "I think he lost control of himself to some extent."[68] From eyewitness accounts, it seemed that of the lower ranking officers on the ground, some tried to maintain order, while others chose not to, or failed in spite of good intentions. Journalist Michael Wolfers, writing almost a year later, pointed to the serious disconnect between officers and soldiers of the federal army:

---

[64]   M. Chris Alli, *The Federal Republic of Nigerian Army: The Siege of a Nation*, Lagos, Nigeria: Malthouse Press, 2000, 42. We attempted several times to interview Gen. Alli, but were unable to do so.

[65]   Ibid., 46.

[66]   *Daily Sketch*, "The March on Asaba Bridge," Oct. 9, 1.

[67]   Interview with Patience Chukura, Dec. 10, 2009, Lagos; interview with Grace Monyei, June 28, 2010, Asaba.

[68]   Interview with retired Gen. Ishola Williams, April 14, 2016, Lagos.

> The Nigerian army . . . is in fact two forces. At the top are the supremely elegant officers, men who in their middle twenties are leading thousands of troops. The soldiers, perhaps 18 or 19 years old, are volunteers taken from the towns and villages . . . and sent to fight after two months training.[69]

There can be little doubt that at least some officers actively participated in or condoned the violence. Others probably never had much control over their ill-trained and opportunistic troops; as Ishola Williams noted, the shortage of competent combat officers led to some units being commanded by education or medical officers with no experience in the field – a point that does not absolve them from the responsibility to behave correctly. Furthermore, whatever messages were coming from the FMG about the need to protect Igbos, clearly there were concerns in the army itself about the anti-Igbo sentiments of many soldiers and officers, which Muhammed's leadership had not countered. Federal officer Ike Nwachukwu, whose father was Igbo, noted that after the failed crossing of the Niger, he was taken out of the field and reassigned to Lagos: "I came under suspicion – could it be that I was passing information to the rebel forces?" He said he did not take this seriously, but it was done "to save me from being shot in the back."[70] Civilians, unfortunately, did not have the same protection.

CONTROLLING THE NEWS

The devastation at Asaba was exactly the kind of incident that both the FMG and the British authorities did not want – it was potentially a public relations nightmare. And so it became important to make sure that the full extent did not become widely known. This was actually not difficult, given a combination of tight press control

---

[69]   Michael Wolfers, "Nigerian Troops Close in on Ibo Heartland," *The Times*, Aug. 30, 1968, 3.

[70]   Interview with retired Gen. Ike Omar Sanda Nwachukwu, Oct. 11, 2016, Lagos. Cyril Iweze, a federal officer of Midwest Igbo origin, also described his difficulties in leading troops who were suspicious of his ethnicity (interview, April 13, 2016, Lagos).

within Nigeria, and inattentive and compliant international news media at the time.

War reporting generally was weak and inadequate. From the beginning of the war, the FMG had put a tight reign over all reporting and information from the war zone, making it illegal for anyone, including international news sources, to divulge information deemed detrimental to federal authorities.[71] In August 1967, for instance, playwright Wole Soyinka was arrested and imprisoned for two years as a spy after he met with Ojukwu in an attempt to broker peace. During the early months of the war, the domestic press maintained a consistent, if sparse narrative: even after the setback of the Midwest invasion, the war was going well, would likely end soon, and that although the Igbos were responsible for the conflict, they had nothing to fear in a post-war Nigeria. During the month of October, the pro-government *Daily Times* reported only a handful of war-related stories, none mentioning any specifics about the ongoing military action. Gowon had broadcast to the nation on October 1, stating that Biafra was on the brink of collapse; he now planned for an end to the war and for reconciliation with all Igbo people. *Daily Times* journalist Dan Abasiekong, writing on the day of the Asaba massacre, noted, "Gowon has shown the way Nigerian hearts have been warmed by his latest gracious gestures to the Ibos."[72] Abasiekong continued that the Igbos "are still bona fide members of the Nigerian family, their frequent delinquent acts and misdemeanours notwithstanding."[73] Nevertheless, he concluded that no matter how well they were treated the country should be prepared for "hostility and treachery" from many implacable Igbos.[74]

[71]   John J. Stremlau, *The International Politics of the Nigerian Civil War, 1967–1970*, Princeton: Princeton University Press, 1977; Sylvanus A. Ekwelie, "The Nigeria Press under Military Rule," *International Communication Gazette*, 25, 1979, 219–232.

[72]   Dan Abasiekong, "How to Bring the Ibos back into Our Fold," *Daily Times* (Nigeria), Oct. 7, 1967, 5.

[73]   Ibid., 5.

[74]   Ibid.

Another newspaper, the *Daily Sketch*, gave more coverage to the military action, with a distinctly pro-government position, telling the story of the triumphant progress of the Army through the Midwest. On October 6, the *Sketch* reported the capture of Asaba, and noted that "civilians in the liberated areas ... are known to be giving their full support to the Federal troops now in their midst."[75] This was followed up on October 9 with a front-page photo of Muhammed and several officers on the Asaba Bridge: "victorious Federal troops, happy and contended (sic) ... on an inspection tour, following reports that the rebels had planted explosives there with a view to blowing it up."[76] Shortly after this photo was taken, the bridge was indeed blown up. The same story went on to report "disorder in the East," with the Biafrans apparently rising up against Ojukwu. Over the next week or so, the *Sketch* maintained the consistent theme of the imminent collapse of Biafra, reporting on "Ojukwu's world of fantasy,"[77] a "rebel army mutiny,"[78] the premature news that Onitsha had fallen, and even that Ojukwu ("Nigeria's Hitler") had been captured.[79]

Clearly the goal of the Nigerian press in late 1967 was to support the government and look toward the end of the war. Foreign media outlets were invoked to bolster the case that the Igbo had nothing to fear, and should quickly end the war. For instance, on October 6, an uncredited story in the *Daily Times* liberally quoted a *New York Times* editorial urging the government "to demonstrate a will and capacity for the national reconciliation and reconstruction it has promised"[80] The *New York Times* mentioned Gowon's conduct code: "He told the troops they were not fighting a war with a foreign enemy, nor were you fighting a religious war or Jihad." On October 7,

---

[75]   *Daily Sketch* (no byline), Oct. 6, p. 1.
[76]   *Daily Sketch* (no byline), "The March on Asaba Bridge," Oct. 9, 1.
[77]   *Daily Sketch* (no byline), "Ojukwu's World of Fantasy," Oct. 11, 1.
[78]   *Daily Sketch* (no byline), " Rebel Army Mutiny," Oct. 12, 1
[79]   Sina Bamgbose, "Ojukwu Captured?" *Daily Sketch*, Oct. 13, 1 and back page.
[80]   *Daily Times* (no byline), "The Ibos Miscalculated in Seceding – Says American Newspaper," Oct. 6, 1967, 3. The writer is quoting an unsigned editorial, "Way to Peace in Nigeria," Oct. 6, 1967, *New York Times*.

another uncredited story noted that "influential foreign newspapers have ... drawn attention to the stark fact that the game is up ... "[81] The story quoted extensively from the UK's *Guardian*, which praised Gowon and the "remarkable prowess of the Army," and a week later, the *Daily Times* cited the Italian *Corriere della Sera*, which blamed Ojukwu's "blind determination" for the downfall of the Igbos, while Gowon was "scrupulous, fair, absolutely free of political ambition."[82] The story also quoted Permanent Secretary Philip Asiodu telling a press conference in Germany that the government's goal was reconciliation: "there is no question of massacring Ibos in the captured areas." Asiodu did not then know that his younger brother, Olympic athlete Sydney Asiodu, had been killed in Asaba a few days earlier.

By October 27, the *Daily Times* was reporting that the Midwest military governor had decreed it would now be an offense to refer to the people of the Midwest Igbo-speaking areas (Ika, Asaba, and Aboh) as Igbo, stressing their distinction from Biafra, and "appealed to the people to learn to forgive and forget ... "[83] Shortly after, on November 17, the *Daily Times*, while reporting the troubling presence of "Biafran spies," was noting "the atmosphere in Asaba remains calm, with life gradually returning to normal."[84] Apparently, many civilians were returning, "doing serious cleaning in their homes which they abandoned at the sight of federal troops." Furthermore, the Asaba market is well stocked and open, with federal troops constituting 60 percent of the buyers. Meanwhile, "a Red Cross team that arrived about a month ago is still carrying out relief operations." Left unsaid is why homes need "cleaning," why the majority of trade involves soldiers, or indeed why relief operations are required in the liberated town – a point to which we will return in Chapter 4.

---

[81]   *Daily Times* (no byline),"Ibos Were Victims of Ojukwu Propaganda, Says UK Paper," Oct. 7, 1967, 2.

[82]   *Daily Times* (no byline), "Ibo Blindness Killed Peace Moves: Italian Paper," Oct.13, 1967, 7.

[83]   *Daily Times* (no byline), "Now No More Ika Ibo – By Order," Oct. 27, 1967, 8.

[84]   Iredia Osifo, "Five Rebel Spies Held in Asaba," Nigeria *Daily Times*, Nov. 17, 1967, 1.

It was somewhat ironic that one of the most common actions of the Nigerian press was to regularly invoke international media calls for the Biafrans to surrender, since most of the foreign press was in itself dependent on secondhand government sources for its coverage and very few independent journalists were able to see any action firsthand. Internationally, the Vietnam War and conflicts in the Middle East were seen as much more pressing, as well as easier to understand, and there was a widespread belief that the war would be over very quickly. In the United States, some concerns had been raised early in the conflict. On July 21, *New York Times* reporter Lloyd Garrison described brutal killings of civilian villagers as the troops drove toward Nsukka,[85] while 10 days later, *Newsweek* cautioned that "there are likely to be some pretty nasty massacres despite the little code-of-conduct booklet."[86] In general, however, the war was not being closely followed by the US press; when it began, Secretary of State Dean Rusk declared that Nigeria was "part of Britain's sphere of influence."[87] Unlike events in Congo a few years earlier, neither the United States nor the Soviet Union saw Nigeria as vital to their strategic interests, which made the Nigerian Civil War the first post–World War II conflict that did not evolve into a confrontation between the two superpowers, thus muting its international impact.[88]

In contrast, as we have noted, Nigeria was important to British interests, and the UK media were especially important in defining the story of the war, both to Nigeria and the world, since in the immediate post-colonial period they were extremely influential among elite Nigerians.[89] Unfortunately, they largely bolstered the official British position. For instance, at the same time as some US media were

[85] Lloyd Garrison, "Biafran War Refugees Describe How Nigerians Killed Villagers," *Toronto Globe and Mail* (*New York Times* News Service), July 21, 1967, 8.
[86] John Barnes, "Nigeria: A Time for Slaughter," *Newsweek*, July 31, 1967, 39.
[87] De St. Jorre, *The Brothers' War: Biafra and Nigeria*, Boston: Houghton Mifflin, 1972, 179.
[88] John J. Stremlau, *The International Politics of the Nigerian Civil War*, 1967–1970, Princeton: Princeton University Press, 1977.
[89] A.B. Akinyemi, "The British Press and the Nigerian Civil War," *African Affairs*, 71:285, 1972, 408–426.

questioning the behavior of the Nigerian troops, the *Observer* was describing the importance of Gowon's code of conduct.[90]

Indeed, the British press mostly relied on official Nigerian sources and hearsay accounts, a result of a combination of Nigerian censorship, lack of resources, laziness, and perhaps also pressure from their own government, whose goal was to avoid public discussion of civilian losses. Bill Norris, Africa correspondent for the *Times* of London, was one of the few British journalists to go into the field during 1967, tailing the federal troops through the Midwest, together with Independent Television News (ITN) reporter John Parker. They did so after defying a ban on traveling outside Lagos by manufacturing a fake letter of authority to carry with them.[91] According to Norris, most other reporters "stayed in Lagos and took briefings from the British Consulate [who] lied through their teeth throughout."[92] British journalist John De St. Jorre, who later wrote one of the most detailed accounts of the war, also wrote of Nigerian censorship and the "obstructionism of some of the top civilian and military officials in Lagos," adding wryly that "I remember one British weekly journalist mustering 3,000 words of lively copy, which was later published, when he was no nearer Biafra than Lisbon."[93] The FMG made it clear that any foreign journalist who visited Biafra would be declared *persona no grata* in Lagos. Thus the BBC's experienced West Africa correspondent Angus McDermid, who had been planning to cover both sides and had made early reports out of Biafra, was forced to remain in Lagos when he returned there.[94]

His replacement in Biafra, Frederick Forsyth, arrived in the east in July 1967. He recalled that his briefing described the secession as a "small bush uprising" and that Ojukwu had no real Igbo support.

90   Walter Schwarz, "Why Nigeria's War Splits Hawks and Doves in Whitehall," *The Observer*, Aug, 27, 1967, 4.
91   Bill Norris, "Media Ethics at the Sharp End," in David Berry, ed. *Ethics and Media Culture: Practices and Representations*, Oxford: Focal Press, 2000, 325–338.
92   Phone interview with Bill Norris, Dec. 14, 2011.
93   de St. Jorre, *Brothers' War*, 354
94   McDermid, quoted in Paul Harrison and Robin Palmer, *News Out of Africa: Biafra to Band Aid*, London: Hilary Shipman, 1986, 10.

"The Nigerian army was an absolutely magnificent fighting force which would sweep effortlessly through this rabble of Ibo tribesmen ... I was to file a summary of this 10-day war."[95] For a short time, BBC radio reported from its correspondents in both Biafra and Lagos. However, Forsyth's reports contradicted the official narrative and enraged British High Commissioner David Hunt. Forsyth was summoned back to London and told that "the BBC was extremely dissatisfied" with his reporting, after which he resigned. He recalls, "I knew there was a conspiracy of silence way back in October 1967 ... There was a brutal and callous cynicism operated by my government ... "[96] Forsyth later returned to Biafra, where he became perhaps the best-known apologist for Ojukwu's cause, becoming especially influential during the massive coverage of the famine.[97]

Forsyth's embrace of Biafra brought him great condemnation in London, where his reporting was generally dismissed as propaganda.[98] Meanwhile, the British government continued to exert influence over the country's press corps in direct and indirect ways. Bill Norris noted that reporters were regarded as potentially valuable sources of information to their government, and he described how he was approached by the military attaché at the British High Commission, who asked him to gather information on troop strength, combat-readiness, morale, and "the quality of officers and NCOs" – all for a fee.[99] Norris declined, but others undoubtedly accepted; indeed, British FCO

---

[95]   Forsyth, quoted in Harrison and Palmer, *News Out of Africa*, 11–12.

[96]   Ibid., 16.

[97]   See Frederick Forsyth, *The Making of an African Legend: The Biafra Story*, London: Penguin, 1969.

[98]   In 2015, Forsyth revealed that for the last year of the civil war, he was an unpaid informer for MI6, the British intelligence agency. His explanation was that MI6 wanted to find out if the reports of starvation in Biafra were accurate, given that many in the government were dismissing these reports as Biafran propaganda. According to Forsyth, he believed that confirming the accounts was important in countering the government's support for what he called "the Nigerian dictatorship." See Frederick Forsyth, *The Outsider: My Life in Intrigue*, London: Putnam, 2015.

[99]   Norris, "Media Ethics at the Sharp End," 329.

records have frequent references to information provided by journalists, including ITN's John Parker.[100]

While it certainly cannot be assumed that most journalists were
government informers, it is apparent that, at least until the famine story
became inescapable, the British press generally supported the government position. Colin Legum, for example, a highly respected journalist
and Africa expert, had written stories highly critical of the pre-war
treatment of the Igbo, but believed secession was "a nonsense which
wouldn't work," and that a fast end to the war was needed.[101] Indeed, an
important element in the pro-FMG position was that full support would
ensure a short conflict and would minimize casualties on both sides,

And with access to the fighting forbidden, most foreign journalists were too far from the action to know what was happening. All
these factors combined to ensure that the news media completely
missed the most significant single civilian massacre by FMG soldiers.
Even the few independent-minded journalists who did report from the
front – notably Bill Norris of the *Times* and Alfred ("Fred") Friendly
Jr. of the *New York Times* – were unaware of what happened at Asaba.
Norris passed through Asaba in mid-October, sending back photos of
the damage and noting that the town appeared to be largely
abandoned,[102] but he had no idea that a systematic massacre had
occurred.[103] This is perhaps less surprising when one realizes that
journalists' route (under guidance from the federal forces), took them
along the main road out to the Cable Point district and on to the
bridge, where Norris and others observed troops lobbing mortars
across the Niger. No reporters appear to have ventured off the main
road into the quarters. At Cable Point, Norris's camera captured
images of heaps of scattered property and women picking through

[100]   For instance, an FCO telegram noted, "we have been told by Parker, ITN reporter
         (protect source) who is usually reliable that six South African mercenary pilots have
         arrived at Kano," Aug. 21, 1967, UK National Archive, Telegram 2003, FCO 38/284,
         file 112.
[101]   Quoted in Harrison and Palmer, *News Out of Africa*, 27.
[102]   Some of these photos were published in Bill Norris, "War across the Niger,"
         The Times, Oct. 24, 1967, 14.
[103]   Telephone interview, Bill Norris, Dec. 14, 2011.

FIGURE 3.2 A woman combs through abandoned belongings looted from homes, Cable Point, Asaba. Photo by Bill Norris, October 1967, courtesy of *The Times*.

the debris, which he attributed to families having abandoned their homes, rather than widespread looting (Figure 3.2). Both ITN and Associated Press also had crews briefly filming in Asaba/Onitsha at the same time, and the images they broadcast of the Niger Bridge and abandoned property are virtually identical to those of Norris.

Likewise, the *New York Times's* Alfred Friendly had reported directly from Benin City when federal troops retook the city, mentioning the civilian reprisals against Igbo people.[104] Later, he reported that everyone in Asaba had fled as federal troops advanced:

> the bodies of two that did not leave in time lay near the main road. Vultures picked at the skeletons sprawled amid the pathetic rubble of panicky flight: empty, battered suitcases, and ruined bedding. Bullet scars pocked the façade of every house on the main street.[105]

---

[104] Alfred Friendly Jr., "City Shows Scars," 1.
[105] Alfred Friendly Jr. "Battle Continues for Nigerian City," *New York Times*, Oct. 13, 1.

West Africa correspondent "Griot" (most likely the magazine's Nigeria expert, Kaye Whiteman) gave a very similar account, clearly reporting from Cable Point, the area nearest the bridge, rather than from inside the town itself. The picture is of an abandoned town with a few unfortunate deaths, rather than the devastation that had occurred. Beyond these stories, no contemporary accounts of the fate of Asaba can be found.

WHAT DID THE BRITISH GOVERNMENT KNOW?

Exactly when the British government became aware of the extreme violence stemming from the Midwest action is not clear. As we have noted, the FCO records point to a continuing concern that Nigerian troops would commit atrocities, with the Wilson government seeing the potential for a groundswell of public opposition to the support of the FMG. To make matters worse, the British government was frustrated about the lack of information coming out of the Midwest. On September 1, a confidential letter from the British High Commission in Lagos had expressed this frustration. The writer noted that the FMG's publicity machine has been poor and misleading from the beginning, but now, in the aftermath of the Midwest invasion, "the areas of untruth have been extended ... there is an uncomfortable aura of exaggeration if not deliberate falsehood."[106] Even in Lagos, the lack of communication from the field, created by the autonomy (and in the case of Muhammed, the insubordination) of field commanders, meant that news spread slowly. According to Philip Asiodu,

> ... when the things happened in Asaba, there we were in Lagos. We didn't really get proper reports. The people who perpetrated it knew what they did was criminal ... they must have done their best to suppress reports coming out.[107]

---

[106]   Confidential letter from G.D. Anderson in British High Commission, Lagos, to Patrick H. Moberly, West and General Africa Department, Commonwealth Office, Sept. 1, 1967, UK National Archive, FCO 38/284, file 144.

[107]   Interview with Philip C. Asiodu, Oct. 8, 2009, Tampa.

Asiodu made frantic attempts to get news of his brother, but it was not until he visited Asaba toward the end of the war that he concluded Sydney must be dead. His body was never found, and it is not known for certain how he died.[108] There is evidence that attempts to inform people outside Asaba of the massacres were systematically suppressed by troops in the field. Akunwata Okocha, for example, wrote to the International Red Cross in October describing what had just happened. After his letter was intercepted by the military, he was arrested, tortured, and incarcerated in the notorious Kirikiri Prison in Lagos.[109] As we have noted, Celestina Isichei's letter to her brother in Oxford only made it out through the help of a sympathetic soldier.

Inevitably the FMG did find out, of course. Several witnesses report that a few weeks after the massacre, Col. Robert Adeyinka Adebayo, Military Governor of the Western Region, visited Asaba and was appalled at the destruction, although we have not found independent verification of this visit.[110] Philip Asiodu confirmed that government officials received no formal or detailed accounting of what happened, although he heard many informal reports from people who had escaped Asaba, and it was clear that widespread killings had happened. As a member of Gowon's inner circle,

> I participated throughout the crisis and civil war. And there was a small group of officers who met every night with the head of government, in the principal staff of the army headquarters, to review situation reports and hand out decisions ... So, I immediately had to address a memorandum to the head of government and say, "Look here, here is what has happened. We can't allow this to continue, because it'll destroy the whole hope of trying to keep one country."

---

[108]   Our interviewee, Emmanuel Onukwu, reported that he was in his house in Cable Point on October 6, along with Sydney Asiodu and others. Some decided to try to cross over the river to Onitsha, but Sydney left to return to his home in the same area. He was never seen again. Interview with Emmanuel E.K. Onukwu, Dec. 15, 2009, Asaba.

[109]   Interview with Akunwata S.O. (Sylvester) Okocha, Dec. 13, 2009, Asaba.

[110]   E.g. Interview with Akunwata S. Okocha; Interview with Luke Enenmoh.

According to Asiodu, "Some action was taken immediately, by the military government in Benin, which was in charge of the Midwest – action taken to try and reopen schools, relief materials, stop any further indiscipline." Asiodu later added that he facilitated

> a Delegation of people from Asaba and other places in Asaba Division ... to meet Gen. Gowon in Dodan Barracks to re-affirm their loyalty to One Nigeria and receive assurances that they were indeed accepted by him and the Federal Military Government as loyal citizens of Nigeria. Gen. Gowon received the Delegation well and expressed sympathy for those who had lost their dear ones and those who were suffering harassment, and assured them of protection.[111]

Asiodu was not the only one who attempted to address the situation in the weeks following. On February 1, 1968, Anthony Ukpabi Asika, Administrator of the new East Central State (and an Igbo from Eastern Nigeria), wrote a typed memo titled "For Discussion with the Commander in Chief," which addressed various issues pertaining to the "liberated areas of East Central State" (formerly in the Midwest region). Under a section titled "the case of Asaba," Asika proposed three responses. The first was originally titled "Admission of Tragedy," although the words "admission of" have been crossed out by hand and replaced with "the." The second two points are "investigation and publicity of results" and "restitution in forms of pensions to widows, orphans and other dependents now."[112] It does not appear that any of these actions were taken. This was perhaps not surprising since Asika, an Igbo from Eastern Nigeria was often in a precarious position, "attacked by a virulent Biafran Radio as the arch-quisling of all time, held in suspicion by many on the Federal side."[113]

---

[111] E-mail to Elizabeth Bird, Oct. 26, 2016.
[112] Copy of memo provided by Emeka Keazor, author of a biography of Asika, who obtained it from his papers (personal communication, July 2014).
[113] John de St. Jorre, *Brothers' War*, 380

Years later, in a speech of apology to Asaba, Gowon himself said that he knew nothing about the massacre until the 1990s: "it is not something that I would have approved ... I was made ignorant of it, I think until it appeared in the papers."[114] He repeated this assertion in 2016:

> Such a report was never made to me by anyone ... Do you think if I had known about such a thing at that time, I would not have done something about whoever was responsible?[115]

The Asika memo and Asiodu's accounts point to the fact that, in spite of Gowon's denials, some at the highest level of the FMG did know about widespread killings in Asaba within weeks, even if the horrific details of the organized massacre were not fully understood. Asika himself was cited as the source for a January 1968 article in the London *Observer*, describing how 700 people in Asaba had been killed as a result of a "misunderstanding," a point to which we will return.[116]

Undoubtedly publicity about the Asaba atrocities would have been a significant embarrassment to the FMG, which continued to maintain the position that the war was being conducted in accordance with the Code of Conduct, and the Igbo had nothing to fear. The same month that Asika essentially proposed coming clean about civilian deaths in the Midwest, the FMG published a glossy booklet about the Midwest liberation.[117] The publication described the Biafran army as an entity "whose record of plunder, pillage, robbery, vandalism, deprivation of civil liberties and other excesses is without parallel in our

114   Austin Ogwuda, "Gowon Faults Setting Up of Oputa Panel," *Vanguard News*, Dec. 09, 2002, available online at: https://groups.yahoo.com/neo/groups/Naija-news/conversations/topics/2517

115   Interview with Gen. Yakubu Gowon, Oct. 10, 2016, Abuja.

116   Colin Legum, "How 700 Ibos Were Killed by Mistake," *The Observer*, Jan. 21, 1968, 21.

117   Federal Military Government of Nigeria, *The Nigerian Crisis and the Midwest Decision*, Benin City, February 1968. Accessed at University of Oxford, Weston David Reading Room, reference C05. R00564.

history,"[118] and argued that the goal of the Biafran invasion was "the subjection of the entire people of Nigeria to perpetual Ibo rule."[119] It noted that when Murtala Muhammed entered Benin," his troops were embraced as liberators (which indeed they were by many), "and Midwesterners again started to breathe the air of freedom."[120] This echoed a speech given by Gowon on December 23, 1967, in which he decried the "malicious propaganda amongst our detractors" that had raised fears of annihilation among the Igbo, declaring that "Ibo-speaking parts of the Mid-West are fast recovering from the ravages of the rebel incursion."[121] As we noted earlier, there is no doubt that Gowon knew about the insubordination and volatility of Muhammed, just as the British did, but as he told an interviewer in 2007, his tenuous hold on power made it difficult to control him, and he was reluctant to remove him.[122]

The British government, while trying to keep pressure on Gowon behind the scenes, also continued a "business as usual" approach, standing firmly behind the FMG.[123] The authorities in London were clearly getting minimal information from the Midwest war front. The Nigerian media were publishing nothing negative, and the FMG's tight controls over foreign journalists actually seeing action were effective. The daily government reports, which depended heavily on local sitreps from commanders in the field, were sketchy at best. An October 7 sitrep noted that the Second Division had "secured Asaba 5 October ... by a direct attack astride the main Benin/Asaba road by the 6th brigade."[124] This was followed on October 9 by a report that "Federal 2 Division firm in Asaba by first light 6 October." It also

---

[118]   Ibid., 3.

[119]   Ibid., 7.

[120]   Ibid., 11–12.

[121]   Federal Ministry of Information, Lagos, "General Gowon Restates Objectives of War against Rebellion" (press release), Dec. 23, 1967, UK National Archive, FCO 38/285, file 273.

[122]   Michael Gould, *The Biafran War*, 69.

[123]   See John W. Young, *The Labour Governments 1964–1970, Vol. 2, International Policy*, Manchester: Manchester University Press, 2004.

[124]   FCO Daily Sitrep 74, Oct. 7, 1967, UK National Archive, FCO 38/285, file 193.

confirmed that the Niger Bridge had been blown on the eastern side that same day.[125] By October 11, there was "nothing to report" from the Midwest,[126] while by October 12, Biafran troops were reported back in force at Onitsha, shelling across the river to Asaba.[127] While there were reports of mob violence and confusion in Onitsha, nothing untoward was noted in Asaba. For a few days between October 7 and 12, there were several communications about a supposed "truce" that was being negotiated directly between the people of Ontisha and Murtala Muhammed, agreeing that they "will not be molested provided they permit his troops free movement through the town."[128] While the context of this is missing, and it was apparently dead by October 12 when Biafran troops settled firm into Onitsha, one might wonder whether the news of violence and mayhem in Asaba might have spurred local leaders in Onitsha to propose the truce.

Nevertheless, accounts were beginning to circulate about disastrous civilian losses soon after October, and eventually, these caused concern for the British government. One important catalyst was the handwritten letter sent by Celestina Isichei to her brother Patrick, a Catholic priest studying in Oxford. With the loss of his brothers, Emmanuel and Osi, Patrick learned that he was his mother's only surviving son.[129] Shocked and distressed, he made the letter available to Dame Margery Perham, then an Oxford professor and perhaps Britain's leading expert on West Africa, a scholar much respected in government circles. A typed copy of the letter was

---

[125]   FCO Daily Sitrep 75, Oct. 9, 1967, UK National Archive, FCO 38/285, file 194.

[126]   FCO Daily Sitrep 77, Oct. 11, 1967, UK National Archive, FCO 38/285, file 198.

[127]   FCO Daily Sitrep 78, Oct. 12, 1967, UK National Archive, FCO 38/285, file 199.

[128]   FCO Daily Sitrep 74, Oct. 7. Also, Sir David Hunt, in a "restricted memo" to Eric Norris, Foreign and Commonwealth Office, noted a possible ceasefire between Onitsha and Muhammed: "The Onitshans sent a message to Col Muhammed, who had just captured Asaba, asking him not to fire; he at once agreed (contrary to his blood-thirsty reputation) and they agreed to avoid all hostilities." He noted that this "not confirmed but credible ... the Ibos, like every African tribe, are riddled with factions and clans and there will always be one lot who don't want to persevere in a lost battle," UK National Archive, FCO 38/284, file 201.

[129]   Patrick and Celestina had additional siblings from their father's first wife.

made; it is now among Perham's papers in Oxford.[130] In response, Perham wrote a letter to *The Times*, published on October 31. She decried the lack of attention being given to Nigeria, and wrote,

> An Ibo clergyman brought me a letter today from his sister
> describing how in their family town, where there was no fighting,
> the government troops collected all the men including her young
> brother and used a machine gun upon them.[131]

With federal forces now pushing into the most heavily populated areas of Biafra, she noted that people might argue that Ojukwu should surrender and save his people. "But if the Ibo believe that the government forces are aiming at extermination ... they will not surrender and a long guerilla war of terrible brutality might ensue." She acknowledged that the Biafrans were not blameless in their behavior during the Midwest invasion, but "unless General Gowon and his council can control the conduct of their troops what hope can there be that ... the Ibo people can be won back to make an effective part of a reunited Nigeria?"

This letter was quickly followed on November 2 by a rebuttal from Sir Bryan Sharwood Smith, former Governor of Northern Nigeria and a firm supporter of the federal cause. He expresses his concern with Perham's letter, and urged that judgment on massacres should be reserved "until vouched for by responsible, independent witnesses."[132] He argued that such independent accounts should not be hard to find: "If they are true then those responsible should be pilloried. But if they are not true, as has been the case with other stories, then much harm can be done to future relations between Nigeria and this country." Smith acknowledged the excesses of the 1966 pogroms, but "No doubt can exist, too, of the sincerity and urgency of General Gowon's determination ... to limit the impact of

130   Celestina Isichei, letter to Patrick Isichei, Oct. 21, 1967, University of Oxford, Papers of Margery Perham, MSS Perham, 412/2/4.

131   Letters, *The Times*, Oct. 31, 11.

132   Letters, *The Times*, Nov. 2, 1967, 11.

war on innocent people and of his desire to bring the Ibo back to the conference table."

The case for the FMG continued with a letter from B.O. Ogundipe, from the Nigerian High Commission in London, who declared that "no iota of truth can be found in Dame Margery Perham's allegations ... "[133] Rather, he claimed, Midwesterners "had been brutalized by the rebels," and that after they were "liberated" by the federal forces, they had wanted revenge but had been calmed down by the newly appointed Military Administrator. He described supposed atrocities by the Biafrans: "Perhaps this is what Dame Perham mistakenly attributed to the Federal troops!" Dismissing all her allegations as "wild rumors," he reiterated Gowon's determination to bring the Ibo back into the Nigerian fold.

This series of exchanges ended with a letter published on November 30, written by Richard J.H. Matthews, an academic at Oxford. He asserted that Perham's allegations were true; he had read "no fewer than five hand-written letters confirming wanton rape and massacre of the Ibo civilian populace by Federal soldiers." He noted that one letter listed 18 victims by name, and "another gives an official Lagos Government figure of 702 killed at Asaba." He described additional letters, adding "it is noteworthy that many of those killed have been students or young professional men. There can be no doubt as to the truth of these matters." He concluded that perhaps the High Commissioner "will reconsider his contention that such reports contain 'no iota of truth.'"[134]

The British Government was clearly paying close attention to this discussion; copies of all four letters are archived in the FCO war records. Handwritten and initialed comments from several officials accompany the photocopy of the Matthews letter, dated from the day

---

[133]   Letters, *The Times*, Nov. 1, 1967, 11.

[134]   Letters, *The Times*, Nov. 30, 1967, 11. Matthews (now a resident of Switzerland) confirmed that Nigerian friends in Oxford showed him these letters, one of which referred to the "official Lagos government" figure (which would suggest the FMG knew details of the massacre). However, he had not kept these letters nor made copies of them at the time (phone call with Elizabeth Bird, Oct. 27, 2016).

of its publication through to December 6. One such comment reads: "Moderation and balance are qualities unknown to the partisans of either side in this war. But I fear that Mr. Matthews' letter carries more conviction than Brig. Ogundipe's denial."[135] All through this period, the British government records show a continuing concern about civilian casualties, with particular apprehension about Murtala Muhammed, who after his abortive attempts to capture Onitsha by means of an amphibious attack across the Niger, was becoming increasingly unpredictable and insubordinate. He ran his campaign as a virtually independent warlord; an eyewitness report published in mid-October described his headquarters as resembling "the court of some medieval warrior king, with flags strung over the porch and vehicles, instead of horses, churning up the mud outside."[136]

Muhammed was not the only commander who authorities in Lagos had difficulty controlling; during late 1967 and early 1968, the British government noted with dismay the tendency of all three Division commanders to operate autonomously, especially in terms of arms procurement, which the British government was trying to coordinate centrally: "The three field commanders seem to purchase whatever they fancy ... and are acquiring the status and habits of warlords."[137] However, concerns about Muhammed's unpredictability were especially strong, as they had been since the beginning of the war. In early December he had attended a meeting of military commanders in Lagos but, according to a memo from the British High Commission Lagos, had "reportedly refused to accept movement orders for the troops under his command, and had walked out of the meeting in dudgeon and had not returned." The memo continued that Muhammed is "insubordinate and dangerous," which "reminds one of the risks which Gowon is taking by refusing to discipline this young, headstrong, ruthless and tribalistically

---

[135]   UK National Archive, FCO 38/285, file 249.
[136]   Griot, "Roundabout: The View from the Bridge, Asaba,"1357.
[137]   Confidential memo from D.C. Tebbitt, Feb. 2, 1968, UK National Archive, FCO 38/ 270, file 420.

minded officer."[138] Concern about Muhammed continued into early 1968, as his troops went into action on the eastern shore of the Niger: "Muhammed has an ugly reputation and there is no doubt that in Asaba, as well as in Benin and Agbor, his troops rounded up and shot large numbers of Ibo in cold blood."[139] The underlying fear continued to be that as excessive civilian casualties become known, British and international public opinion would be roused.

Indeed since Asaba, word had been spreading in Britain that confirmed many of the government's worst fears, as with increasing desperation, various groups were trying to be heard. In early November, the *Guardian* published a brief article reporting on a Biafran press conference in which staff "distributed copies of a letter from an Ibo girl in Midwest Nigeria describing the slaughter by Federal troops of two other brothers."[140] But nothing more was heard; as Patrick Isichei recalled in 2015,

> We were struggling for someone, somewhere in the world to hear the story ... nothing that we did would bring it to the limelight. It was as if the whole world had turned against us and we were alone ... because of the almighty oil.[141]

Surviving letters in Perham's papers show that her high status made her the focus of such efforts, with many forwarding communications to her, hoping that she could convince the authorities to act, or at least get the word out to influence public opinion. For instance, on October 28, Andrew Osula, representing the Organisation for the Advancement of Africans (based in London), wrote to H.M. Burness, Information Officer of the Church Missionary Society (CMS, which had long been active in Asaba): "The war has reached its

[138] Memo from G.D. Anderson to P.H. Moberly, West and General Africa Department, Dec. 14, 1967, UK National Archive, FCO 38/285, file 259.
[139] Michael Newington (British High Commission), memo to Peter McEntee, West and General Africa Departments, Jan. 20, 1968, UK National Archive, FCO 38/285, file 292.
[140] Commonwealth Staff, "Inquiry Urged into Nigerian "Atrocities," *The Guardian*, Nov. 8, 1967, 5. We assume this was a copy of Celestina Isichei's letter.
[141] Interview with Father Patrick Isichei, Asaba, Oct. 6, 2015.

climax ... The peoples of the land – leaders, even the church, have lost control of the situation ... this is a danger!!!" He goes on: "we have appealed to the British Prime Minister to awaken the interest of the British and other Governments in the Nigeria crisis."[142] An October 31 letter from T.G. Brierly, Oxfam's field director for Western Africa, noted,

> a tragedy of appalling dimensions is unfolding .... Who can blame the Ibos for refusing to believe the Federal Government's honeyed words that they have nothing to fear? ... Reliable sources estimate that, following the Federal 'liberation' of the Mid-West, at least 700 Ibo civilians (including women and children) were slaughtered in Benin, over 1000 (mostly men) in Warri and Sapele, and over 2,500 in Asaba.[143]

CMS Officer Burness backed up Perham's assertions in a letter to Sir Gawain Bell (a former colonial administrator in Nigeria), dated November 3, citing "a source on which complete reliance can be placed":

> Between October 3 and 6, many people were killed in Asaba town. 1,000 reckoned as a low estimate ... On the second evening they came back to collect a present for the Federal O.C. to take it to him as a mark of respect and submission. Next morning a group, estimated as between 200–400, walked up the main road to seek an interview – met by a sergeant and a squad of soldiers – told him their business and handed over £170. He received this money and turned a machine gun on them. Many other people were hunted and killed. The soldiers for these several days were ruthless and apparently unrestrained and corpses lay everywhere.[144]

[142]   Andrew Osula, letter to Miss H.N. Burness, Oct. 28, 1967, University of Oxford, Papers of Margery Perham, MSS Perham, 412/4/82.

[143]   T. G. Brierly, letter to K.A. Bennett (Oxfam), Oct. 31, 1967, University of Oxford, Papers of Margery Perham, MSS Perham, 412/4/83.

[144]   H.N. Burness, letter to Sir Gawain Bell, Nov. 3, 1967, University of Oxford, Papers of Margery Perham, MSS Perham, 412/4/37.

Burness pointed to the potential consequences of the Asaba atrocities:

> Anyone concerned with this situation should not underestimate
> the atmosphere of fear which is at present making it impossible for
> the Ibo people to believe in the "sincerity and urgency of the
> determination of General Gowon and his associates to limit the
> impact of the war on innocent people" ... they believe that if they
> surrender, they will be shot down like the people at Asaba in the act
> of offering their token of respect and submission. And so they
> choose to die, fighting like the 2000 at Calabar – and not to consider
> any suggestion of sitting down at the conference table.

She concluded: "We are desperately concerned at the needs to arouse public opinion in this country to some awareness of what is going on ... "[145]

Burness wrote to Perham herself on October 31, responding to her published *Times* letter and noting how similar stories had reached CMS. She was preparing a letter to the *Observer*, "drawing attention ... to the gap between General Gowon's assurances to the Eastern Ibos and what seems to have actually happened in the Mid-West," and noting that this "must have had more effect on the attitude of the Eastern Ibos than any words from Lagos." Her conclusion, however, was resigned: "we have no confidence that HMG is prepared to take any action – rather the contrary." She attaches a Christian Council of Nigeria statement October 26, decrying "reports of indiscriminate killings," stressing that the Council is not taking sides, and ending "one is overwhelmed by the suffering and futility of it all."[146]

Finally, a handwritten letter from a Nigerian Igbo academic living in London thanked Perham for her *Times* letter, which "shows the outside world a picture of what federal victories have meant for us so far."[147] He described hearing from family about "destruction of Ibo

---

[145] Ibid.

[146] H.N. Burness, letter to Margery Perham, Oct. 31, 1967, University of Oxford, Papers of Margery Perham, MSS Perham, 412/2/37.

[147] I.O. Okonjo, letter to Margery Perham, Oct. 31, 1967, University of Oxford, Papers of Margery Perham, MSS Perham, 412/4/127.

life and property in Benin and in Asaba Division," with "dispropor-
tionate damage in Asaba ... what we are waiting for with bated breath
is to know exactly how many dear relatives we have lost ... " He noted
that "the revulsion which your article is bound to engender in the
civilized world will induce General Gowon and his council to translate declarations of good intentions toward Ibos ... into concrete
realities," since "There is no doubt that General Gowon is anxious
to have world opinion on his side."

However, the efforts to bring these events to public attention
turned out to be futile; the suffering of Asaba engendered no revulsion
in the "civilized world." Neither the London nor Lagos government
acknowledged any issues, and the compliant press either did not know
or did not care.[148] As de St. Jorre commented, "the press and the
lobbies ... were indistinguishable."[149] Furthermore, and echoing
O'Brien's earlier criticism about the lack of interest in the 1966
pogroms, de St. Jorre pointed to the racism inherent in coverage of
all African conflicts: "Black Africans, their sovereignties and their
sensibilities, were clearly not taken seriously ... By and large, the
old rule-of-thumb for African reporting – one dead white equals
a hundred dead blacks – held good in all its many ramifications."[150]
While it is hard to prove a direct connection between deep-rooted
racial attitudes and the indifference to suffering that characterized
Western attitudes to the war, a kind of casual racism permeated
much international reporting, whether from Britain, the US, or elsewhere. This was visible in the routine use of such terms as "Ibo
tribesmen," which became the default way to describe Biafrans, and
a tendency to use "tribalism" as a convenient explanation for the war
itself. A not untypical example from *Newsweek* once described a "call

[148]   The main exception to the complete silence on Asaba was the more independent
Guardian, which as well as reporting on the distribution of Celestina's letter, briefly
mentioned that Asaba had been "devastated" and that this "threatens to make the
false prophecies of Radio Enugu come true after all," ("Compromise –or Ruin for Both
in Nigeria," Nov. 10, 1967, 10). However, no details are provided.

[149]   de St. Jorre, *Brothers' War*, 356.

[150]   Ibid., 355.

to arms" broadcast by Ojukwu over Radio Biafra, that "thundered across Nigeria's secessionist Eastern Region ... like the throb of primitive drums ... directed at Biafra's Ibo tribesmen."[151]

Patrick Isichei sadly commented years later about the impact of this indifference, especially on the part of Nigeria's former colonists: "It changes your opinion about things ... Up until then I was all for what is sworn by the British – law and justice, and fairness, and straight-forwardness ... "[152]

The first (and only) press report specifically to address the Asaba killings appeared in January 1968, in the *London Observer*, as we have noted earlier. In this story, the widely respected Africa correspondent Colin Legum acknowledged credible reports of previous massacres, and confirmed that federal troops took part in the killing. As he noted, "there are no war correspondents on either side," and thus he is relying on second-hand reports. Some details are consistent with eyewitness accounts, including a mention that some of the civilians decided to welcome the troops with drumming and dancing. However, he reports that another group of "implacably hostile" Igbo attacked troops by surprise as they "began to relax with the entertainment provided for them."[153] "The soldiers' instinctive reaction was to scent 'Ibo duplicity and perfidy,'" and "in this blind mood of anger all Ibo males were rounded up and shot." Legum gave his source as East Central State Administrator Anthony Asika, who described the event as "a genuine misunderstanding." The story was headlined, "How 700 Ibos Were Killed by Mistake," acknowledging that the Federal Government did know what had happened. The story, however, provides an excuse by blaming the Igbos for supposedly attacking the troops – an event for which we have found no corroborating evidence. Legum did acknowledge that the episode, along with a massacre in Onitsha, "dramatically reinforced fears of genocide," but the account, by marking the event as exceptional and provoked, served to reinforce

---

151   *Time*, "Drums of Defeat," 90:14, Oct. 6, 1967, 70.
152   Interview with Patrick Isichei.
153   Colin Legum, "How 700 Ibos Were Killed," 21.

both the Lagos and London positions that civilian deaths were minimal and unusual.

Maintaining that position was important to head off increasing pressure to stop arms sales. Several months previously there had been suggestions that the threat of an arms cut-off could be used to force federal authorities to control the behavior of their troops; by the end of the year, the goal had become to maintain secrecy about escalating sales, as the British worried about a possible loss of influence if other powers moved in as suppliers. In early December, the government took "the extraordinary step of diverting to Nigeria a consignment of new-model armoured cars that had been intended for the British army – which was forced to wait 12 to 15 months for replacements."[154] Even as they were working to keep the Asaba atrocities under wraps, the British authorities were also focused on "spinning" this continued escalation. Thus on December 19, 1967, the head of the Commonwealth Office news department advised on how to head off press scrutiny, noting that "new orders for large quantities of material clearly raised difficult questions." Discussing whether to maintain a position that nothing had changed, he wrote, "If the actual facts become known such as line would undoubtedly damage our reputation for credibility with the Press."[155] Three days later, a confidential memo was issued on how to deal with press questions in the event that journalists "get wind of the new order being shipped out," although "we should not volunteer any information of the details of the orders." One concession to the realities of the escalating sales was "we should not try to maintain a distinction between offensive and defensive weapons."[156]

[154]   Philip Alexander, "A Tale of Two Smiths: the Transformation of Commonwealth Policy, 1964–70," *Contemporary British History*, 20:3, 2006, 315.

[155]   D.D. Condon, Head of News Department, memo to Commonwealth Office, Dec. 19, 1967, UK National Archive, FCO 38/269, file 383.

[156]   T.J. Allison, Note to Press Officers, Dec. 22, 1967, UK National Archive, FCO 38/269, file 388.

At the same time, there is evidence that Britain continued to pressure Gowon to remove Muhammed because of the continuing accounts of atrocities (see Chapter 4), and he was eventually removed from the combat zone in May 1968. However, by then both Britain and the FMG seemed to have successfully avoided any public outcry about excesses in the field, with media attention and public concern having shifted to the starvation crisis.

BIAFRAN RESPONSE

Just as the series of letters of Margery Perham had warned, while the authorities in Lagos and London downplayed the events in Asaba, the Biafrans saw them as the prelude to an even greater disaster – all-out genocide. At the onset of the war, fear of genocide, in the wake of the massacres of Igbos in the north and west, was a key factor in the decision to secede. At the same time, Ojukwu had also positioned secession as essentially a struggle for political self-determination. Following the failed invasion of the Midwest, the central theme of Biafran propaganda became that the war was a defensive struggle against federal troops bent on the mass slaughter of Igbo people, and this rhetoric of genocide became one of Biafra's most effective tools to stiffen the resolve of the Igbo in the East.

Asaba was not the only killing of civilians committed during the first few months of the war. Witnesses in Asaba also mentioned violent killings in nearby small communities such as Ogwashi-Ukwu, Ibusa, and Igbodo, all of which were largely ignored in media and official reporting. However, the October 7 Asaba massacre, with its evidence of planning and coordination, sent a uniquely chilling message to people in Biafra, who feared that if federal troops would massacre so many of those who remained loyal to Nigeria, simply because of their ethnicity, they would do far worse to Igbos who had defied the government and seceded.

Alfred Obiora Uzokwe, in a memoir of childhood in Biafra, describes how the news of the massacre reached his mother, who was a member of the Gwam family from Asaba: "She was crying uncontrollably and reeling on the floor ... I wondered why God would let such calamity befall us."[157] Obiora's grandfather, G.W. Gwam, plus two uncles and several other relatives, died in the massacre, leaving his father bereft and angry as he tried to console his wife: "He blamed Britain in his prayers for aiding and abetting the federal troops; he blamed Czechoslovakia; he blamed Egypt and all those supporting the Nigerian troops and causing this suffering ... I simply despised Yakubu Gowon and abhorred his lieutenants."[158]

For some from the Midwest, the massacre was the catalyst that led them to throw in their lot with Biafra. In 1967, Joseph Anene Okafor was a final-year student at St. Patrick's College, Asaba, preparing for university entrance: "Many of us west of the Niger did not feel we were really part of what was happening in the Ibo heartland ... it was a fight between Gowon and Ojukwu ... if the Feds enter Asaba we would welcome them, being part of Nigeria."[159] However, Joseph's elder brother, Nwadu, a civilian worker in Benin City, was killed by federal troops there. Worried about the advance to Asaba, Joseph and his father left for the East right before the bridge was blown. He had no intention to fight for Biafra, but "the massacres in Asaba were several murders too many," and at that point he signed up. "I would say that the incident was more compelling than any other thing to join the army."[160]

And for those already committed to Biafra, the Asaba massacre was clearly pivotal. Philip Onyekeli, a Midwest Igbo, began fighting for the FMG, but later reluctantly joined the Biafrans, as we describe in Chapter 1.[161] He was assigned to a military training school in Umuahia, where he heard about Asaba. The news was "a turning point in the feelings of a lot of us, that these people were just brutal."[162] The deliberate assembly and slaughter of civilians who

[157] Alfred Obiora Uzokwe, *Surviving in Biafra: The Story of the Nigerian Civil War,* New York: Writers Advantage, 2003, 70.
[158] Ibid., 70–71.
[159] Joseph Anene Okafor, e-mail to Elizabeth Bird, Aug. 26, 2014.
[160] Ibid.
[161] Interview with retired Gen. Philip Onyekeli, April 16, 2016, Lagos.
[162] Ibid.

had come to pledge support was "unheard of in modern warfare."[163]
He recalls that "it changed their thinking. If anyone was thinking
there was going to be peace ... there was not going to be any peace.
It had to be full-scale war."[164] Simon Uchenna Achuzia, the young son
of Biafran Col. Joseph Achuzia, then living in Onitsha, also recalled
the dreadful news about Asaba: "the game changed," in terms of how
Biafrans felt about the war.[165] Indeed, the impact of Asaba continued
to resonate throughout the war; in August 1968, the *New York Times*
reported a conversation with a Biafran civil servant who explained
why they were fighting on against such overwhelming odds:
"We know what happens, even if we don't fight back. At Asaba,
every man and boy was shot and dumped in the river. The missionaries saw it."[166] In October 1967, the fall of Enugu had led to much
speculation that Biafra would soon seek peace; if there had been widespread confidence that there would be no reprisals, it is possible this
might have happened, with countless lives saved. Instead, in the wake
of the Asaba killings, Biafran fear and resolve hardened.

At the same time, Ojukwu and his government tried to capita-
lize on what they hoped would be widespread revulsion at the killings,
launching into a full-scale effort to make an international case for
genocide. In February 1968, the Joint Consultative Assembly of
Biafra sent a long document to the UN Committee on Human
Rights, listing multiple atrocities, starting with the 1966 pogroms
and continuing through the Midwest invasion. In requesting that the
war be ruled genocide, it noted that "Asaba was one of the centers of
mass killings of the natives," and it gave detailed accounts of murder
and rape, with one witness estimating 2,000 killed.[167] A second, much

---

[163] Ibid.

[164] Ibid.

[165] Interview with Simon Uchenna Achuzia, March 14, 2014, Asaba.

[166] Lloyd Garrison, "Biafrans Accept Risk of Defeat," *The Times* (from *New York Times*), Aug. 3, 1968, 3.

[167] Joint Consultative Assembly of Biafra, letter to Third Committee of the United Nations on Human Rights, Feb. 15, 1968. The document cited multiple instances in support of the genocide argument, including (in Appendix D) the testimony of Mr. J. Dike Ofili of Asaba, who described rape and killings in the town. Clearing

briefer letter, written a few days later to UN General Secretary U Thant, cited many of the same examples in making the case for a ruling of genocide, arguing that the 1966 pogroms constituted "a genocide of an enormity only equaled in recent times by the experience of Jews from the Nazis."[168]

CONSEQUENCES

However, the attempts to bring attention to civilian casualties gained little traction, with the successful British efforts to downplay these events. N.U. Akpan, Biafra's Head of Civil Service, wrote in his memoirs that Biafra, as arguably the most Westernized region of Nigeria, had initially placed great faith in Britain and that, early in the war, the British could have brokered peace: "the British government ... could have found a way to end the war without compromising their policy ... if they had really wanted to."[169] Instead, it was not until mid-1968, when the war had essentially entered its new phase and was being played out under the glare of much more international scrutiny, that Britain felt compelled to act, as we shall see in our next chapter.

And so the war dragged on for more than two years after the slaughter at Asaba. In Asaba itself, the remaining and returning civilians settled into a sometimes uneasy peace, with soldiers and civilians coexisting, as the eyes of the world focused on the suffering across the Niger River. Asaba remained little more than a footnote in the history of the Civil War. In 1970, de St. Jorre described the massacre as "inexcusable," but essentially dismisses it as an aberration.[170] This position was maintained in later accounts; for

[168] House for Nigeria/Biafra Information, "Nigeria/Biafra Information Collection," Reel 5. Center for Research Libraries, Chicago.
M.T. Mbu, Commissioner for Foreign Affairs and Commonwealth Relations, Republic of Biafra, to His Excellency U Thant, Feb. 24, 1968. Accessed in Clearing House for Nigeria/Biafra Information, "Nigeria/Biafra Information Collection," Reel 5. Center for Research Libraries, Chicago.

[169] Ntieyong U. Akpan, *The Struggle for Secession 1966–1970: A Personal Account of the Nigerian Civil War*, London: Cass, 1972, 151.

[170] De St. Jorre, *Brothers' War*, 285. De St. Jorre essentially restates Legum's 1968 explanation that the massacre "was sparked off by a Biafran attempt to kill a Nigerian officer and organized by a bitterly anti-Ibo Midwesterner." However, in

instance Kantowicz, in his 1999 historical overview, concludes that "during the fighting, civilians and some Nigerian soldiers slaughtered Ibos at the cities of Asaba and Onitsha, but these massacres were exceptional and were not ordered by the Nigerian commanders."[171] The most recent history, by Michael Gould, barely mentions Asaba.[172]

These omissions, however, have led to a widespread underestimation of the importance of Asaba in the progress of the war. Certainly, the extent of the organized killing remained unique, even as often brutal actions continued with federal advances. A thriving town, never part of the secession, had been deeply traumatized and its inhabitants scattered – a disaster for the people themselves. However, its significance lies beyond the immediate suffering of its people – both in what it did not precipitate, and also in what it did. This early in the war, Asaba could have been a deep embarrassment, both to the Nigerian government and its allies in London. If the tragic, personal stories that remain fresh even 50 years later had been broadcast to the world's living rooms when they happened, it is certainly conceivable that Britain's position would have been seriously undermined. In late 1967, Commonwealth Secretary Arnold Smith had argued for a peacekeeping force that would monitor the war and try to speed up a peace, but to no avail. Had the full truth been known then, his argument would surely have been stronger. British authorities knew that atrocities had happened and discussed options that might have produced an earlier peace, but eventually decided that total support of the FMG, to preserve both the unity of the country and British economic interests, was the only option. In turn, the realization that such actions could happen with impunity undoubtedly emboldened elements in the Nigerian military, especially in the Second Division.

his usually meticulously footnoted book, de St. Jorre offers no source for this account. His book does expressly acknowledge the contributions of Legum, with whom he worked at the *London Observer*.

171   Edward R. Kantowicz, *Coming Apart, Coming Together: The World in the 20th century, Vol. 2*, New York: Eerdmans, 1999, 244.
172   Michael Gould, *The Biafran War*.

In late March 1968, for example, Muhammed's forces committed another major atrocity – the massacre of about 300 civilians, including women and children, who had gathered to pray in Onitsha cathedral as the federal army moved in to finally take the town.[173] Like the massacre at Asaba, this event received little international press coverage, aside from a brief mention in the *Times* a month later.[174] Thus the combination of news management and control in both Lagos and London, no doubt facilitated by international indifference to the plight of Africans killing Africans, ensured that the war continued.

Meanwhile, Asaba "proved" to Biafrans that their fears of genocide were true and that their only option was to fight to the death, a point the British themselves understood, even as they hoped that the Biafran reverses would precipitate a rebellion against Ojukwu and a subsequent surrender.[175] As Donald Tebbitt, a senior Foreign Office official on Nigeria, noted in November 1967 as a peacekeeping force was being discussed, "Fear for their lives is the mainspring of Ibo resistance and this is where a peace force could have a part to play."[176] An unnamed official added a handwritten comment: "I can see no reason why the Ibos should 'see the flaws' in the theory that the Northerners might show them no mercy. Not much seems to have been shown in Benin and Asaba."[177]

In 1970, when the war ended, the once-dreaded extermination of Igbos did not materialize. Beginning during the war, and continuing until today, scholars, activists, and others have disagreed about whether it was a war of genocide against the Igbo, using first civilian massacres and then starvation. Heerten and Moses offered the most comprehensive and measured recent discussion of this question, focusing primarily on the question of intent – that true genocide is usually understood to include a systematic attempt to wipe out

---

[173]   De St. Jorre, *Brothers' War*, 188.

[174]   William Norris, "Biafrans' Ordeal by Air Attack," *The Times*, April 25, 1968, 8.

[175]   Donald Tebbit, summary of report by Col. Robert E. Scott, defense advisor in British High Commission, Lagos, Nov. 24, 1967, UK National Archive, FCO 38/285, file 247.

[176]   Ibid.

[177]   Ibid.

a people, based primarily on their identity. They point to the complexities of Biafra, such as the fact that Biafra comprised many other ethnic groups who also suffered, while Igbos still living elsewhere in Nigeria were not targeted. This indicates that the intent of the war was indeed to end secession and preserve Nigerian unity, not wipe out the Igbo. At the same time, the methods used were often horrific and inexcusable: "On these terms, the Biafra case, with the blockade representing an attack on the entire population, seems to occupy a grey zone between degenerate warfare and genocide."[178] Few now argue that Gowon's government ever had deliberate genocidal intent, and there is no evidence that he ordered or condoned killings at Asaba or anywhere else.[179] Nevertheless, it is clear that hatred for Igbos did drive some of those who served in his name, and that his policies and leadership were unable to contain those genocidal impulses. In a chaotic and undisciplined theater of war, the people of Asaba suffered more than any other community west of the Niger; their suffering continued throughout the war, and the scars have not yet healed.

[178]   Lasse Heerten and A. Dirk Moses, "The Nigeria–Biafra War: Postcolonial Conflict and the Question of Genocide," *Journal of Genocide Research*, 16:2–3, 2014, 190.

[179]   See for example Bartrop, "The Relationship between War and Genocide"; Gould, *The Biafran War*.

4   Surviving the Occupation

The Nigerian Civil War had begun with weeks of rapid action. The federal advance and occupation of the Eastern city of Nsukka followed by the Biafran counteroffensive in the Midwest had created in both sides the belief that the conflict could be brought to a quick and definitive resolution through lightning advances and conclusive military victories. For federal authorities, the prospect of a swift conclusion was bolstered by the recapture of the Midwest and the occupation of Asaba. Murtala Muhammed's goal was a dramatic and decisive victory, and internationally the expectation was that the war would be over before the New Year of 1968.

However, as we have seen, Muhammed's failures at Asaba dispelled any illusions of a quick victory, and the actions of his troops against civilians had created new resolve and new recruits for Biafra. The conflict became a war of attrition marked by small skirmishes, while the economic blockade started the deadly work of starvation. In the words of Axel Harneit-Sievers, it was a war to be won "by the side that could, on the long run, mobilize more human, military and economic resources that the other."[1]

While Muhammed was bogged down in Asaba, the Federal First Division under Col. Mohammed Shuwa had occupied the Biafran capital city of Enugu, while the Third Marine's Commando Division, under Gen. Benjamin Akundele captured the Eastern city of Calabar, eventually sealing off Biafra's border with Cameroon. With the island of Bonny, which controlled access to the Atlantic, firmly in federal hands, Biafra was now completely encircled and landlocked.

---

[1]   Axel Harneit-Sievers, "The People, the Soldiers, and the State," in Axel Harneit-Sievers, Jones O. Ahazuem, and Sydney Emezue, *A Social History of the Nigerian Civil War: Perspectives from Below*, Enugu: Jemezie Associates and Hamburg: Lit Verlag, 1997, 46.

Between October and April, the war dragged on, especially in the Asaba-Onitsha zone, with the Biafrans in control of Onitsha.

Meanwhile, the Biafrans were trying to gain international attention for their claims of genocide against civilians, with little success. British authorities continued to express private anxieties about Murtala Muhammed, with the fear that news would emerge about civilian casualties. This was compounded by concern about the actions of Col. Benjamin Akundele (known as the "Black Scorpion"), whose troops had reportedly massacred civilians in and around Calabar when that city was taken in October, including "all the male inmates of the mental hospital."[2] By January 1968, the British were writing that Akundele was "widely believed to be mentally unbalanced and has undoubtedly instated something like a reign of terror in Calabar."[3]

Muhammed's stalemate was finally broken in December 1967, when the Sixth Brigade of the Second Division, bolstered by reinforcements, crossed the Niger River further north at Idah and advanced on Onitsha, finally capturing it after several attempts. The intention was to eventually link with the First Division at Enugu. However, Muhammed's penchant for indecisiveness and poor communication continued, and it was not until late March 1968 that troops headed toward Enugu, traveling in a long convoy with about 6,000 troops. On March 31, near the town of Abagana, Biafran troops ambushed the column. A homemade rocket missile (known as *ogbunigwe*) hit a truck carrying gasoline, which exploded and set off a chain reaction that destroyed many vehicles, killed possibly thousands of federal troops, and allowed the Biafrans to capture large amounts of equipment.

Abagana was the last Biafran success in the war, slowing down the Nigerian advance into Biafran territory. By then, the pressure from

2   Memo from Michael Newington in British High Commission to Peter McEntee, West and General Africa Departments, Jan. 28, 1968, UK National Archive, FCO 38/285, file 292.
3   Ibid.

Britain to remove Muhammed was intense; even then, Gowon was reluctant. According to Gowon's wartime Federal Commissioner of Information, Anthony Enahoro, who worked closely with the British government, "If there was anyone that Gowon feared so much, it was Murtala Muhammed."[4] Muhammed was eventually reassigned out of the war zone in May 1968; Enahoro explained that this was not only because of the humiliating defeat at Abagana, but also because the British were again threatening to curtail arms sales. Enahoro claimed that he threatened to leave the cabinet if Muhammed was not removed. Eventually Gowon agreed, on condition that Enahoro be the one to confront him: "At the meeting of the Federal Executive Council I confronted Muhammed with elaborate evidence complete with photographs. He was livid. He could not refute them so resorted to calling me all sorts of names ... Needless to say, I was instrumental to his withdrawal from that sector ... "[5] Muhammed was reassigned to Signals Division, and never saw combat again.

LIFE UNDER OCCUPATION

In Asaba, as October drew to a close and the main war action was elsewhere, many had found refuge in nearby bush, or in small towns in the area; others had gone to Biafra and did not return until the war ended in 1970. Everything of value had been stolen or destroyed, and the once thriving town was a ruin. In late October an official British government account stated that while a total of 8,000 troops were stationed in Asaba, the "whole civilian population has left the town" (clearly something of an exaggeration).[6] A month later the same source reported that things had improved slightly with "some 5–600 civilians (few of them male) now in Asaba. Market women conducting brisk business. Bulk of civilians live in refugee camp outside town." The town however continued to present a desolate scene: "Asaba

---

4   McLord Obioha, "Why FGN Used Hunger against Ibos: Interview with Anthony Enahoro," *The Nigerian and Africa*, March 1998, 10.

5   Ibid.

6   FCO Daily Sitrep 92, Oct. 31, 1967, UK National Archive, FCO 38/285, file 217.

reported badly damaged with destruction worst at Cable Point and places nearer Onitsha. Most buildings in town have suffered, some buildings in centre of town gutted by fire."[7]

While federal authorities encouraged people in the "liberated areas" to return to their homes British officials recognized "[o]f course discipline is appallingly bad, and the troops do not behave themselves when drunk."[8] It is no surprise then that conditions remained dire in Asaba. Streets were empty as the remaining inhabitants stayed in what was left of their damaged houses and began to rebuild their lives. This was a slow and agonizing process, and for the next year, life in Asaba was difficult and constrained. Free movement was forbidden, and people had to obtain a pass to shop at the market or tend their land in the nearby agricultural areas.[9] In the immediate aftermath, those who had remained in Asaba, or who trickled back as things settled down, were focused primarily on survival. Many returned to what was left of their houses, gradually making them habitable. Igwemma Osakwe described how after the destruction of their home, his family subsisted in a room in another partly built house while gathering thatch and building materials from elsewhere.[10] Others subsisted in refugee camps established in local schools, such as St. Patrick's College, joining other displaced refugees from surrounding areas.[11] Rehabilitation groups were formed, and people tried to rebuild their lives as best they could. Red Cross worker Frank Ijeh, for example, tried to care for the

---

[7]   FCO Daily Sitrep 112, Nov. 29, 1967, UK National Archive, FCO 38/285, file 243.
[8]   Michael Newington (British High Commission), memo to Peter McEntee, West and General Africa Departments, Jan. 20, 1968, UK National Archive, FCO 38/285, file 292.
[9]   See Egodi Uchendu, *Women and Conflict in the Nigerian Civil War*, Trenton, NJ: Africa World Press, 2007. A focus group participant (male, 32, unemployed) described how his father lost his farmland, and all his crops were destroyed; another participant, male, retired army officer, 58, described working on the family farm with little water, no money, and the need for a pass to move around. Four focus groups were conducted in Asaba, March 14, primarily concerned with the short and long-term effects on the community. Most of the 20 participants were not born until after the war, although one group included three individuals in their 50s.
[10]   Interview with Igwemma Osakwe, Dec. 12, 2009, Asaba.
[11]   Uchendu, *Women and Conflict*.

injured and sick: "There was no hospital, no clinic, nothing. But I set up one in my house."[12] He remembered that the Headmistress of Asaba Girls Grammar School, Jane Backhouse, was among those who helped, bringing him drugs and supplies, and generally helping out. Later, after a trip back to Britain, Backhouse's sympathies apparently changed; Luke Enenmoh described how when she returned, "she appeared to be singing a different tune ... dismissing events that happened in her presence ... denying that there was such a general massacre."[13] He believed she "was adopting a kind of British government view, to play down the whole thing," a view that seems plausible given the British approach discussed in Chapter 3. Thus during these months immediately following the massacre, Asabans were caught in an impossible situation, struggling to survive while under occupation from soldiers who distrusted their every move.

RAPE: THE SPECIAL BURDEN OF WOMEN

During the period of military occupation, for women and girls, the fear of rape was ever-present, especially with so few men to protect them. As Tuba Inal noted, "throughout history, it is almost impossible to find a war where rape did not happen,"[14] yet it was only in the late twentieth century that rape began to be recognized as one of the most devastating crimes of war.[15] Our older male informants typically referred to rape not as a violation of women, but as a challenge to men's rights over "their" women, for the shame it brought on husbands whose wives or daughters were raped in front of them or

---

[12] Interview with Frank Ijeh, Dec. 13, 2009, Asaba.

[13] Interview with Luke Enenmoh, Oct. 10, 2014, London.

[14] Tuba Inal, *Looting and Rape in Wartime: Law and Change in International Relations*, Philadelphia: University of Pennsylvania Press, 2013, 4.

[15] The 1977 Additional Protocols to the Geneva Conventions offered the first legal protection against rape in wartime, and in 1998, the Rome Statute defined rape explicitly as a war crime. The 1993 efforts to document 40,000 cases in Bosnia-Herzegovina represented the first systematic recording of rape "as a weapon of war." See Michelle Hynes and Barbara Lopes-Cardozo, "Observations from the CDC: Sexual Violence against Refugee Women," *Journal of Women's Health and Gender-Based Medicine*, 9:8, 2000, 819–823.

abducted by soldiers.[16] Emmanuel Mordi described how soldiers commandeered his family compound and brought women there to be raped: "My aunt, about 65 years old at that time was ejected from her room which was then utilized. We were in an adjoining room."[17]

In our interviews, both male and female participants described the widespread rape and forcible "marriages" to soldiers, while also vividly showing how shameful and difficult it was to acknowledge this at the time:

> Oh, yeah, there were rapes. I came by enough girls that were forcibly married by soldiers. I have an auntie who was forcibly married by a soldier. After, he left the woman with the children … Children were raped, even old women were raped … They treated us like animals.[18]

Josephine Onyeneman described how she managed to avoid a forcible "marriage" at the age of 13, through the strong will of her grandmother. Soldiers came to her house and tried to take her away:

> I refused. My grandmother … said I am too small to marry now. Why would they force me? … My grandmother said, a soldier killed your father, killed your brother, it is a shameful thing to go marry them. So my grandmother pushed me inside in a room … there I am staying … I am afraid. I am afraid.[19]

Many others were not so fortunate:

> The family we stayed with, their daughter was abducted by soldiers … taken from Asaba … and brought back to her father after a week. When she came back, she was a different girl … she wouldn't talk to anybody, she was very weepy … We got to hear later that the child was taken by one of the officers and used for a week … But, you

---

[16] See also Jyotsna Mishra, *Women and Human Rights*, New Delhi: Kalpaz, 2000, for a discussion of rape as humiliation of the male enemy.
[17] Emmanuel Mordi, e-mail to Elizabeth Bird, July 22, 2016.
[18] Interview with Nkemdelim Maduemezia, June 23, 2010, Asaba.
[19] Interview with Josephine Onyemenam, June 23, 2010, Asaba.

see, we come from a culture where talk like rape is taboo – a girl says she's been raped, getting married is like an impossibility. So lots of girls had been raped and not said anything.[20]

In these accounts there was no doubt as to who bore the physical and emotional scars of the experience: "One of our sisters, one of the army officers took her away and dumped her ... At that time he has impregnated her and then he moved away."[21] Emeka Okonkwo, a boy of six in 1967, observed something he did not understand at the time:

I can remember my mom and one other lady, a soldier man was pointing at them ... And my mum and her was kneeling down, begging. After some time my dad took us to the sitting room. And later my mom came and joined us again ... when I told my mom what I witnessed, she was shocked that I could remember such.[22]

Another male interviewee spoke of the long-standing trauma experienced by a female relative:

After the killing of people in Asaba ... They started raping the women. They come to the house. They say they heard gunshots around, that the women are hiding the soldiers. They take them away, then they bring them back later. These girls come back, they cannot talk ... One of my relatives, when she sees me, she says, "Fabian, do you remember what happened when they came to take us away?" She told me, "I have not discussed this. I have never mentioned it to my husband." She is feeling bad that she wants to tell him. I said, "Listen, it's your deal. If you want to tell him, tell him." She says, "I want you to tell him." So, we went out ... he said he'd never heard, and when he got home, they cried. Anyway, at the end, that was a way for her to forget, because she's been carrying it in her mind all along.[23]

---

20 Interview with Gertrude Ogunkeye, Dec. 11, 2009, Lagos.
21 Interview with Ken Eneamokwu, June 28, 2010, Asaba.
22 Interview with Emeka Okonkwo, June 28, 2010, Asaba.
23 Interview with Fabian Oweazim, Oct. 10, 2009, Tampa.

While we heard no first person accounts of rape it is clear that the practice was pervasive. Several women described how as young girls, they were disguised as older women or given babies to carry, in an attempt to ward off would-be rapists. Victoria Uraih recalled, "I carried my younger brother at the back, and my grandmother gave me her dress ... so that I would look like an old woman. The same thing with my sister, and my cousin."[24] In addition, their stories pointed to the fact that, contrary to many survivors' reports that only males died, many women were killed in the massacres and occupation, often after resisting the soldiers' advances. Luke Enenmoh, one of the few mature men remaining in Asaba at the time, described how difficult it was to protect women, although Captain Matthias was again remembered for trying to help:

> Some of us saw soldiers dragging women and we couldn't say anything because we were too scared we would be killed ... One girl ... her mother came to our village and said her daughter was taken. At that time, Captain Matthias was around and ... he followed me with some soldiers, we went and rescued the girl. And he took the girl to his headquarters and said, stay here. I understand later that a major, a Nigerian major came there and requested that that girl should come with him, and so Captain Matthias couldn't help it because he was his superior officer.[25]

In the last few years, many studies have appeared of the traumatic effect of wartime rape.[26] For women, the experience of rape must somehow be incorporated in their daily lives as they continue to function as mothers and providers, often in silence.[27] So many years later, it is probably impossible to capture the suffering of women in Asaba, yet the literature from more recent events can act as surrogate.

[24]   Interview with Victoria Nwanze (née Uraih), May 3, 2012, Asaba.
[25]   Interview with Luke Enenmoh.
[26]   E.g. Wenona Giles and Jennifer Hyndman, eds., *Sites of Violence: Gender and Conflict Zones*, Berkeley: University of California Press, 2004.
[27]   Veena Das, *Life and Words: Violence and the Descent into the Ordinary*, Berkeley: University of California Press, 2007.

As Inal writes, "For centuries ... the physical pain of women has been translated into a social pain through the meanings attached to rape."[28] In Asaba, the mass rapes have indeed left a palpable legacy in the community at large, which we shall explore in more detail in our final chapter.

CHALLENGES TO SURVIVAL

While many other communities throughout Nigeria and the secessionist Biafra suffered great loss of life in the war, few lost so many key people in such a targeted way. On entering Asaba, while federal troops killed people indiscriminately, they also singled out influential men, as we have noted, and many more elders and titled men were in the forefront of the Ogbe-Osowa massacre. Few families did not suffer the loss of one or more of their members, some up to 40 men and boys; witness Charles Ugboko noted, "some women went crazy, they just couldn't bear it ... Some lost all their sons, plus husband."[29] In addition to the personal anguish experienced, these losses had a profound impact on the political structure and traditional family support system. For instance, Assumpta Mordi's uncle, Daniel Mordi, was the recognized family head. A prominent figure, he ran a successful stenography school; his impressive home and its telephone (the first in Asaba) stood as symbols of his influence. Like many Asaba leaders, he was a strong proponent of Western education, and family members turned to him for guidance and to settle differences. Assumpta, a small child in 1967, was living temporarily away from Asaba with her immediate family, but described how usually cousins from the same extended family of polygynous marriages lived together "like brothers and sisters. All the children ate according to age grades, and the wives took turns to cook."[30] Daniel Mordi died at Ogbe-Osowa, along with his brothers Gabriel and Benedict and at least one cousin; after that, "everything fell apart." Daniel's wives

---

28   Inal, *Looting and Rape in Wartime*, 60.
29   Interview with Charles Ugboko, Dec. 12, 2009, Lagos.
30   Interview with Assumpta Mordi, Oct. 7, 2011, Asaba.

struggled to keep the children in school, as they had lost not only him but also his brothers who would normally step in to help. The two surviving junior brothers, including Assumpta's father, were overwhelmed and could not take care of them all. The family never returned to its former prominence: "my family with that glory and all that is all gone . . .. We never really recovered."

Many other families were equally devastated. Emmanuel Chukwara lost four brothers – Eddie, Christian, Dennis, and Samson – as well as his mother, Mgbeke, and father, David. He survived because he had taken his wife and children to safety as the troops arrived:

> There is no house . . . that did not suffer the killing. There are places you have three doctors, all killed. Father, mother, everybody. In my mother's case, the senior brother was killed, the next sister was killed, the junior ones, about five of them . . . I was the only man in the house where you have more than 30 people . . . I was responsible for my children, for the children of my relations, too.[31]

Emmanuel described how heavy this burden became for him, as a man who would never normally have this level of authority, and how many family members, himself included, were never able to receive the education that once would have been expected.

As noted by anthropologist Victor Uchendu, the extended family, often including the descendants (through the male line) of one great-grandfather, was (and still is) the building block of Igbo society.[32] Senior males are the lynchpins, but all males are highly valued: "Following from mutual dependence, is the value placed on the importance of man. Man is valued above all things in Igbo society. The society demanded, and still demands, a large family, a demand that makes polygyny a desirable goal and the position of ancestors a dignified one."[33] Influential men would likely have two or more

---

[31]   Interview with Emmanuel Chukwara, December 15, 2009, Asaba.
[32]   Victor Chikezie Uchendu, "Ezi na ulo: The Extended Family in Igbo Civilization," *Dialectical Anthropology*, 31:1–3, 2007, 167–219.
[33]   Uchendu, "Ezi na ulo," 216.

wives and many children; in addition to having responsibility for them, they were also expected to provide leadership to their full and half-brothers and their families, and to assist with education and other needs. Such men would also be expected to provide for the widows and children of men who died. This hierarchical kinship structure is an essential foundation for local community cohesion; as Elizabeth Isichei points out, it incorporated

> the authority of the family head, Diokpa ... over the extended
> family, the authority of the governing age-group, Oturaza, over the
> whole town, and the limited and specific duties and the personal
> prestige of individuals holding particular titles. The Diokpa was the
> oldest man of the oldest surviving generation in a family. Each
> quarter, as well as each component family, acknowledged
> a Diokpa's authority. He was regarded with reverence, for he
> embodied the authority of the ancestors.[34]

The disruption of traditional support mechanisms within families led to spirals of decline that affected generations, a point to which we will return in our final chapter. Young women and men born well after the war blame the massacre for their generation's hardship and lack of prospects; if "those who were supposed to lift Asaba up were not taken away" life would have been very different for their descendants and for the entire community.[35]

At the same time, the loss of so many men meant that a huge burden fell on women, as they faced the task of rebuilding their families' lives alone. Felicia Nwandu describes her return to Asaba after a few weeks in the bush:

> We have no home to enter. Our house was burnt down. Everything.
> In fact, you know, the bags they put rice and beans, that is what we

[34]   Elizabeth Isichei, "Historical Change in an Ibo polity: Asaba to 1885," *Journal of African History*, 10, 1969, 422–423.
[35]   Male, 34, single, fashion designer, focus group participant, March 14, 2014, Asaba.

tied, because there was no clothes, there was nothing for us to hide our nakedness.[36]

The family lived as refugees in their own community:

> We suffered . . . later we saw some Christian organizations, they give us salt . . . you just put your finger in the salt like this (*swirls finger*) and then put it in your soup so you can get that taste. A lot of children *kwashiorkor*, people were dying just like that. We ate rat, lizard, all these things . . .[37]

At times, religious groups stepped in. Emma Okocha, for example, described how after the death of his father, his mother felt unable to care for him, as the youngest of several surviving brothers. She handed him over to a Catholic nun, who then raised him.[38] Aged 14 in 1967, Martina Osaji lost her father and up to 40 other male relatives. Her mother was a refugee in Biafra, so Martina was taken in by a Catholic priest who had studied under her father, until her sister finished secondary school and could take care of her.

However, in families that were able to rebound, women were the key. With the breakdown of traditional patterns of responsibility, some women took on roles that would have been unthinkable before, as in the example of the Uraih family. Before the war, Asaba indigene Robert Uraih was a successful tailoring contractor in Kano, Northern Nigeria, where the family lived in the *Sabon Gari*, the "strangers' quarters" assigned to non-indigenes. All Robert's 10 children were born in Kano, and visited Asaba only during the summer holidays, spending time with grandparents in the family home. Ify Uraih described their life in Kano: "My father was quite well-to-do. We were comfortable. We had stewards; we had a driver who was taking us to school."[39] Ify Uraih remembered life as peaceful, with his father an ardent supporter of a united Nigeria. When the 1966

---

36   Interview with Felicia Nwandu, June 28, 2010, Asaba.
37   Ibid.
38   Interview with Emma Okocha, Oct. 13, 2009, Tampa.
39   Interview with Ify Uraih, Oct. 9, 2009, Tampa.

FIGURE 4.1 The Uraih family in Kano in 1962, celebrating the
admittance of oldest son Ben (sitting far right) to medical school in Britain.
Sitting: Paul (killed at Asaba in 1967), baby Robert, Mrs. Veronica Uraih,
Victoria, Ben. Standing: Anthony, Ify (on stool), Lucy Chineze, Emma
(killed in 1967), Ubaka. Father Robert Uraih and son Medua not present.
Photo courtesy of Ify Uraih.

pogrom began, the oldest son Benjamin was in university in Britain;
the rest of the family fled to Asaba, leaving almost everything behind,
and hoped to wait out the crisis in a safe haven (Figure 4.1):

> It was difficult for him to believe that Nigeria would one day go the
> way it did . . . Even when Biafra was declared, he did not believe in it,
> and he told us that this thing will pass . . . we must remain in
> Asaba . . . federal troops will not harm us.[40]

Robert and two of his sons, Paul and Emma, were killed on October 7,
and another son, Medua Gabriel, was gravely wounded. Ify Uraih, then
15 years old, also survived, crawling out from among the bodies of the
dead, as we describe in Chapter 2. Later, Robert's wife, Veronica, then
49 years old, found the bodies of Robert and Emma, and she dragged

[40]   Ibid.

them in a wheelbarrow back to the family house for burial. Paul was never found, although until the end of the war, Veronica held out hope that he had escaped and would return home.

Thus Veronica, who had lost nine members of her own natal family, was devastated. Her first challenge was to take care of her wounded 18-year-old son, Medua Gabriel, who was unable to walk for weeks. Soldiers were billeted in the family house, where she lived with her surviving children, the youngest a toddler. She found herself with no choice but to take on the role of family leader. Robert had been the patriarch, with many extended family members beholden to him, and with his death, those family members turned their backs on her and her children, refusing to help:

> I think it was not out of wickedness and such ... It was because there was no money. They didn't even have money to train their own children. It was my father helping them. So, when it happened, they couldn't get their share.[41]

Life had been turned upside down:

> If you look at it, for a woman who was not a working mother because she was being provided for, all of a sudden turned to be a trader, a working woman, to fend for her children – not only one but about six. Life has to change greatly.[42]

Although she had lost almost everything, the family home remained standing, if damaged, and Veronica was determined to ensure her children succeeded. She became a trader, and her children also hawked goods when they could. Tradition had dictated dependence on the extended family, but with this support system in tatters, the Uraihs formed their own tight-knit unit: "It taught me a lesson – mind your business .... Because you don't know who is your friend, who is

41   Interview with Victoria Nwanze.
42   Interview with Medua Uraih, May 3, 2012, Asaba.

not . . . So we had our own relationship amongst ourselves."[43] All the Uraih children went on to higher education, including the girls:

> Her eyes were red, she would say this smoke that is making me cry now will never touch my daughters . . . They must go to school . . . as long as I'm alive none of my daughters will suffer. So that had been her determination.[44]

In Asaba, as in Igbo society generally, when a woman dies she is returned for burial to her natal family. Many years later, when Veronica Uraih died in her nineties, her children insisted she be buried in the Uraih family house, recognizing her central role in their survival and success. We heard other stories like hers; the resilience of such women was striking. Again, relief workers reports point to the way the people of Asaba, especially women, worked hard to rebuild their shattered homes and lives:

> While we were in the area we saw some of the most imaginative examples of self-help projects and cooperatives of any of our trips. These included rabbit raising, piggeries, poultry farms and fisheries . . . We were impressed with their foresight and initiative as they prepared for a return to normal life even while the military situation could not permit mobility and continuity.[45]

Esther Nwanze summed up the determination of women, describing how she lost everything, but managed to protect and feed her family: "Women . . . women of Asaba they are fighters. I was one of them. Even now, I still fight."[46] And, as noted by Egodi Uchendu, women's new independence began to undermine traditional male dominance in a way that resonates today.[47]

[43]   Interview with Chineze Uraih, May 3, 2012, Asaba.
[44]   Interview with Victoria Nwanze (née Uraih).
[45]   Report of Bradford and Jean Abernethy: "AFSC relief efforts for war sufferers in the federally reoccupied areas of Nigeria, Sept – Dec. 1968," Archives of American Friends Service Committee, Philadelphia, USA, 3–4.
[46]   Interview with Esther Nwanze, Oct. 7, 2011, Asaba
[47]   Uchendu, Women and Conflict.

THE "SECOND OPERATION"

In 1968, as Nigerian forces advanced into Biafran territory, with their already precarious lines of communication stretched dangerously, they became easy targets for lightly armed and highly mobile Biafran guerrillas who often enjoyed the support of the local population. Igbo-speaking parts of the Midwest along the Niger's west bank, including the areas around Asaba, experienced intense guerrilla activities marked by continued sabotage, ambushes, and raids by small groups of irregular forces.[48] Asaba residents officially professed support for "One Nigeria," and undoubtedly most just wanted to be left alone. A few, including women, took a more active role in support of Biafra, sometimes for very personal reasons. Patricia Akaraiwe, for example, was a 27-year-old mother of four who had been living in the northern city of Kano before the war. Her husband, Joseph Akaraiwe, was killed in the anti-Igbo riots in September 1966. Fearing for the lives of her family, she fled to Asaba, where she found refuge with her husband's parents. Having lost his income, she began to trade, leaving the children with her in-laws and traveling 80 miles north to the Midwestern town of Auchi, where she would buy salt and fish for resale in Asaba. In early October as federal troops approached Asaba, she packed her children up and fled across the still-standing Niger Bridge to the Biafran side in Onitsha. There she joined the Biafran army as a spy, citing her anger at the unpunished murder of her husband. For the next two years, together with another woman, Patricia would cross back to Asaba, collect information on troop movements and then report back to the Biafrans. She only stopped when the woman she spied with was arrested, tortured, and forced to reveal details about the operation.[49]

Activities such as these made life very difficult for the federal troops, whose punitive control of civilians was partly spurred by the constant fear of "saboteurs" who might aid the Biafrans in their regular hit-and-run incursions into the Midwest. Frank Ogosi

---

[48] Harneit-Sievers, "The People, the Soldiers, and the State," 79.
[49] Interview with Patricia Akaraiwe, June 28, 2010, Asaba.

remembered the ominous sight of the "Biafran Babies" overhead, which could often signal trouble to come: "Small aircrafts fashioned from Volkswagen engine over there ... Each time that they saw this Biafran Baby coming to drop bombs, they start killing in the town."[50] On Easter weekend in April 1968, federal troops retaliated against the constant harassment, once again venting their anger on the civilians of Asaba in what is known locally as "the Second Operation."

The new flurry of violence affected those who either had remained or had returned to Asaba in hopes of rebuilding their lives following the October massacres. Families once again awoke to soldiers knocking on their doors, demanding that saboteurs should be handed over, and killing people at random. Catherine Igbeka was nine years old, and the horror of what happened to her family remains a vivid memory. As anti-Igbo violence erupted in the North, Catherine moved from Kaduna to Asaba with her 11-year-old sister Patricia, where they lived with her father, Martin Igbeka, and his wife. When federal troops first arrived in Asaba in October 1967, Catherine witnessed the killings and looting that followed, but her immediate family survived unscathed. After the danger appeared to have subsided her father, who had fled to the bush, returned home and "things settled down" for a while. As most of the fighting had now moved east across the Niger, the family believed the worst was over and both sisters returned to school, which had reopened. Early in the morning of April 17, the family heard a woman screaming in the street that federal troops were killing children. While Catherine and the rest of the family cowered in the house, her father went to talk to the soldiers standing outside:

> The next thing we heard was they were firing into our house when he opened the door ... We heard just the shots ringing into the parlor ... as I looked to the door, my dad was alive but his skull was in pieces. There were pieces of his skull all over the place. As a child what I thought was oh, he shouldn't die. He is still alive but what do

---

[50]   Interview with Frank Ogosi, Dec. 15, 2009, Asaba.

FIGURE 4.2 S. Elizabeth Bird interviews Felix Onochie, who is showing a photo of his brother Emmanuel, killed in the "second operation." Photo by Fraser Ottanelli.

we do with these pieces? . . . When I picked up one of the pieces, big piece of skull and I thought "oh God how do we attach this." They pushed me into the house. My only help, gone.

With the help of a neighbor, Catherine and her sister quickly washed, clothed, and then buried her father's body behind the family home.[51]

Felix Onochie described how his brother Emmanuel died during the same operation (Figure 4.2). Before the war, Emmanuel was a teacher in Warri, but returned to Asaba in early 1968. When the troops resumed their searches through the town, he hid in the ceiling of the house: "One of my townsmen came out and joined with the troops, shouting, 'Come out here, come out here! We have seen you! . . . If you come out on your own you'll be saved.'" Emmanuel and others who had come out as requested "were marched to the city center along here where they were all gunned down."[52]

51 Interview with Catherine Nkendelim Igbeka, London, UK, Oct. 10, 2014.
52 Interview with Felix Onochie, June 28, 2010, Asaba.

Witnesses recalled that soldiers again began going house to house, pulling out men and boys and shooting them. In addition, they started to force everyone out of their homes and began setting fire to houses throughout the town.

> My grandmother, she was very old, about 85 ... And when these federal troops came to occupy my father's house, she refused, and said, you killed my son, you drove my son away, and you want to occupy his house? And then she was beaten up mercilessly ... and then they used the head of the gun to break her waist. She never walked till she died ... They pushed her away, burned the house ...[53]

As they attempted to purge Asaba of any possible Biafran sympathizers, soldiers forcibly evacuated civilians still in the town to the grounds of St. Patrick's College (SPC) (Figure 4.3). The college was already established as a refugee camp for homeless people from Asaba and the surrounding area, and the arrival of additional families swelled the numbers still further. Even at the camps, males perceived as being

FIGURE 4.3 Refugee camp at St. Patrick's College, Asaba, 1968. Photo by Brad and Jean Abernethy, courtesy of AFSC.

[53]   Interview with Onyeogali Okolie, Dec. 13, 2009, Asaba.

of military age were not safe. Anthony Egbuiwe reported, "When were assembled at SPC, they were picking us out one by one ... and killing them ... I saw a soldier pierce a dagger into somebody's buttocks, and dragged him out."[54] Patrick Obelue, who as a young boy had helped bury the dead of the October killings, also witnessed soldiers arrive at SPC, seize young men, and execute them. According to Egbuiwe, when the young men were assembled, machine guns were mounted around them. Another mass execution seemed to be pending, when Father Hugh Conlon, a Catholic priest at St. Joseph's Church, arrived and begged the Brigade Commander to spare them, which he did. Even after that, Patrick Okonkwo recalled that every so often, soldiers would come to the camp to round up older boys, who were removed in trucks. Whether they were then conscripted or killed he did not know, but "they never came back."[55]

While some were able to leave after a few weeks, many were confined on the grounds for months sleeping outdoors on the bare ground, since most of the former classrooms were filled to capacity. After hurriedly burying their father, Catherine Igbeka and her sister found themselves at SPC, among those sleeping outside and standing on line for hours for food: "You have to queue to get your own portions. If you get your own relief you give out to the other people, so ... you can all share."[56] According to Anthony Egbuiwe, the occupants suffered from sickness and malnutrition: "Many died of cholera outbreak and lack of sanitation" (Figure 4.4).[57]

The refugees in the camp were fed mainly by foreign relief organizations.[58] In another report to the American Friends Service Committee in August 1968, David Scanlon and Christian Hansen

---

[54] Egbuie's account is reported in Ifeoha Azikiwe, *Asagba Prof. Joseph Chike Edozien: His Thoughts, Words, Vision*, Bloomington, IN: Authorhouse, 2015, 284.

[55] Interview with Patrick Okonkwo, June 27, 2010, Asaba; interview with Patrick Obelue, Dec. 12, 2009, Asaba.

[56] Interview with Catherine Igbeka.

[57] Azikiwe, *Asagba Prof. Joseph Chike Edozien*, 284.

[58] Interview with Catherine Igbeka; interview with Peter Ojogwu, Dec. 14, 2009, Asaba.

FIGURE 4.4 Portions of meat laid out for refugee meals. Two cows were slaughtered each day, yielding portions for more than 2,000 people. Refugee camp, St. Patrick's College, Asaba, 1968. Photo by Brad and Jean Abernethy, courtesy of AFSC.

described conditions in the SPC camp, where they witnessed "extreme malnutrition" and a complete lack of medical care. Scanlon noted that six or seven refugee teachers were trying to offer classes:

> There are probably about 400 children in the camp/school. They have no books, paper, pencils; the teachers are trying to recall the subject matter that they would be covering in an ordinary class . . . I have

never seen teachers trying to teach without any materials/ supplies ... I have nothing but admiration for these teachers ...[59]

While holding most of the population at SPC, federal soldiers set out to torch the town. Many homes had been damaged or destroyed the previous year, but the 1968 operation resulted in much more widespread destruction. Felix Ogosi recalled that most houses had thatched roofs, and were easily set ablaze: "As we got to the SPC, we all were there, only to see smoke everywhere as we look back. The whole town was in smoke everywhere, giving the impression that the town was now under fire."[60]

MEANWHILE, IN THE MIDWEST

Asaba was not the only community to suffer as a result of the continued Biafran incursions into the Midwest. The "Second Operation" was part of an organized federal attempt to clear Biafrans out of the area once and for all; troops moved into the small towns of Ibusa and Ogwashi-Ukwu around the same time.[61] John Kunirum Osia, then a priest serving Ibusa, recalled that as the troops moved in, many people fled into the bush:

> The pervasiveness of fear, the charged military atmosphere and suspicion, rendered futile any attempt of the elders to organize and govern Ibusa as they used to do. They were apprehensive, panicky and could not do anything that might offend the sensitivity and sensibility of the Nigerian soldiers. Fresh in their minds was, of course, the massacre of our people at Asaba in October 1967 ... There was dusk-to-dawn curfew which in of itself created more problems for people.[62]

---

[59] Transcript of tape recorded by David Scanlon and Christian Hansen, Aug. 15, 1968; summary of recommendations to American Friends Service Committee, no page numbers. In archives of AFSC, Philadelphia.

[60] Interview with Felix Ogosi, Dec. 13, 2009, Asaba.

[61] Ibusa, also known as Igbuzo, is about eight miles west of Asaba, while Ogwashi-Ukwu is another eight miles west along the same road.

[62] Osia's recollections are taken from the transcript of an interview he gave to *Ndi Anioma Times*, which he shared in a personal communication, Nov. 24, 2014. The interview

Father Osia helped set up two large refugee camps in the area, where displaced people were kept away from town, as they had been in Asaba, and he was the only person exempt from the curfew. Once he was detained by a federal officer who did not know his status, and became yet another person who owed his safety to Captain Matthias, who was now regularly in Ibusa:

> Fortunately for me, Captain Matthias was passing by around 7:15 pm and stopped at the guard room when he saw my Peugeot 404 van. He asked what I was doing in the guard room [and] inquired which officer ordered that I be detained. The soldiers said "Major Yar'Adua." He ordered that I be released immediately and apologized.

Matthias continued to be a professional presence among the often undisciplined troops in the area. Luke Enenmoh recalled how he led a delegation from Asaba to Ibusa, to stress to the soldiers that they were not harboring saboteurs, and that people should be encouraged to return from their refuges in the bush. At Ibusa, he encountered a situation in which Matthias had locked up some women who had been caught coming into town at night, in defiance of the curfew. They were suspected of helping Biafran infiltrators, and things were very tense. Enenmoh spoke with the women and learned that they had been coming back and forth from the bush to care for a prominent elderly man. He had then died, and the women came back to help bury him:

> I said please sir ... you are asking people from the bush to come out and so forth. If you let them go back, they can be your messengers, they will tell those people that everything is okay, they are safe. And they will be coming home. He said, you think so? So he set them free. I was touched.

was later reprinted online, dated Feb. 13, 2016: http://emekaesogbue.blogspot.com/20 16/02/my-wartime-experience-with-anioma-rev.html. We had hoped to interview him, but he died Dec. 23, 2014.

Accounts like these are in stark contrast to the story of what happened at Isheagu, another nearby town. It had become an active trading center, and had also experienced Biafran incursions, which came to a head in May 1968, not long after the "Second Operation" in Asaba. Patrick Idahosa, the commanding officer at Isheagu, wrote in his memoir that his troops repelled a Biafran raid, but then in action "that did not meet my approval," they "went berserk and burned down a part of the town."[63] According to Idahosa, the following day, Biafran leader Ojukwu broadcast to his people that this incident again showed that "the Federal government was fighting against all Ibos no matter where they came from."[64] While Idahosa described "clearing" Isheagu, he did not acknowledge any civilian casualties, just as he did not acknowledge his role as one of those who had gathered civilians for execution in Asaba.[65]

The people of Isheagu remember the events rather differently, as described in a locally produced booklet.[66] The writers acknowledged that local people were involved in trading goods to Biafra, while hiding the proceeds and thus angering occupying troops. After the Biafran incursion in the early hours of May 2, "most inhabitants deserted the town and ran to some neighbouring towns or to their farms."[67] Soldiers encouraged them to come back; those who did were lined up and shot as collaborators. The writers list 187 men who were massacred in this event; according to Egodi Uchendu, the town was then razed, and "remained unoccupied till the end of the war."[68] Isheagu was the subject of a brief, anonymous Associated Press story almost two months later, in which Idahosa, who before the war had been trained in counter-insurgency training at Fort Bragg, North Carolina, described how "federal troops, moving abreast in a straight

[63]   Patrick E. Idahosa, *Truth and Tragedy: A Fighting Man's Memoir of the Nigerian Civil War*, Ibadan. Nigeria: Heinemann Educational Books, 1989, 111.
[64]   Ibid.
[65]   See Chapters 2 and 3.
[66]   Okonkwo and Okolie, *Isheagu and the Nigerian Civil War, 1966–1970*, printed in Lagos, no date.
[67]   Ibid.
[68]   Uchendu, *Women and Conflict*, 99.

line, marched methodically through the half-mile-long village firing automatic weapons."[69] Idahosa denied that any civilians were killed: "This was a good, well-done job." This assessment was not questioned. Like the much larger killing in Asaba and the killing of civilians in the cathedral at Onitsha (described in Chapter 3), the fate of Isheagu went largely unnoticed. However, its effect was to allow those troops who were so inclined to continue with impunity, while keeping local civilians in terror and further solidifying the resolve of the Biafrans to fight on.

REBUILDING ONCE MORE

After about three months at SPC, many families left the camp, but for many this was only the beginning, as they returned to find their homes destroyed and their belongings once again looted. As we have noted, international relief organizations had begun to provide assistance in late 1967, and this had expanded to a significant presence by 1968, as the townspeople began to rebuild after the "Second Operation." Foreign relief organizations provided life-saving support, including the International Red Cross, Caritas, Catholic Relief Services, and American Friends Service Committee (Quakers). Families would line up outside the Catholic Mission to receive precious supplies of dried milk, flour, and other basics (Figure 4.5). The relationship between the community and the military continued to be tense at best; David Scanlon and Christian Hansen, representatives of the AFSC who visited the area to determine emergency relief needs, wrote in August 1968:

> People are confined in the town by the military government as it is feared they might ... give help to the Biafrans ... Medical supplies are simply not there. Theoretically people could go to the doctors attached to the military but after the ... killings that have taken

---

[69]   *Sumter Daily Item* (North Carolina), June 24, 1968, 9A. This story does not seem to have been widely picked up; one must assume that the Fort Bragg connection led to its being deemed newsworthy in North Carolina.

FIGURE 4.5   Families line up outside the Catholic Mission to receive food and other supplies, Asaba, late 1968. Photo by Brad and Jean Abernethy, courtesy of AFSC.

place in the town the people are petrified and are afraid to go near the army at all. And they would have to go through army lines to get to the military doctor.[70]

They noted that people in the town were still required to get permits from the military to move about, and that farming and commerce had been come to a halt, further exacerbating the food shortages.

Indeed, the records of relief organizations indicate the exceptional and long-lasting nature of Asaba's suffering, one noting in 1969, "UNICEF reports the Midwestern region normalized, except for Asaba."[71] Another reported in August 1968 that

> During the fighting around Asaba, 60% of the homes were leveled and destroyed ... People are actually living in what were former latrines which have been merely covered over with a layer of dirt.[72]

[70]   David Scanlon and Christian Hansen, summary of recommendations to American Friends Service Committee. Aug. 15 1968, archives of AFSC, Philadelphia.

[71]   International Red Cross Committee, "Food and Relief Situation," April 24, 1969, 22.

[72]   American Friends Service Committee, "Nigeria/Biafra Relief," Oct. 10, 1968 (no page numbers). In archives of AFSC, Philadelphia.

The extent of the destruction is indicated by Asaba's removal in 1969 from the government's official list of Nigerian towns.[73]

Fear was still a constant part of life for Asaba, as well as for other nearby communities dealing with possible Biafran incursions. Even with the bridge closed, the river was not a barrier to regular movement between Biafra and the Midwest, as the spying activities of Patricia Akaraiwe show. There was also a brisk trade going on across the river, using canoes and other available craft, as women all over the Midwest tried to make a living by acquiring much-needed commodities, sometimes obtained from soldiers, and trading them to Biafra to raise money to feed their families. Nevertheless, throughout 1968, Asaba remained in dire straits, exacerbated by disputes between relief agencies and the federal authorities. In early December, an Associated Press story, which was picked up in several US newspapers, reported that 8,000 people in Asaba were facing famine, with Fathers Conlon and Osia saying that food was about to run out. The Nigerian authorities, as part of an ongoing dispute with the International Red Cross over accusations of spying for Biafra, had just expelled the last five IRC workers in Asaba:

> Five hundred tons of food and medical supplies are locked in
> a warehouse here, but the key is 280 miles away in Lagos, held by
> Robert C. Koepp, a former Peace Corps member.[74]

The disputes led to protests: "The camp blossomed with signs saying 'white men go home.'"[75]

Things finally began to improve for Asaba only as the war itself went increasingly badly for Biafra. The destruction of the convoy at Abagana was essentially the last military success for the secessionists, and the federal troops continued to close in around the shrinking enclave. By June, the Second Division, now under Col. Ibrahim

---

[73]   Egodi Uchendu, "The Growth of Anioma Cities," in Toyin Falola and Steven J. Salm, eds., *Nigerian Cities*, Trenton, NJ: Africa World Press, 2004, 153.

[74]   Arnold Zeitlin (Associated Press reporter), "8,000 Ibo Tribesmen to Lack Food," *Gettysburg Times*, Dec. 10, 1968, 12.

[75]   Ibid.

Haruna, was firmly in control of Onitsha. There was a significant garrison at Asaba for the rest of the war, tasked with fending off incursions and neutralizing saboteurs, but the town was suffering less and was able to focus on rebuilding. Some of the major schools, such as SPC, had closed after the first operation, but had reopened briefly in early 1968. The headmaster of SPC, US–born Marianist brother Roman Wicinski, was killed around the time of the second operation, most likely by Biafrans, and the remaining Marianist missionary staff who had been running the school left. As things settled back after people left the SPC refugee camp, an Emergency Grammar School, run out of the Catholic Mission, opened to serve students from all of the shuttered schools.[76] Later, other schools reopened, although many could not afford to attend. For some of them, "there would be little tents where people would learn how to type," and with relief agencies' assistance, some funding was made available to help fatherless children pay fees and return to school.[77]

Meanwhile, across the Midwest, official actions were being taken to assert loyalty to Nigeria. On May 11, 1968, the British High Commission in Lagos sent a batch of five letters back to London, all from leaders in Midwest towns, and all addressed to the Deputy High Commissioner at the British Embassy in Benin City. These followed demonstrations in several communities, featuring banners urging "Midwest People Arise and Defend your Fatherland ... One United Nigeria!" One of these letters, written on behalf of the "entire people of Asaba, Aboh, and Ika Divisions," expresses "our utter disgust and condemnation of the Rebels and their collaborators for their devilish attempts to dis-integrate Nigeria." While acknowledging that some in the area may have expressed support for Ojukwu earlier, "it must be made clear that the majority of the people ... DID NOT support this plot." The letter ended: "Long Live Nigeria. Long live Gowon ... May the Anglo-Nigerian British relationship flourish." In forwarding the letters, the writer wryly noted that "the demonstration was by no

---

[76]   Interview with Fabian Oweazim.
[77]   Interview with Catherine Igbeka.

means spontaneous ... no doubt part of the current public relations campaign!"[78]

By mid-1968, the war had also entered a new era of international awareness, which kept attention away from the Midwest while Asaba's slow recovery continued. As we have seen, the Biafrans had tried hard to gain international attention to the abuses against civilians, but with impending starvation now looming, this crisis became the focus of a very effective Biafran public relations campaign that finally drew international attention. Photojournalist Gilles Caron made three visits to Biafra for *Paris Match* magazine, the first in April 1968, when he covered the "ignored war," including documentation of action not far from Asaba.[79] Biafran authorities, now working with American-owned Swiss public relations firm Markpress, invited journalists into the country, and in June a contingent of British reporters arrived and began reporting heartbreaking stories from hospitals, refugee camps, and marketplaces hit by apparently indiscriminate federal bombing.[80] The photos of Don McCullin, who reported for several UK and international media outlets and who intended his images to stir readers' consciences, had a particularly strong impact.[81]

The massive media coverage led to major efforts across Europe and the United States to send aid to Biafra, as well as to increasing pressure on governments, especially in the UK, to stop supporting the Nigerian FMG. The British government had successfully avoided consequences from the early excesses against civilians, but was now coming under increasing pressure, needing "not only to defend arms

[78]   M.J. Newington, letter (with supporting documents) to Peter McEntee, WGAD, May 11, 1968, UK National Archive, FCO38/270, file 474.

[79]   Claude Cookman, "Gilles Caron's Coverage of the Crisis in Biafra," *Visual Communication Quarterly*, 15, 2008, 227.

[80]   Paul Harrison and Robin Palmer, *News Out of Africa: Biafra to Band Aid*, London, Hilary Shipman, 1986; Kevin O'Sullivan, "Humanitarian Encounters: Biafra, NGOs and Imaginings of the Third World in Britain and Ireland, 1967–70," *Journal of Genocide Research*, 16:2–3, 2014, 299–15.

[81]   David Campbell, "Cultural Governance and Pictorial Resistance: Reflections on the Imaging of War," *Review of International Studies*, 29, 2003, 57–73.

sales to the FMG, but also to indicate that it would stop supplying arms if the FMG appeared to be slaughtering Igbos."[82] The proposed solution was the creation of an International Observer team, which would visit Nigeria to investigate claims of atrocities against civilians. The FMG was extremely reluctant to allow this, but agreed after being given an ultimatum by the British government threatening the withdrawal of arms support.[83] The team, comprised entirely of ex-military men from the UK, Poland, Canada, the United Nations, and the Organization of African Unity, traveled to Nigeria several times between September 1968 and January 1970, visiting villages that had been retaken by federal troops, as well as refugee camps (including in Asaba). They did not visit areas still under Biafran control and thus had little to say about the starvation in Biafra itself, focusing primarily on whether civilians had been killed by advancing troops. The make-up of the observer teams, as well as their impartiality has been widely questioned; as Suzanne Cronje noted, "at the very least the team should have included international jurists and professionals experienced in the investigation of crime and the recording of evidence, not to speak of social workers, medical men and people capable of telling an Ibo from a non-Ibo."[84] The visits were carefully controlled by the FMG, and some stage-managing clearly occurred. For instance, Cyril Iweze, a Midwest Igbo serving on the federal side, noted that when international observers arrived, he was always called for interview; "the Federal government wanted to use me as an example, that he's an Igbo man, yet he's fighting for our side."[85] In a series of reports, the observers claimed to have found no evidence of untoward civilian deaths, and generally praised the conduct of the troops. Their findings were widely reported in the press; for instance, the *Times* of London wrote that "international observers ... found that Ibo people were

---

[82] Karen E. Smith, "The UK and 'genocide' in Biafra," *Journal of Genocide Research*, 6:2–3, 2014, 253.

[83] Ibid.

[84] Suzanne Cronje, *The World and Nigeria: The Diplomatic History of the Biafran War 1967–1970*, London: Sidgwick and Jackson, 1972, 84.

[85] Interview with retired Gen. Cyril Iweze, April 13, 2016, Lagos.

afraid of Federal soldiers because of Biafran propaganda" but that these fears were unfounded.[86] Again, a year later, the *Times* reported that there was no evidence of any atrocities. Specifically, a Polish member of an international observer team informed the *Times* reporter, "we have been unable to find one single trace of mass killings of Ibos."[87] The fate of Asaba, and the other victimized Midwest communities, was even more effectively buried.

Meanwhile, the FMG was also stepping up its efforts to convince the world that the war was being fought honorably. Throughout the war, the government had highlighted cases in which federal soldiers had been punished for inappropriate actions; as early as October 17, 1967, British authorities were informed that "one Federal soldier found in Bwa Bank Agbor was summarily executed for looting on orders of Col. Muhammed."[88] But the main push to demonstrate adherence to the conduct code came later, as more eyes turned to Biafra; in a particularly well-publicized incident in 1968, a Nigerian officer had been caught on film killing an unarmed, bound Biafran prisoner. Michael Nicholson, a British ITN reporter, smuggled the footage out of the country, where it was shown on television, causing great embarrassment in Lagos. Nicholson knew the name of the officer: "I had to then identify this lieutenant and he was court martialed and he was then shot – tied up to a tree, blindfolded and then executed."[89] The execution, on Sept. 6, 1968, was filmed as evidence of justice being done.[90] And in August 1968, the FMG had invited Margery Perham to come to Nigeria, where she visited recaptured areas and ultimately was convinced both of Gowon's honorable intentions toward the Igbo and the need for Ojukwu to surrender in order to save thousands of lives. In an immediate post-war assessment, she

---

[86]   Michael Wolfers, "Nigeria Observers Find No Evidence of Genocide," *The Times*, Oct. 4, 1968, 8.

[87]   Julian Mounter, "No Evidence of Genocide in Nigeria," *The Times*, July 21, 1969, 5.

[88]   FCO Daily Sitrep 82, Oct. 17, 1967, UK National Archive, FCO 38/284, file 206.

[89]   Audiotaped interview with Michael Nicholson, 2002, archived in Imperial War Museum, London, Ref. 21537.

[90]   *The Times*, "Execution of Nigerian Officer Filmed," Sept. 4, 1968, 1.

recalled the account of the massacre at Asaba, writing that while troubling, it was the kind of "isolated incident" that is inevitable in war.[91]

However, by 1969, the killing of civilians, whether in "clearances" of villages or through bombing, had almost become beside the point; these actions had not induced widespread public outrage, as we describe in Chapter 3. Patrick (Paddy) Davies, a member of the Biafran propaganda team who later wrote a thesis about the issues, noted the failure of Biafra's early propaganda campaign, which was three fold – pogrom and genocide, religious warfare, and oil/economic war. "All three relatively impacted on the world stage, but ... did not motivate any external mobilization."[92] In contrast,

> famine ... achieved what religion, genocide and pogrom, and oil, did not. Famine has struck countless communities throughout history, but the impact had always been local and gone largely unnoticed in the rest of the world. In this case, the isolation was swept aside because the media was made to take interest – an excellent case of manipulative persuasion.[93]

Some have argued that the very success of the Biafrans' PR campaign was ultimately responsible for many more deaths, as the images of suffering sparked outrage and foreign aid. As reporter Nicholson remarked, "[they were] very powerful images, and it kept the war going. ... Had it not been for us, the Biafran cause would have died much earlier ... We are pawns, aren't we? ...."[94]

Biafra went through its agonizing death throes throughout 1969, its territory shrinking into the small Igbo heartland. Meanwhile, Asaba began to experience some semblance of normal

[91]   Margery Perham, "Reflections on the Nigerian Civil War," *International Affairs* 46, 1970, 237.

[92]   Patrick Ediomi Davies, "Use of Propaganda in Civil War: The Biafra Experience," doctoral thesis, Department of International Relations, London School of Economics and Political Science, June 1995.

[93]   Ibid., 182.

[94]   Interview with Michael Nicholson.

life, even while still under occupation. Some farming resumed, although Asaba never returned to an agriculturally based community, and small businesses and markets developed, often catering more to soldiers, who had ready cash, than to locals. Some troops took seriously the task of "winning the hearts and minds" of the residents, and relationships became more cordial. Some Asaba women willingly married soldiers; for instance in 1968, Dorothy Dumnodo Okafor-John, who had witnessed her brother's death in Benin City, met and married Chris Alli, an officer among the occupying forces. Recalling their courtship and long marriage, Alli later wrote: "What an irony of fate, and a paradox of the Nigerian experience!"[95] In 1969, Maryam Okogwu, daughter of Chief Leo Okogwu, who was killed on October 7, married army officer Ibrahim Badamasi Babangida, who years later became the military head of state (in 1985). Of Captain Matthias, who set the standard for professional conduct toward civilians, little more is known. He remained in and around Asaba and Ibusa for some time, managing his sector humanely and peacefully, as we have seen.[96] According to one survivor, he may have been killed by another soldier later in the war, possibly in a fight over a woman.[97]

Violence by soldiers, while now more contained, still erupted, as it did in an event that sent shockwaves through the town – the murder of the *Omu* of Asaba, Mgboshie Okolie, in 1969. The *Omu* is the highest-ranking female leader; she must be post-menopausal and is elected by rotation among the quarters, in the same way as the *Asagba*. Her primary role is to regulate the market, but she has an esteemed place in traditional culture, and is the only woman with the title of *Eze*, a red-cap chief. According to Egodi Uchendu, the *Omu* was "clubbed to death in her home and physically mutilated afterwards by two federal soldiers from the military unit stationed in [Asaba]," apparently because she refused to cooperate with orders she considered

---

[95]   M. Chris Alli, *The Federal Republic of Nigerian Army*, 54.
[96]   Interview with Luke Enenmoh.
[97]   Emmanuel Mordi, personal online communication with Elizabeth Bird, Oct. 10, 2015.

incompatible with her role as a community leader.[98] Celestina Isichei recalls that during one of her visits to her mother from her new home in nearby Ogwashi-Uku, she heard about the *Omu's* murder: "the soldiers had tried to kill her by shooting her and they couldn't, so they set her house ablaze and then they killed her. *Omu's* house was kind of a sacred place that people ran to, and she was believed to be very powerful."[99] The murder of this prominent leader was seen as a particular affront and violation – "a slap in our face."[100] Her death is still remembered today, and a statue of her stands at a prominent road junction.

By the end of the war, in January 1970, more people had returned to Asaba. Relief agencies were still active, and reconstruction and rehabilitation efforts began in earnest. In the decades since, Asaba has persevered and grown. Often led by women, many families showed astonishing resilience, and have risen again. But Asaba has never forgotten.

[98] Uchendu, *Women and Conflict*, 127.
[99] Interview with Celestina Isichei-Isamah, Oct. 10, 2014, London.
[100] Male, 28, unemployed, focus group participant, March 14, 2014, Asaba.

5 Reclaiming Memory in an Age of New Media

For the people of Asaba, the official concealment and misrepresentation of the massacre has left them with a sense of anger and unresolved grievance, not only for the personal loss of so many loved ones, but also for the shared trauma experienced by the whole community. Repeatedly, survivors and witnesses spoke of the need for "justice"; some demanded reparations and judicial processes, others felt the need for a formal memorialization process, which we will address in our final chapter. However, survivors overwhelmingly expressed a basic need to be recognized and acknowledged – indeed, for the broader Nigerian society simply to believe that this event really happened. As Minow writes, one of the most destructive consequences of such atrocities is "the destruction of remembrance ... as well as ... lives and dignity."[1] As one interviewee recounted,

> Nobody seemed to know about it. Even in the ... military history books, there's no mention of it. It has got to be part of our history, because if you don't have a history, you cannot go ahead in life."[2]

Many interviewees told us they had rarely spoken of the massacres outside their families, because they thought they would not be believed, like survivor Ify Uraih:

> I kept it all buried in my heart. When I went to school in Lagos and the war had ended ... I was talking about the civil war with a group of Yoruba classmates, and I told the story. One of them,

---

[1] Martha M. Minow, *Between Vengeance and Forgiveness: Facing History after Genocide and Mass Violence*, Boston: Beacon Press, 1998, 1.

[2] Interview with Gertrude Ogunkeye, Dec. 11, 2009, Lagos.

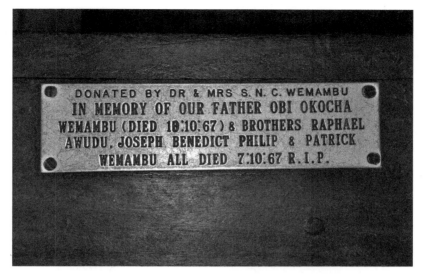

FIGURE 5.1   One of several commemorative family plaques in St. Joseph's Catholic Church. Photo by Fraser Ottanelli.

whose father was a magistrate, looked me in the eyes and said I was a liar, that it could never have happened. I took a knife, and I almost killed him. I was going to be expelled from my school because his mother ... thought the principal brought in some ex-Biafran soldiers to kill their children ... Fortunately for me, the principal was a Catholic reverend father, and he happened to have known a little bit about what happened. So, he managed to solve the problem.[3]

Others marked the deaths of loved ones in private family ceremonies, or they installed small memorial plaques in churches (Figure 5.1). Many such plaques adorn the pews in St. Joseph's church, often noting the deaths of several family members on one date, although with no mention of the circumstances. Many families lost all personal documents and photos in the destruction of their homes, while some

---

[3]   Interview with Ify Uraih, Oct. 9, 2009, Tampa.

treasure the few images that survive, sharing them with children and grandchildren. Chuck Nduka-Eze, whose mother Rose was killed, told us that only one photo of Rose, holding his older brother as a baby, survived. Nduka-Eze superimposed a photo of himself as a toddler on the original image, thus creating a visual memory of the family together (Figure 5.2). While there was pressure to play down the past, some survivors refused. Patience Chukura, who lost her husband, as well as his father and two brothers, recalled that she would place a memorial notice in the newspaper every year:

> You can't believe that at one time I put in the papers, "In memory of Eddie Chukura, who was killed on the sixth of October." Somebody phoned me to say, "Why must you say he was killed? Why don't you let it go; it means that you are reporting the federal troops, reporting the soldiers." And I said, "Well, the man was killed. He didn't die a natural death." So it made it difficult for us.[4]

As Hodgkin and Radstone have remarked, "A memory that is accepted as public knowledge has recognition, acknowledgement; other memories do not."[5] This acceptance into national public knowledge is at the core of Asaba's wish to bring their story out of the local and into the national and global arenas, which has become the logical step that follows the documentation of the suppressed history.

Jan Assmann makes a useful distinction between everyday "communicative memory" and "cultural memory."[6] Everyday memory is a collection of individual recollections and stories, and it is heavily influenced by firsthand experiences and accounts. Many people in Asaba maintain individual or family memories, but these have rarely moved beyond the local. In contrast, cultural memory "consists of objectified culture, that is, the texts, rites, images, buildings, and monuments which are designed to recall fateful events ... As the officially

---

[4]   Interview with Patience Chukura, Dec. 10, 2009, Lagos.

[5]   Katharine Hodgkin and Susannah Radstone, "Introduction: Rethinking Memory," *History Workshop Journal*, 59, 2005, 132.

[6]   Jan Assmann, "Collective Memory and Cultural Identity," *New German Critique*, 65, 1995, 125–133.

FIGURE 5.2 Composite photo showing Rose Nduka-Eze, killed in Asaba, holding her older son Anthony, and with younger son, Chuck, superimposed. Courtesy of Chuck Nduka-Eze.

sanctioned heritage of a society, they are intended for the *longue durée*."[7] Assman notes that "The ... crystallization of communicated meaning and collectively shared knowledge is a prerequisite of its transmission in the culturally institutionalized heritage."[8]

---

[7]   Wulf Kansteiner, "Finding Meaning in Memory: A Methodological Critique of Collective Memory Studies," *History and Theory*, 41, 2002, 182.

[8]   Assman, "Collective Memory and Cultural Identity," 130.

In Asaba, even the beginning of formal recognition of the massacres was a long time coming, and the story lived on primarily in communicative memory. Early attempts to have annual commemorations collapsed under pressure from central government, and many people were afraid to speak out.[9] Indeed, active attempts to revisit war grievances were widely discouraged; perhaps understandably, the immediate impulse after the war was to reconcile and bring the union together, inspired by Gowon's famous pronouncement that in this conflict there would be "no victor, and no vanquished." And as experience elsewhere shows, the pressure to forget is often as much part of the post-conflict transition as the impulse to remember, with the insistence on memory perceived as "opening old wounds." In considering Asaba, we are reminded of Trouillot's often-quoted statement on how history is created:

> Silences enter the process of historical production at four crucial moments: the moment of fact creation (the making of sources); the moment of fact assembly (the making of archives); the moment of fact retrieval (the making of narratives); and the moment of retrospective significance (the making of history in the final instance).[10]

As we have shown, all these crucial moments are pertinent to Asaba – the record that was never created, the development of a flawed and incomplete narrative, and the failure of "official" history to acknowledge the events.

BREAKING THE SILENCE, LAYING THE GROUNDWORK

As the numbers of direct witnesses began to dwindle, and as some survivors gained more prominent positions, there was a growing sense of urgency that work was needed to inscribe the story of the Asaba massacres into the "officially sanctioned heritage" of

9   Interview with Msr. Emmanuel Chukwumah, June 28, 2010, Asaba.
10   Michel-Rolph Trouillot, *Silencing the Past: Power and the Production of History*, New York: Beacon Press, 1995, 26.

Nigeria.[11] The opportunity to disrupt the official silence came with the 1994 publication of *Blood on the Niger*, the first book devoted entirely to the Asaba events.[12] Written by Nigerian journalist Emmanuel "Emma" Okocha, who, as a small child, lost his father at Asaba, the book is based partly on survivor testimony, and it received attention both in Nigeria and the diaspora. Unfortunately, the book is problematic as a reliable historical account; it is haphazardly sourced, poorly edited, and often confusingly written.[13] It seems to be based on a combination of firsthand interviews (none of which are referenced) and secondhand reports culled from the papers of the author's uncle, Akunwata (Sylvester) Okocha, who was a witness. In addition, Okocha frequently embellishes the narrative with fanciful details drawn from his imagination. The book led to some controversy within the Okocha family; according to the elder Okocha's son, the family considered filing legal action for the unattributed appropriation of the older man's work.[14] However, Akunwata (Sylvester) Okocha decided that the public dissemination of the story was more important than issues of family ownership. His only public statement about the issue appears obliquely in his own self-published book about the history of Asaba, where he writes about "minors who have stolen my research works and hurriedly went to press ... after interviews with me or taking my publications."[15] However, an understanding of this context is helpful in reading the book, as it clarifies often puzzling aspects of the sometimes incoherent narrative.

In spite of these shortcomings, Emma Okocha's work was crucial in bringing the story of the massacres to a broader audience, and he has rightly received a significant degree of recognition in

---

[11]   Kansteiner "Finding Meaning in Memory," 179–197.

[12]   Emma Okocha, *Blood on the Niger*, New York: Triatlantic Books, 1994.

[13]   In our work, we do not use Okocha's book as a source, although we have interviewed some of the individuals whose accounts also appear there.

[14]   Interview with Pastor Chris Adigwe Daniels Okocha, Oct. 10, 2015, Asaba.

[15]   Akunwata S.O. Okocha, *The Making of Asaba: A Compendium of over Sixty-Five Years of Patient Research within and without Africa*, Asaba: Rupee-Com Publishers, 2013, iv.

Asaba. Furthermore, an important contribution by Okocha and others was to bring the Asaba events to the attention of the Nigerian Human Rights Violations Investigation Commission (HRVIC, better known as the Oputa Panel), established by President Olusegun Obasanjo in 2001. As Nigeria emerged from years of military rule, the panel was set up as a mechanism of transitional justice to consider the history of human rights abuses from 1966 to May 1999, of which civil war events were part. Evidence presented to the panel included the Ohanaeze Petition, a lengthy document describing abuses against the Igbo from the 1966 coups on into the war, which included detailed affidavits made in 1969 by several Asaba survivors, originally used to petition the United Nations (see Chapter 3). In addition, a group of survivors testified directly, including Emma Okocha and others we have subsequently interviewed. In defining the role of the HRVIC, Obasanjo presented the classic transitional justice perspective, stating that the Commission "was established to demonstrate his administration's determination to heal the wounds of the past (...) for complete reconciliation based on knowledge of the truth in our land."[16] An official goal was to somehow use the findings to achieve forgiveness and reconciliation, both through prosecutions and peace-building initiatives. The commission held hearings in several locations across Nigeria, creating significant public interest. Unfortunately, it was underfunded and faced a huge task; it eventually dissolved amid ethnic wrangling, and its report was suppressed, although it is now available on the Internet.[17] No prosecutions or peace-building initiatives were ever mounted.

However, since HRVIC testimonies were broadcast on television and widely discussed in the press, the Oputa Panel brought visibility to civil war (and other) atrocities. One of the star witnesses for Asaba was Ify Uraih who, as we describe in Chapter 2, lived

---

[16]   Hakeem O. Yusuf, "Travails of Truth: Achieving Justice for Victims of Impunity in Nigeria," *The International Journal of Transitional Justice* 1, 2007, 272.

[17]   Nneoma V. Nwogu, *Shaping Truth, Reshaping Justice: Sectarian Politics and the Nigerian Truth Commission*, New York: Lexington, 2007.

through the Ogbe-Osowa massacre that killed his father and brothers. Nneoma Nwogu, in her analysis of the Oputa Panel, points to the Asaba testimonies as at one level, "a success story":

> Dr. Uraih's relief came with his opportunity to tell his story not just before the HRVIC but before a country who listened through radios and television. By this opportunity, his victimization was made real, and as Soyinka suggests, "acknowledged."[18]

Furthermore, the Oputa Panel set the stage for more survivors to agree to write and speak publically. Scholars began to do important research, the most significant being the work of Egodi Uchendu. Her interviews with women, conducted in 2000–2001, shed new light not only on Asaba, but also on the neglected wartime experience of women in the entire Anioma region.[19] Geographer Stanley Okafor contributed to a volume on the war and its aftermath, offering a short but vivid personal account of his experiences as a boy in Asaba during the massacres.[20]

Another landmark occurred in 2002 when Gowon made a public apology to the people of Asaba, saying he had not ordered the massacre and knew nothing about it until years later.[21] While there is no evidence that Gowon did order it, his second claim seems disingenuous, as we noted in Chapter 3, since it is apparent that the FMG was aware of excesses against civilians in Asaba, even if all the details were not immediately known. However, his speech was an important symbolic moment; an apology constitutes an acknowledgment, which can be the first step toward reconciliation, since it "involves the admission that ... wrongful acts were committed, that such acts

[18] Nwogu, *Shaping Truth, Reshaping Justice*, 62.
[19] Egodi Uchendu, *Women and Conflict in the Nigerian Civil War*, Trenton, NJ, Africa World Press, 2007.
[20] Stanley I. Okafor, "The Nigerian Army and the 'Liberation' of Asaba: A Personal Narrative," in Eghosa E. Osaghae, E. Onwudiwe, and R. Suberu, eds., *The Nigerian Civil War and its Aftermath*, Ibadan, Nigeria: John Archers, 2002, 293–299.
[21] Austin Ogwuda, "Gowon Faults Setting Up of Oputa Panel," *Vanguard News*, Dec. 09, 2002, available online at: https://groups.yahoo.com/neo/groups/Naija-news/conversations/topics/2517.

should not have been committed, and that those who committed them were responsible for having done so."[22]

CULTURAL MEMORY IN A NEW MEDIA AGE

Historically, the Oputa Panel and its collapse coincided with the rise of the Internet and "new media," and this opened new doors to a public consideration of history. In an age of "old media," the massacres at Asaba were very effectively contained, both in terms of scholarly and public record. The lack of journalistic coverage at the time was crucial in both respects. As Barbie Zelizer writes, in the modern world, "[t]he story of the past will remain in part a story of what the media have chosen to remember, a story of how the media's memories have in turn become our own."[23] Here, Zelizer emphasizes the ability of journalists to make active decisions about what to cover, in common with Zandberg, who notes, "Journalists choose which stories or facts have importance. They select facts, construct them into cultural-interpretative frames, and thus give them meaning."[24] The same might be said for scholars, and the scholarly narrative on Asaba is similarly impoverished. In the case of Asaba, as we note in Chapter 3, the options for unfettered media coverage were essentially closed, and the narrative of Asaba that emerged (such as it was) was inaccurate and helped serve the interests of both Lagos and London. This narrative in turn affected scholarly war histories.

With the collapse of the Oputa Panel, and following the publication of a new edition of *Blood on the Niger* in 2006, new media sites began to emerge as places where memory work might happen. Multiple online forums connect the extensive diaspora with those in Nigeria, and new contestations of memory began to develop. Of course, with the migration of the story to the virtual world, it

---

[22]   Trudy Govier, *Taking Wrongs Seriously: Acknowledgment, Reconciliation and the Politics of Sustainable Peace*, Amherst, NY: Humanity Books, 2006, 15.

[23]   Barbie Zelizer, *Covering the Body: The Kennedy Assassination, the Media, and the Shaping of Collective Memory*, Chicago: University of Chicago Press, 1992, 214.

[24]   Eyal Zandberg, "The Right to Tell the (Right) Story: Journalism, Authority and Memory," *Media Culture and Society* 32:1, 2010, 7.

inevitably mutates, and the potential to generate heat increases dramatically. In February 2009, for example, the neutral discussion site Nigerian Village Square reposted a piece written some years earlier by Nigerian commentator Lawrence Chinedu Nwobu about Murtala Muhammed, in which he is described as the "Butcher of Asaba." Nwobu wrote,

> In a rain of blood, tens of thousands of innocent youths, some of them just 6 years old were lined up on the streets of Asaba and executed in cold blood on the direct orders of Murtala Muhammed. The Asaba massacre ... remains one of the bloodiest ... in the history of the African continent.[25]

The "tens of thousands" description is clearly an exaggeration, but Nwobu's commentary has appeared many times, and these figures have been repeated in subsequent Internet forums, as a narrative develops that is independent of the personal memories of survivors. The discussion that followed Nwobu's post on this occasion points to the complexities of developing a new collective memory that is historically plausible and honors the dead without inciting an urge for revenge. Many forum posters commented that they were hearing this for the first time; some picked up on Nwobu's call for action, while others argued against the value of such memories. For example, "Draftman" wrote

> When are we going to stop the finger pointing ... let's look at all the killing that Lt. Col. Ojukwu did, he has blood on his hand too ...
> The war is over, and the Biafra agitators lost, so let's move on.

"Agidimolaja" then wrote a long account of the events leading up to Asaba, concluding, the "Asaba massacre did not just happen, one thing led to another." "Tony" weighed in:

---

[25]   Lawrence Chinedu Nwobu, "Remembering Murtala Muhammed: The Butcher of Asaba," Feb. 19, 2009, online at www.nigeriavillagesquare.com/forum/articles-comments/29729-remembering-murtala-muhammed-butcher-asaba-2.html.

> War ... does not give anyone the right to target and
> indiscriminately kill civilians as Murtala ... did ... this is why there
> is an international criminal court in the Hague to try people guilty
> of war crimes and crimes against humanity ... You would scream to
> high heavens if your people were the victims ... Your Nigeria that
> you claimed to have fought for is a shameful disgrace of a nation
> where injustice and massacres is the order of the day.

Discussions like these could be found in Nigerian Internet forums
during the first decade of the twenty-first century, pointing to the way
that new media have been able to bring previously silenced histories
to light, while also opening the door to inflamed passions, exaggeration, and unsubstantiated claims.

COLLABORATION, MEMORY, AND ORAL HISTORY

This new era of open discussion acted as a catalyst for the community
effort to recover the history of the massacres in a more systematic
way, which in turn led to our involvement as researchers. As Irwin-
Zarecka noted, "to secure a presence for the past demands work –
'memory work' which addresses the 'infrastructure' of collective
memory, all the different spaces, objects, 'texts,' that make an engagement with the past possible."[26] Around 2007, Asaba leaders wished to
embark on some serious memory work, essentially hoping to help
"recalibrate" the national memory, and they formed a committee
made up of US- and Nigerian-based members, including several survivors and witnesses. Their intent was not to inflame, but to work in
the spirit of Hoffman, who argues that the "long afterlife of loss" may
afford the next generation the ability not only to validate the suffering
of the past, but to use that memory constructively in the future. She
argues that "it is necessary to incorporate loss into a vision of life."[27]

[26] Iwona Irwin-Zarecka, *Frames of Remembrance: The Dynamics of Collective Memory*, New York: Transaction Publishers, 13.
[27] Eva Hoffman, "The Long Afterlife of Loss," in *Memory: Histories, Theories, Debates*, ed. Susannah Radstone and Bill Schwarz, New York: Fordham University Press, 2010, 414.

They looked for an active academic partnership with scholars who would find the challenge rewarding.

Blood on the Niger author Emma Okocha, then based in the United States, made the initial contact. At first, the committee was interested in the possibility of conducting a forensic examination at Asaba, and Okocha contacted a forensic anthropologist at our university. She had existing research interests elsewhere in Nigeria, and was able to visit Asaba in 2008.[28] In 2009, we hosted an Asaba Symposium at the University of South Florida, attended by scholars, survivors, and members of the diaspora community in Florida. Some survivors made public statements about their experience, and our first survivor testimonies were privately recorded. Soon after, it became apparent that forensic research would not only be too costly and complex, but could also offend local sensibilities. A cultural anthropology/history collaboration seemed most appropriate, and we made our first visit to Asaba in late 2009. Here we met formally with the *Asagba* (traditional ruler) of Asaba, Joseph Chike Edozien. Dr. Edozien had a long professional career at the University of North Carolina, Chapel Hill, and as a former academic, he appreciated the importance of systematic research. Our work in Asaba could not have happened without his blessing. Eventually our Community Advisory Board, chaired by Dr. Uraih, was formed; it includes Chuck Nduka-Eze, the lawyer who presented the Asaba case at the Oputa Panel, as well as several prominent Asaba leaders, many of whom lost family members in the massacres.

In developing this community-based research, we always had two important points in mind. First, we had to negotiate the complexities of being "outsiders" who nevertheless want and need to work closely with the community. Particularly sensitive issues arise when outsiders become involved, and we are mindful of the problematic

---

[28]   For a brief description of that early phase of the research, see Erin H. Kimmerle, "Forensic Anthropology: A Human Rights Approach," in Natalie R. Langley and MariaTeresa A. Tersigni-Tarrant, eds., *Forensic Anthropology: An Introduction,* Boca Raton, FL: CRC Press, 2012, 424–438.

issues raised when Africans' history is reconstructed by non-Africans.[29] However, experience also shows there are times when outsiders may be able to break through the political gridlock and facilitate a more open discussion of tragic events in a nation's history. In the case of France, for instance, it took Paxton's pioneering work on Vichy to legitimize a national debate on wartime collaboration.[30] Cole and Barsalou argue that the participation of outsiders is "vital" in post-conflict situations; the experience of the Oputa Panel, which degenerated into ethnic wrangling, suggests that this is a highly appropriate context in which to offer objective outsider research.[31] At the same time, they caution that such interventions require sensitive and truly collaborative relationships with host communities. Our task as outsiders was to assemble and present an accurate account of the atrocities in Asaba, which would be a significant intervention in the established narrative of the war, while also offering our community partners a foundation on which to build their own transitional justice efforts. Second, it became important to underline the independence of our research – that our account of Asaba would be driven by our scholarship, not by any prescribed community agenda. Community leaders strongly supported this position for a key reason – they are well aware of the potentially volatile nature of the work, and the danger of any research being dismissed as propaganda. We understood that some in Asaba hoped eventually to use our evidence in human rights initiatives, and we have made our interviews available to them for such purposes. Once again, to have any value, our findings must be seen to be independent. Thus the role of the Community Advisory Board, and the many friends we now have in Nigeria, has been to facilitate the logistics of setting up interviews, and offer practical assistance during our many visits to Asaba – not to

---

[29]   See, for example, Chinua Achebe, *Home and Exile*, New York: Random House, 2000.

[30]   Robert O. Paxton, *Vichy France: Old Guard and New Order, 1940–1944*, New York: Knopf, 1972.

[31]   Elizabeth A. Cole and Judy Barsalou, "Unite or Divide: The Challenges of Teaching History in Societies Emerging from Violent Conflict," *United States Institute of Peace, Special Report* 163, June 2006.

shape the nature of our narrative. We have not requested or been offered any research funding from our Nigerian partners. The developing community relationship has had the occasional hitch; for instance, we and the Advisory Board soon parted ways with Emma Okocha, once it became apparent that his agenda reflected a more activist approach that required a particular, less-nuanced narrative.

On our part, it has been important to cast our net as widely as possible with relation to sources and viewpoints, and also to reflect constantly on the process of our research. For instance, our understanding of the specifics of the October events draws heavily on oral accounts, which potentially may be perceived as flawed and subject to the distortion of memory. As Radstone notes, "it is now widely accepted that personal accounts of the past do not necessarily offer direct access to that past."[32] Alessandro Portelli cautioned that "memory is not a passive depository of facts, but an active process of creation of meanings,"[33] a point that has been taken up by the burgeoning interdisciplinary field of "memory studies" in recent years.[34]

It soon became apparent to us that even at the community level we were dealing with two types of memory. A shared community memory about the Asaba atrocities and their contemporary salience clearly exists, and our interviews reveal elements of this. It is a honed-down narrative that is told widely and taken for granted, especially from people who were not physically present; we have often heard it during casual conversations in Asaba. This narrative is focused almost entirely on the October 7 Ogbe-Osowa parade itself, which is typically framed as a horrendous betrayal that was completely unexpected,

[32] Susannah Radstone, "Reconceiving Binaries: The Limits of Memory," *History Workshop Journal*, 59, 2005, 135.

[33] Alessandro Portelli, "What Makes Oral History Different?" in Robert Perks and Alistair Thomson, eds., *The Oral History Reader*, London: Routledge, 2016 (1979), 54.

[34] For a recent review of oral history as method, see Alistair Thomson, "Four Paradigm Transformations in Oral History," *Oral History Review* 34:1, 2007, 49–70. For a useful discussion of the field of memory studies, see Karen E. Till, "Memory studies," *History Workshop Journal*, 62, 2006, 325–341.

given the goodwill gestures and clear loyalty of the people – joyful marchers were brought together, and then mowed down without warning, in a grotesque dance of death. An important element is the death of elders, leaders, and important community members. During our many visits to Asaba and in conversation with people with Asaba roots, we came to expect an almost ritualistic recitation that went something like this:

> Our people came out joyfully to welcome the troops; we wore the *akwa ocha* and we "danced One Nigeria." Without warning, the terrifying Northern troops surrounded us, separated men from women, and turned the guns on our men. We were loyal Nigerians, and were unfairly singled out. And we have never recovered.

We became used to hearing this core narrative; people seemed to feel the need to explain the story to us, even when we clearly knew it already. Almost by definition, shared community memories of this kind are self-serving – they present a narrative that advances the agenda of the community in some way. Indeed, this local collective memory does important symbolic work. It marks out Asaba as being especially badly hit, and supports the notion of exceptionalism that characterizes many Asaba people's senses of identity. It offers explanation for things that have gone wrong in the community, a point we address more fully in Chapter 6.

We would not and do not argue that the core collective narrative is incorrect. But consistent with the usual process of memory construction over several decades, it is incomplete and over-simplified. This raises an important question: can oral history get beyond this, and be an effective way to get closer to what actually happened? Traditionally, historians shied away from the use of survivor testimony, citing the unreliability of memory. More recently, a more anthropologically inspired approach has argued that closer attention to the multitude of voices and memories can actually deepen our historical narratives, as memory is incorporated into accepted history.[35] Portelli, while offering cautions about the constructed nature of memory, simultaneously argued vigorously for the value of oral history. He noted that the richness and specificity of the method does produce valid accounts of past events, especially when these have been silenced in traditional histories, arguing that "historical work excluding oral sources (where available) is incomplete by definition."[36]

Indeed, we argue that it is the oral history method *itself* (supplemented by additional documentary sources) that has revealed the more nuanced, complete picture that demonstrates both the limitations of the core local narrative and the sparse documentary record. Eyewitnesses were interviewed alone and in many locations – Asaba, Lagos, London, Benin City, Ibadan, even Tampa. Significantly, many mentioned that they had rarely, if ever, told their stories before, some even to their own families. Their accounts often offer harrowing details, and taken together, they paint a much more complex picture of the horrors that unfolded, as we report in Chapters 2 and 4. Different interviewees focus on specific events they experienced, sometimes filling in the gaps in others' accounts, but there is remarkable consistency across their stories. As a result of these interviews, we know that the killings started days earlier, shortly after the troops arrived, and that the Ogbe-Osowa parade was not a joyful welcome, but a last-ditch attempt to stop the killing. We know that killing went on sporadically for days or even weeks later, and that many additional victims perished as a result of the "Second Operation" in early 1968. We know that contrary to common "knowledge," the victims included some women, and that many "ordinary" Asabans – farmers, laborers, fishermen – died with the doctors, lawyers, and civil servants who are often celebrated. We know that the people of Asaba were not in one mind about loyalty to Nigeria; there certainly were Biafran

[35]   See, for example, James E. Young, "Between History and Memory: The Voice of the Eyewitness," in Ana Douglass and Thomas A. Vogler, eds., *Witness and Memory: The Discourse of Trauma*, New York: Routledge, 2003, 275–283.

[36]   Portelli, "What Makes Oral History Different?" 56.

sympathizers among them. However, with the exception of one self-identified spy, we found no suggestion that Asaba civilians were actively working for the Biafran cause, and the consistent eyewitness accounts give the lie to the idea that pro-Biafran violence provoked the attacks on civilians. And finally, in contrast to an often one-dimensional depiction of the evil Northern perpetrators presented in contemporary local summations, we learned that many of the soldiers in Asaba were not from the North, and that their actions were in no way uniform. While some behaved with unspeakable brutality, others became saviors and protectors of civilians, a point to which we will return.

In advocating for oral history, we do not argue that simply assembling enough accounts will produce the "truth" of an event. "Human memory is not a sealed box containing a pure record of events, uncontaminated by the outside world; individual memories are themselves formed in constant interaction with the cultural sphere."[37] Memories are always edited and reframed, and mutate over the course of decades. Memories of events seen through the eyes of a child will necessarily differ from those experienced as a teenager or adult. Nevertheless, we agree with Portelli that oral history deserves its place as a key tool in the recovery of stories that have long gone untold. And, like him, we believe that when oral history is a central method, it "changes the writing of history," fore-grounding the voices of participants, and destabilizing the omniscient voice of the historian.[38]

COLLABORATING IN MEMORY CONSTRUCTION

Having established the independence of our research, and being convinced of the importance of bringing our findings out of the academic world and into the public sphere, we began an active process of intervention into the "memoryscape." As defined by Phillips and Reyes', the "memoryscape" is "a complex landscape upon which memories

---

[37]   Radstone, "Recovering Binaries," 131.
[38]   Portelli, "What Makes Oral History Different?" 57.

and memory practices move, come into contact, are contested by, and contest other forms of remembrance... [and] are unsettled by the dynamic movements of globalization and ... new practices of remembrance."[39] For academics, the impulse to intervene in established narratives is a familiar dimension of scholarship; our goal was certainly to offer new insights and interpretations to the academic discourse on the Nigerian Civil War. We wanted to contribute to the scholarly dimension of the memoryscape by necessarily rethinking some of the textual histories that frame accounts of Asaba, through scholarly publications. And we are convinced that serious attention to oral history and memory is key strength of our scholarly intervention.

However, as our work developed, it became apparent that the new media environment, with its possibilities for a new era of active memory work, begs for a more active participation in public discourse, in addition to academic contributions. Furthermore, and in the spirit of the tenets of applied anthropology/public history, we believed it was our ethical responsibility to our partners and interviewees to make our findings public and accessible. Ross, who studied the after-effects on people who testified to the South African Truth and Reconciliation Committee, noted that public testimony can be both cathartic and traumatic, and if nothing happens as a result of disclosure, people may understandably feel betrayed.[40] Karen Till argued that "a major shortcoming of memory studies is the scholarly isolation from the public engagement of ... memory work," continuing that this is an "embarrassment to the academy."[41] We agree, and we wished to build on the trust we have established with community members, offering them a resource that will not only benefit them, but also the public in Nigeria and elsewhere, facilitating articulation

[39]   Kendall R. Phillips and G. Mitchell Reyes, "Surveying Global Memoryscapes: The Shifting Terrain of Public Memory Studies," in Phillips and Reyes, eds., *Global Memoryscapes: Contesting Remembrance in a Transnational Age*, Tuscaloosa: University of Alabama Press, 2011, 13–14.

[40]   Fiona C. Ross, "On Having Voice and Being Heard: Some After-Effects of Testifying before the South African Truth and Reconciliation Commission," *Anthropological Theory*, 3, 2003, 325–341.

[41]   Karen E. Till, "Memory Studies," 339.

between our scholarly research and the work of those already active in trying to reclaim the memory of Asaba. Our increasingly visible online presence began in 2010 with the project website (www.asabamemorial.org), which includes background information, news, video clips, our publications, and other resources. The site has already become a resource for scholars and the public worldwide; from 2010 through mid-2016, it had been visited almost 10,000 times, with 7,800 unique visitors. In 2010, we began a blog (www.asabamemorial.wordpress.com) that chronicles our travels in Nigeria, discussing the research in a more informal setting and inviting comments. To date, this blog has attracted over 21,000 visits.

As our work developed, our goal became to intervene in the larger memoryscape through utilization of media. One step, for example, was to rewrite the Wikipedia entry on the massacre, drawing from our published work and referencing that work extensively. Essentially we agree with Pentzold, who argues that online media may constitute the "memory places" in which active memory work is done: "Wikipedia is not only a platform to constitute and store knowledge, but a place where memory – understood as a particular discursive construction – is shaped."[42] Since the initial rewrite, the entry has been edited several times by others, who have created new links and honed a few points (http://en.wikipedia.org/wiki/Asaba_massacre). We have noted that it is frequently now referenced as an authoritative source during online discussions. We spoke to reporters in Nigeria and the US whenever the opportunity arose and also contributed a piece to the widely read Nigerian newspaper, *ThisDay*, which was reposted on several other online news sites.[43] Two years later, the piece was republished in *Vanguard* newspaper (without our consent), generating

---

[42]   Christian Pentzold, "Fixing the Floating Gap: The Online Encyclopaedia Wikipedia as a Global Memory Place," *Memory Studies*, 2:2, 2009, 264. Pentzold is invoking the influential work of Pierre Nora, "Between Memory and History: Les Lieux de Mémoire," *Representations*, 26, 1989, 7–24.

[43]   S. Elizabeth Bird and Fraser Ottanelli, "Revisiting the Asaba Massacre," *ThisDay* (Nigeria), Oct. 5, 2014, 94.

almost 500 comments that ran the gamut from supportive to vitriolic.[44]

Our broader forays into social media began when we posted a link to our first published article on the massacres to a popular Nigerian diaspora discussion board with over a million subscribers (www.nairaland.com). Most post using screen names, and rules of behavior are fairly loose. Discussions cover everything from music to fashion, but politics and history are perennial subjects. The sensitivity of our work, as well as the continuing contestation over memory, immediately became apparent, and the subsequent tracking and analysis of online memory work has become an important part of our ongoing research. After one member posted a note of appreciation, a second member, "Dudu Negro," posted the following:[45]

> ... go to page 4 of this amateur research product and read some of the reasons why the war happened. Ibos said because dem sabi English language pass Hausa and dem sabi business so Nigerians hate dem ... The biggest problem we have as a people is the ability to tell ourselves the truth and act on it. Bunch of goats!!

"Monkeyleg" responded:

> I find no blame in the writers article, and I for one will accept the account of what happened as truth. It is a real shame that up to this very date 40yrs post the civil war, anti Igbo sentiments still exists ... So where have we grown as nation, how do we represent difference from the past? No wonder we are still making the same mistakes we made 50yrs ago. For those familes who suffered this brutal wicked incident, maybe at last thier stories will be told and heard.

---

[44] See www.vanguardngr.com/2016/10/revisiting-1967-asaba-massacre/.
[45] In all online discussions quoted directly, original spelling and punctuation are retained.

"Dudu Negro" responded with, "Can an Ibo ever open his mouth and present true perspective of events without exaggerating it falsely to score points?" After that, the discussion turned into several pages of ethnic name-calling; the massacre itself was forgotten. We have faced similar reaction in other forums, demonstrating that our "unbiased outsider" stance is by no means universally accepted. Reminding us again about the problematic issues raised when outsiders intervene, we noted that in his negative reaction, Internet commenter "Dudu Negro" also wrote that "White people dont understand this culture or the root of our issues but come here and speak to a people who sell them lies and they publish that as work of historical record."[46]

Nevertheless, we have continued to try to harness the potential of new media to spark the kind of intertextual memory work that is needed. As part of the 2012 Asaba Memorial Day, we showed a short (21-minute) video, using our interviews and available historical photos and documents. We had originally created this video as an aid to use in academic presentations, and it was made using very basic Moviemaker software. However, after encouragement from Advisory Board members, we decided to post the video through Vimeo with a link to the website, and we were quite startled when the video received over 4,000 hits over the next few days. Someone then posted it on YouTube; by 2016 it had been viewed more than 20,000 times on those two sites alone. We have also tracked its many repostings on Nigerian and diaspora sites, with one Facebook posting resulting in 13,000 viewings, and another close to 30,000, while the new traffic on our website shot up. While not exactly viral by global standards, this strategy brought the kind of visibility that conventional scholarly outlets could not. As Drinot notes, sites like YouTube "constitute sources through which to examine the interplay between the history (in the sense of historiography; i.e. history produced by professional

---

[46]   This exchange happened at www.nairaland.com/882413/asaba-massacre-1967-newest-article, Feb. 29, 2012. Last accessed March 28, 2014.

historians) and the collective, and, in turn, transnational or global, memories of a particular historical wound."[47]

As the video made its way across the Nigerian virtual landscape, it was received well by Igbo groups and with scorn by some others. The publication of Chinua Achebe's 2012 Biafra memoir, *There Was a Country*, sparked wide discussion in the online world, as Nigerians revisited the civil war with unprecedented vigor.[48] The Asaba massacre (which Achebe mentions briefly in his book) often comes up in one way or another in such discussions, and our work quickly received notice. In one long thread on Nairaland, in which participants were hotly debating whether the Igbos should make a case to the International Criminal Court for reparations for civilian deaths in the war, the massacre was mentioned, and someone posted our video. In spite of the direct descriptions of the event given by survivors, doubt was still expressed:

> So the ibos want to quickly rush to ICC ... The biafra case was a war, war is not a soccer game. People will die, men will fall and that was what happened to ibos ... and the asaba massacre was brought about by the indiscretion of an itinerant ibo man who thought it is bravery to attack the commander of an army while his army is on top and in charge. What do you expect his soldiers to do? Sing you a lullaby? ... the action of a stupid ibo man caused 700 ibos to be lined up against the wall and shot![49]

We see here how the long-established narrative about Igbo provocation, originating in "old media" in 1968, and repeated in histories, resurfaces as "proof" of Igbo responsibility for the massacre. Others respond with exasperation: "watch the fu**ing video!" writes one contributor.

[47]   Paulo Drinot, "Website of Memory: The War of the Pacific (1879–84) in the Global Age of YouTube," *Memory Studies*, 4:4, 2011, 371.

[48]   Chinua Achebe, *There Was a Country: A Personal History of Biafra*, New York: Penguin, 2012.

[49]   www.nairaland.com/search?q=asaba±massacre&search=Search.

Online media are notoriously problematic, because of the permission they give people to vent, often under the cover of anonymity. In an earlier study of online newspaper comments sections, the first author argued that such forums need to be viewed with caution and not treated as surrogates for audience activity more generally. At the same time, she also noted that not all online forums are the same and that the virtual environment should not be dismissed as a potential site of reasoned discussion.[50] Our experience with the Asaba project supports this position, as we have seen in the more thoughtful way our work has been received in some venues. The Nigeria Nostalgia project, for example, is a Facebook site devoted to memories of Nigeria, especially through photos. Membership is almost 60,000 worldwide, with many (possibly most) in the diaspora, especially the UK and US. This forum, which includes a special subgroup on the civil war, has strict rules of language and behavior, and the slightest signs of ethnic hostility are quickly silenced. The individual who posted our video wrote

- After watching this ... I begin to wonder: Can some wounds ever heal? How do we, as a nation, go about re-uniting the broken "elements" that hold us together?

Some typical comments in the discussion that followed:[51]

- Apart from my parents talking about the Asaba massacres, I did not learn anything about it in school ... We need to present all this atrocities in the light and let it be in a mainstream discussion. Without doing so we will continue in circle and it may actually destroy us as a people
- Thanks for the documentary. Captain Matthias is also the reason why we must tell this story. There is always a remnant of hope among the carnage[52]

---

[50]   S. Elizabeth Bird, "Seeking the Audience for News: Response, News Talk, and Everyday Practices," in Virginia Nightingale, ed., *Handbook of Audience Studies*, New York: Blackwell, 2011, 489–508.

[51]   These comments are taken from a long thread that followed the release of the video in August 2013: www.facebook.com/#!/groups/nigeriannostalgiaproject/permalink/609018385805614/.

[52]   We discuss the key role of Captain Matthias, who was instrumental in controlling violence against civilians, in Chapters 2 and 4.

- Thanks for posting this. Every Nigerian should watch this so we never ever go thru anything like this again
- Thank you for sharing. A little bit of Nigeria's history for sober reflections

We tracked repostings as much as we could, finding the video on many different blogs, such as Jaguda.com, where the blogger noted that

- This documentary gave me the chills, and I'm sure it will too. For those that know already it serves as a painful reminder of our tainted past, and for those that don't it's an eye opener. The best thing we can do as Nigerians is educate ourselves on our past and learn from it so we don't repeat the same mistakes our fore fathers did.[53]

We have now found ourselves invited into the discussion, and the work of recalibrating memory has taken on an additional, collaborative dimension that we are documenting as part of our ongoing exploration of memory.

MURTALA MUHAMMED: PERPETRATOR AS HERO?

An inescapable figure in the evolution of the memory of Asaba has been Murtala Muhammed, commander of the Federal Second Division, which perpetrated the atrocities in Asaba. Prior to and throughout the war, he and General Gowon were at odds, and in July 1975, five years after the war's end, Muhammed toppled Gowon in a coup. On Feb. 13, 1976, during an unsuccessful coup attempt, Muhammed was ambushed in his car in Lagos and was assassinated. Ibrahim Taiwo, his second-in-command at Asaba, close associate, and Military Governor of Kwara State, was killed on the same day near Ilorin in Northern Nigeria. Muhammed was 37 years old and had been in power barely seven months. However, in that short time, Muhammed had become very popular, and his death turned him into a folk hero. He had made his name through a series of decisive acts, widely seen as fighting corruption and trying to restore public

[53]   www.jaguda.com/2013/08/14/video-chilling-documentary-of-a-war-time-massacre-the-legacy-of-the-asaba-massacres/.

confidence in the Federal Government. He also developed policies to curb inflation, and he realigned foreign policy – for example, he announced Nigeria's support for the Soviet-backed Peoples Movement for the Liberation of Angola, straining relations with the United States.[54]

Muhammed's "Nigerianism," which involved non-alignment with major powers, had undoubtedly been one of the reasons for his popularity, and his death brought on an outpouring of grief. Prominent musicians like Sunny Ade recorded songs about him, and hastily produced publications mourned his death in extravagant terms:

> He was the star in our firmament
> Our moon in its reflected glory
> A rarity in his own class
> A genius in his own generation
> When next shall the womb of a Nigerian mother
> Be blessed with another child like this?[55]

Today, the international airport in Lagos bears his name, his portrait appears on the 20 Naira note, and he remains widely revered. Many have questioned whether he would have reached that status had he lived to govern longer, but the fact remains that a revision of his memory is anathema to many Nigerians.

It is thus hardly surprising that he became a central, polarizing figure in the rethinking of civil war history that blossomed after the Oputa Panel and the rise of the Internet. Almost every time his name comes up on Nigerian forums, bitter arguments ensue, with Asaba

---

[54]   A US briefing to Secretary of State Kissinger in 1975 described Muhammed as "an erratic, vainglorious, impetuous, corrupt, vindictive, intelligent, articulate, daring Hausa ... An early ... assessment is that Muhammed [is] anti-American ... [however] Nigerian leadership is far more pro-Nigerian than anti-any cause or country, which is the essence of Nigerianism ... we can probably do little or no political business with the new regime," online at: https://history.state.gov/historicaldocuments/frus1969-76ve06/d208.

[55]   Henry Emezuem Nwigwe, "The Death of Murtala Muhammed: A Lament," April 15, 1976. This extract is from the foreword of a 35-page booklet printed in London. It is one of a collection of similar publications, produced in both Nigeria and the diaspora, held in the Institute of Commonwealth Studies, Oxford, UK.

frequently invoked, as we saw in the 2009 discussion discussed earlier. As an example, we note a discussion that developed on the often contentious message-board, Nairaland.com. In September 2011 a thread was launched, provocatively titled, "Murtala Muhammad was a Loser that took delight in Killing Civilians During War."[56] A member ("Justcash") had reposted a highly critical article about Muhammad, his role in the pre- and post-war coups, and his actions at Asaba. Responses were immediate:

RGP92: Murtala Muhamad have been dead for 35 years now. Please lets forget this and move on

JUSTCASH: The real reason why Nigeria is not making progress is that our history is full of hatred, denials and deception ... It is easy for you to say "Please let's forget" just because it did not happen in your hometown. Maybe, if your grandmother was raped and your grandfather was killed, you will know how it really feels.

SANDEE575: War is war. Anything can happen during wartime ... war crimes is purely an academic definition. Dont declare secession if you dont want war. The oil is for Nigeria not just Biafra alone.

Things escalate:

ALEX14: Ndigbo should never forget all the past atrocities committed against them ... the devilish non-Igbos will always try to shout them down as we (Igbo) try to tell our story. The main strategy for the Igbo nation is not to seek for understanding or forgiveness from the perpetrators ... the aim now is to get even.

PROUDIGBO: The slaughter in cold blood of families; young boys and children is ok in your books b'cos "war is war". You really are a shameless, cold-hearted sack of shi*t ...

JOEYFIRE: Murtala was a failure. Truth is that only in nigeria can a lousy soldier, talentless buffoon become a celebrated statesman. This deranged bloodsucker wasted so many men trying to take onitsha from rag-tag soldiers ...

---

[56]   See www.nairaland.com/762137/murtala-muhammad-loser-took-delight/2. Since those posting use screen names rather than their real names, we also use these in quoting their posts. Original spelling and punctuation is retained.

SANDEE575: I would rather tolerate stupidity than the ibo's treachery.

NDU CHUKS: The great Murtala Mohammed was one of the greatest commanders in the Nigerian Army during the civil war ... It is true that.. some wayward members of 2 Division carried out terrible killings of civilians as punishment for their sympathy for the biafrans. There is no evidence whatsoever that Murtala Mohammed had anything to do with these killings ...

The argument continues in similar vein for some time. As with other discussions, once our Asaba Memorial work started to become known, it began to be invoked as authoritative evidence, for instance in the calmer and more thoughtful Nigeria Nostalgia Project. Even though the site has strict rules about civility and ethnic name-calling, feelings can run high, especially when it comes to the civil war. Muhammed has featured frequently, as in this discussion. In October 2013, a member posted a photo of Muhammed near Benin City in 1967, shortly before his troops moved into Asaba.[57]

Immediately, another member asked, "Wonder how many comments this is going to generate?"[58] Indeed, the conversation continued for more than a year, until December 2014, generating over 500 comments and more than 35,000 words. After some preliminary discussion, some members questioned Muhammed's actions as president, and another described his war record as "dismal." Some back and forth (much longer than presented here) followed:

- As always, people trying re-write history. Murtala was HERO. He ... will remain one as long as history is written.
- One man's meat is another man's poison ... He's my poison because of war crimes committed under his watch ... historical facts have shown that his troops conducted massacres ... he was a very poor military officer tactically..

The discussion then refocuses on whether Muhammed was an effective leader, and at times gets quite heated. The administrator

---

[57]   See Chapter 1, Figure 1.1.

[58]   Since NNP members use their real names, we are protecting privacy by shielding their identities in these quoted posts.

stepped in to caution members about civility, but another member retorted:

- So, the Asaba people murdered themselves abi? May they RIP and may those who did it RIH! [Rot in hell]

However, it becomes clear that members were working hard to avoid confronting Asaba directly. One member made a reference to Muhammed's "alleged" crimes, upon which another responded with a link to our project website:

- You were doing so well until "allegedly" – here's www.asabamemorial.org to rip the veneer off of "allegedly"
- Could that be because all potential witnesses became victims?
- It could be. We were not there so we cannot say and no one has come forward to say he saw him do this or that.
- And the Asaba Memorial work? Anyway Niyi, let everyone believe what they want to and then later on in the after life they may get to know.
- In war, people die. In Asaba, people died ... No death is greater than the other. May they all rest in peace.
- For goodness sake, Asaba was different and you know it. It was different in that it was premeditated. It was callous. It was gruesome.
- War is ugly my friends. Very ugly. None of us should in hindsight judge the decisions made by soldiers from the comfort of our keyboards.
- Even during wars, there are crimes, hence the concept of "war crimes." Murdering innocent civilians cannot be excused by war ... In this day and age for any one to hold up any of these as "heroes" make me wonder if we are speaking the same English language.
- No one is condoning ... but a lot was done to reconcile with the Igbos after the war and these comments we now hear are like a slap in the face ...

Members then discussed whether some kind of reparation to Igbos is in order, with some suggesting that everyone suffered in the war:

- History is not taught in our schools! ... not acknowledging the suffering of others is why wounds will never heal ... Now Ndigbo do not want compensation, they want closure which I think a truth and reconciliation commission would address ... Now if you cannot understand this I suggest you revisit the history of the Biafran war. If your position remains unchanged then there is nothing else to be said.

- In this thread, we are focused on MM. He's not the only war criminal (IMHO), but he is the most honored of them all. That is the question.

As comments on both forums suggest, the memory of the civil war is still highly contentious, as we shall discuss further in our final chapter. The figure of Murtala Muhammed is especially problematic – an interrogation of his heroic status is potentially threatening for many – even more, perhaps, than a more general discussion of possible war crimes. The question of his heroic status is at the heart of the continued sense of grievance held by Igbos in general and Midwesterners in particular. From their perspective, the lack of official acknowledgment of his wartime role symbolizes the nation's failure to resolve the divisions that led to war in the first place.

CONCLUSION: MEMORY WORK IN THE AGE OF NEW MEDIA

In an era of "old media," the Asaba massacres were effectively contained and memories silenced, and the full story remained primarily local. In an era of "new media," the memoryscape is potentially transformed, with new ideas and new information free to circulate widely. People were certainly using the opportunity to try to reinscribe uncomfortable histories into the nation's sanctioned memory several years before our work came on the scene, and our research is now actively contributing. Pentzold notes that the web should not be seen as a static "record":

> [it] cannot be understood as one consistent medium like television or radio but rather as an underlying basis that fosters different applications, tools and forms of communicative interaction ...
> The Web presents not only an archive of lexicalized material but also a plethora of potential dialogue partners. In their discursive interactions, texts can become an active element in forms of networked, global remembrance[59]

[59]   Pentzold, "Fixing the Floating Gap," 262.

These are the qualities of the web that have intrigued us as we work to disseminate what we hope is a nuanced and honest account of what happened in Asaba. As Drinot notes,

> Digital artefacts such as YouTube ... offer historians another tool, along with oral history or the analysis of visual sources, to access and analyse collective memories. They enable historians to examine collective memories in an inherently transnational or indeed supranational context; i.e. in the de-territorialized world of the internet."[60]

This "de-territorialized world" has its dangers, of course. For the academic, it represents a loss of control – we can put our work out there with the best of intentions, but we cannot predict what is done with it. And the more actively we become involved, the more unpredictable things become. Our static website and even our blog remain under our control, while allowing readers to comment. However, once the video or written products are posted, and especially once social media sites are included, things change rapidly. Our video may not only be reposted, but also cut and reassembled. It has been appropriated by pro-Biafra resurgence movements in ways we find disturbing. Language from our published work and website has been cut, pasted, and repurposed. Our work has been praised and welcomed, but it has also been reviled and dismissed in ways that are alarming to those used to the slow pace and relative gentility of academic knowledge circulation. Nevertheless, through the unruly process of today's mediascape, the story of Asaba has escaped local boundaries. Martina Osaji, a cousin of Celestina Isichei, was 14 years when her father, Leo Isichei, was shot down in the street. She and her sister dragged his body to their home and buried him with the help of a sympathetic soldier. She explained why her story is important:

---

[60]   Drinot, "Website of Memory," 372.

There is nothing you can do to replace my father – no amount of compensation. I would rather have my father and my other relations. But I want the world to know that this is what happened ... Even my own children don't know ... God knows why I had to survive: for me to have a story to tell. And that is why I'm telling you now.[61]

Today, the new mediated memoryscape brings together the global and the local to create new opportunities for memory work, whose goal is to reclaim silenced histories and perhaps ultimately bring some measure of justice for Martina, her father, and so many other Asaba victims.

[61]   Interview with Martina Osaji, Oct. 5, 2011, Asaba.

6   Trauma, Identity, Memorialization, and Justice

Asaba today, with a population of almost 150,000, is a very different place from the small, sleepy town it had been before the Nigerian Civil War. Since the war, there have been several administrative reorganizations, each adding new states, and in 1991, Asaba became the capital of Delta State, one of the 36 that now exist in the country. It is more visible than ever before in the nation as a whole, and its status has brought a boom in building, an international airport, and other developments. The old core of Asaba, with its five quarters, remains, but most of the agricultural land once held in common has been sold off. And Asaba still bears many scars. These are visible in the derelict buildings that remain unrestored and on the bodies of those who survived. There are also invisible scars, still fresh in the minds and lives of Asabans who have kept alive the memory of the cruel death of their fathers, brothers, and uncles, even as their trauma has remained institutionally unrecognized. As one focus group participant, not born until after the civil war, noted, "You can't talk to your children about Asaba without mentioning the massacre."[1] The war, and the price Asaba paid, has left an indelible mark, and the sense of "unfinished business" is strong. This has led to a desire not only to ensure the massacre is not forgotten, but also to see some kind of justice for Asaba. The question becomes: what would justice look like? The concept of transitional justice, now widely used to refer to post-conflict situations, encompasses "processes and mechanisms associated with a society's attempt to come to terms with a legacy of large-scale past abuses, in order to ensure accountability, serve justice and

---

[1]   Male, unemployed, 32, focus group participant, March 14, 2014, Asaba.

achieve reconciliation."[2] The people of Asaba wish for justice, but their wish is complicated by the uneasy historical and contemporary relationship with the entity known as Biafra. To understand the unique nature of Asaba's claim, we must first explore that of Biafra.

BIAFRAN MEMORY AND POLITICAL RESURGENCE

With the war's end, the name of Biafra was wiped from the official map of Nigeria – even the Bight of Biafra, from which the name was derived, was renamed the Bight of Bonny. Nevertheless, the memory of Biafra refuses to die; indeed, it has enjoyed a political resurgence, and it is against this backdrop that Asaba seeks to define its own memory and its own future.

The war has left a bitter legacy throughout the country, with which Nigeria is still coming to grips. In 1997, Harneit-Sievers et al. wrote that recognition of the war was "a difficult issue," and that over the years it has been marked primarily as a military event, with each successive military government using it as an "opportunity to assure itself of its role as guarantor of national unity."[3] Little attention was given to the profound impact on civilian communities within the conflict zone. Two decades later, with civilian governments now in power, the war is still strikingly absent from official Nigerian collective memory. In 1970, as the war ended, Gen. Yakubu Gowon had famously declared there would be "no victors, no vanquished," and there has been little official appetite for revisiting past trauma. Renowned author Chinua Achebe, who had actively worked for the Biafran cause, noted in the memoir published just before he died that the war "was a cataclysmic experience that changed the history of Nigeria,"[4] and yet, "Why has the war not been discussed, or taught to the young, over 40 years after its end?"[5] He pointed out that the war is

---

[2]   United Nations Secretary General, Guidance note, United Nations Approach to Transitional Justice, March 2010, 2.

[3]   Harneit-Sievers et al., *A Social History of the Nigerian Civil War: Perspectives from Below*, Hamburg: Lit Verlag, 1997, 1.

[4]   Chinua Achebe, *There Was a Country: A Personal History of Biafra*, London: Allen Lane, 2012, 2.

[5]   Ibid.

largely absent from school curricula and other formal expressions of national history and identity; as Akachi Odoemene noted,

> Nigerian government officials discourage the teaching of civil war history in schools … war history is not on the list of courses in the national university history curriculum in Nigeria; it is rather a mere footnote narrowly subsumed in the course "History of Nigeria since Independence." Yet the civil war remains the most significant episode in Nigeria's national history.[6]

This point was also made recently by Wole Soyinka, who told an interviewer, "Officials do not want to confront their own history, especially the history in the making of which they feel uncomfortable but, if you do not confront your past, you are going to mess up your future."[7] Thus for Igbo-speaking people on both sides of the Niger, there is a widespread belief that the war's impact has never been fully acknowledged.[8] In recent years, however, there has been an upsurge of writing about the war, comprising what has been defined as "a memory boom" around experiences of the war, and encompassing academic scholarship, memoirs, and fictional works, such as the influential *Half of a Yellow Sun*, by Chimamanda Adichie.[9]

These new expressions of memory have given potent symbolic support to more overtly political movements that have gained considerable prominence in recent years. These new secessionist movements were rooted in grievances established during the immediate post-war period. Gowon's government, building on the "no victors, no

---

[6]   Akachi Odoemene, "Remember to Forget: The Nigeria-Biafra War, History, and the Politics of Memory," in Chima J. Korieh, ed., *The Nigeria-Biafra War: Genocide and the Politics of Memory*, Amherst NY Cambria Press, 2012, 169.

[7]   Philip Nwosu, "I'm Pro-Biafra –Soyinka," *The Sun* (Nigeria), July 15, 2016, sunnewsonline.com/im-pro-biafra-soyinka/

[8]   See Chima J. Korieh, ed., *The Nigeria-Biafra War: Genocide and the Politics of Memory*, Amherst, NY: Cambria Press, 2012; Raisa Simola, "Time and Identity: The Legacy of Biafra to the Igbo in Diaspora," *Nordic Journal of African Studies*, 9:1, 2000, 98–117; Daniel J. Smith, "Legacies of Biafra: Marriage, 'Home People' and Reproduction among the Igbo of Nigeria," *Africa: Journal of the International African Institute*, 75:1, 2005, 30–45.

[9]   Odoemene, "Remember to Forget," 199.

vanquished" slogan, had decreed that the war would be followed by "reconciliation, reconstruction, and reintegration," designed to bring the Igbo back into a united Nigeria. Nevertheless, from the beginning some government actions seemed to defy this noble goal, such as the "abandoned property" policy that prevented many Igbo from retrieving property they had been forced to leave behind in the war. In the post-war reorganization of states, this affected property both outside and within the former Biafra: "all Igbo-owned property in the newly created Rivers and South Eastern states [would] be forfeited to the Ijaw and other ethnic minority groups who now controlled them."[10] The government also announced a rule that anyone holding cash and assets in Biafran currency could exchange them for no more than a total of 20 Nigerian pounds, a small sum even then. It was an action that "pauperized the Igbo middle class and earned at its expense a profit of £4 million for the Federal Government treasury."[11] Indeed, many saw these policies as a strategy to prevent the Igbo middle class from regaining key roles in business and commerce. In addition, many Igbo civil servants who had left their posts to join Biafra were unable to regain their lost jobs. While in many respects, the post-war reconstruction was a success and was achieved with no violence, the more negative aspects seeded feelings of injustice.

However, it is clear that specifically war-related issues were not sufficient in themselves to breed the new Biafran secessionist unrest. If post-war Nigeria had been a well-governed economic success, things might have developed differently, and grievances might have subsided. Instead, they have magnified, supporting Ukiwo's argument that the resurgence of secessionism can be more fully explained by considering the role of "state violence" – the actions of oppressive military governments that have negatively affected Nigerians of all ethnicities:

[10]   Ike Okonta, "Biafra of the Mind: MASSOB and the Mobilization of History," *Journal of Genocide Research*, 16:2–3, 2014, 367.

[11]   Philip C. Aka, "The Need for Effective Policy on Ethnic Reconciliation," in E. Ike Udogu, ed., *Nigeria in the Twenty-First Century*, Trenton, NJ: Africa World Press, 2005, 49.

The emergence in post-Civil War Nigeria of regimes that turned a blind eye to or appeared impotent amid killings of persons from particular ethnic or religious groups, and trigger-happy heads of state who gave shoot-on-sight orders to soldiers deployed to troubled sections of the country, remain critical to understanding the contemporary waning of the affective orientation of some Nigerians to the Nigerian state ... State violence also exists where the state or its agents may not have been directly responsible for the act but are perceived to have sanctioned the act by their failure to intervene or prosecute the perpetrators of violence.[12]

Military regimes ruled Nigeria from the Civil War era through to 1999. As noted by Ike Okonta, "A key consequence of the economic slump, military dictatorship and Ibrahim Babangida's polarizing policies in the 1980s and early 1990s was the retreat of Nigerians into ethnic, religious and other associations of primary identity."[13] Under these regimes, violent, often ethnically based confrontations took place all over the country.[14] Perhaps the most notorious regime was that of Sani Abacha (1993–1998), which saw numerous civil rights abuses. The most egregious was the brutal persecution of the non-violent Movement for the Survival of the Ogoni People (MOSOP), which fought against environmental degradation by multinational oil companies. Its leader, writer, poet, and environmental activist Ken Saro-Wiwa, was hanged in 1995, bringing international condemnation on Nigeria.

With the return of civilian rule in 1999, the Oputa Panel, the only attempt to provide a reckoning for the decades of abuses, collapsed in acrimony, as we describe in Chapter 5. The result was that the ideal of Nigerian unity was widely threatened. Over the years, militant political movements have emerged in various parts of the

---

[12]   Ukoha Ukiwo, "Violence, Identity Mobilization and the Reimagining of Biafra," *Africa Development*, 34:1, 2009, 12.

[13]   Okonta, "Biafra of the Mind," 358.

[14]   See Ukiwo, "Violence, Identity Mobilization" for a detailed discussion of these many conflicts.

country, such as the Movement for the Emancipation of the Niger Delta (MEND), which fights against exploitation by the oil industry of the people of the Niger Delta, as well as the destruction of the natural environment. Recent years, of course, have seen the rise of the Islamicist Boko Haram, which has carried out terrorist attacks predominantly in the country's North. This situation has offered fertile ground for the dormant seed of Biafran secession to germinate.

The Movement for the Actualization of the Sovereign State of Biafra (MASSOB) has been the most prominent among many groups advocating for a new secession, arguing that the Igbo people have continued to be marginalized in Nigeria. Formed in 1999, after the return to civilian rule, it was initially based on a "Biafra bill of rights" created by its founder, Ralph Uwazurike.[15] Advocating non-violent protests, it employed strategies such as publically displaying Biafran flags and issuing its own currency and passports, quickly drawing the attention of Nigerian authorities.[16] The most recent, and increasingly prominent, entity is Indigenous People of Biafra (IPOB), created by UK-based Nnamdi Kanu in 2012 after he split with MASSOB.[17] Kanu established a radio station, Radio Biafra, reviving the name of Biafra's most effective wartime propaganda tool, and the station has broadcast around the world. IPOB has also made very effective use of social media; part of its potent message is to frame Boko Haram's activities as a jihad against Christians, while simultaneously reframing the original Biafran conflict as a Muslim-Christian war. The Nigerian Government has had little success in using its broadcasting regulators to shut down the station, but it did arrest Kanu in October 2015 when he returned to Nigeria, sparking protests in the former Biafra. He continues his activism after his release on bail

---

[15] Okonta, "Biafra of the Mind," 356.

[16] Olly Owen, "The New Biafrans: Historical Imagination and Structural Conflict in Nigeria's Separatist Revival," paper presented March 8, 2016, in Changing Character of War series, Pembroke College, University of Oxford, accessible at: www.ccw.ox.ac .uk/news/2016/4/11/the-new-biafrans-discussing-discontent, 2.

[17] See "Confusion, as MASSOB Disowns Radio Biafra Boss, Nnamdi Kanu," *The Vanguard*, Oct. 19, 2015, www.vanguardngr.com/2015/10/confusion-as-massob-disowns-radio-biafra-boss-nnamdi-kanu/.

in April 2017. His supporters do not advocate total independence, but make increasingly visible claims for a restructuring of Nigeria into a "true federal" nation.[18] Pro-Biafra protests have happened in many parts of the East since mid-2015, prompting Amnesty International to condemn the killings of peaceful demonstrators by federal troops at Onitsha, where they were marking the anniversary of secession in late May 2016.[19] According to Olly Owen, the potent combination of a "mythologised historical nostalgia" with current economic and security concerns has fueled the new Biafra movement. The radical Biafra movement has been taken up most avidly by people under 40, many of whom suffer from high levels of unemployment; "Very few of those who actually lived through the civil war in the region show enthusiasm for renewed separatism."[20]

The Biafran separatists argue that successive governments have under-invested in the region, and that the participation of Igbos in top political posts has been carefully controlled, with Igbos still being treated as suspect for their role in the civil war. Furthermore, increased security issues, with a perceived rise in crime and violence, have fed the narrative of protest. And finally, the 2015 national election replaced President Goodluck Jonathan, who enjoyed considerable support in the East, with Mohammadu Buhari, a former military head of state who had fought on the federal side against Biafra, and has now become a symbol of oppression for radical separatists.

ASABA AND THE BURDEN OF MEMORY

At the time of writing, the future of the Biafran separatist movement is unclear. But as Owen argued, "the power of historical memory and myth is such that the issue is unlikely to go away."[21] And as in the war

---

[18]   See for example, Emmanuel Uzodinma, "You Have Made Nnamdi Kanu a Hero, Igbo Youth Movement Tells Buhari," July 12, 2016, dailypost.ng/2016/07/12/you-have-made-nnamdi-kanu-a-hero-igbo-youth-movement-tells-buhari/.

[19]   See www.amnesty.org/en/latest/news/2016/06/nigeria-killing-of-unarmed-pro-biafra-supporters-by-military-must-be-urgently-investigated/.

[20]   Owen, "The New Biafrans," 3.

[21]   Ibid., 11.

itself, Asaba and other former Midwest communities have been drawn into this new political movement, largely against their will. Biafra resurgence movements, just like their secessionist forebears, argue that the "Western Igbo" belong with Biafra; Asaba people certainly participate in pan-Igbo groups and activities, such as those of the dominant organization Ohanaeze Ndi Igbo, but generally do not accept the equation that "Igbo equals Biafra." As the new Biafran movement has blossomed, Asaba's perennial identity as "neither bird nor mammal" still holds.

That sense of being "in-between" has long driven the cultural and political movement for a unique identity – Anioma – for those people once known by colonialists as Western Igbos. Asaba-born Chief Dennis Osadebay, who became the first premier of the pre-war Midwest Region, and others argued for the distinct identity of this group in the 1950s, and it gained traction in the 1970s and beyond. The word itself began as an acronym, derived from the four districts of Aniocha, Ndokwa, Ika, and Oshimili; today, its boundaries correspond with the Delta North Senatorial District of Delta State (Map 6.1).

The movement for creation of a unique Anioma state continues today. Those advocating for Anioma do not seek independence from Nigeria; they maintain their call is a "philosophical affirmation of our self-determination as a people who see themselves at the crossroads of the contemporary Nigerian state."[22]

The complexities of Asaba identity are captured in two starkly contrasting messages that we received in response to our public dissemination of our research, both critical of our characterization of Asaba people. The late Kunirum Osia was an academic and cleric who had ministered in refugee camps in Ibusa and Asaba during the war. Later, he became a passionate advocate for the distinct identity of Anioma, writing the foreword to Don Ohadike's influential book on

---

[22] Kunirum John Osia, "Anioma People Of The Delta," www.anioma.org/.

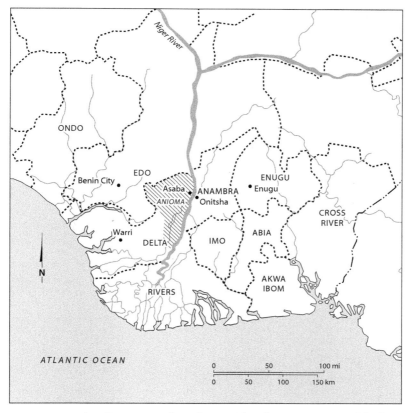

MAP 6.1 Current state boundaries within the area once part of the former Midwest and Eastern Regions, showing the approximate boundaries of Anioma. Cartography by Bill Nelson.

the history of the movement.[23] After reading our first published work on Asaba,[24] he wrote, commending our work but adding:

> Your designation of Asaba as "ethnically Igbo" offends anyone from that part of Nigeria because we are not Igbo. The designation ... was

[23]   Don C. Ohadike, *Anioma: A Social History of the Western Igbo People*, Athens, OH: Ohio University Press, 1994.

[24]   S. Elizabeth Bird and Fraser Ottanelli, "Most Vulnerable Nigerians: The History and Legacy of the Asaba Massacres," *African Studies Review*, 54:3, 2011, 1–26.

a colonial creation because the people never refer nor regard themselves as Igbo. We paid dearly for that faulty designation which we find very offensive. Unfortunately after so many decades of this false designation the people with the help of Chief Osadebay ... christened us "Anioma" ... Prior to colonialism we knew and regarded ourselves as *"Enuani, Oluku mi, Ika, Igala and Ukwuani"* but *never* Igbo" (emphasis in original)[25]

On the other hand, Ifeanyi Adib, an activist for Biafran secession who now resides in Denmark, watched our video online and wrote about a year later:

I think there is some misinformation there, especially where the narrator towards the beginning said that Asaba was never part of Biafra. It was wrong, because Asaba people are the same Igbo/Biafra people only divided by the river "Niger" ... It is understandable in the video that the trauma still remains, and with every sadistic effort to erase Biafra identity from Biafrans, the interviewed put up a show of "loving Nigeria as their country." It was a WWIII that the whole world led by British shamefully fought against innocent Christian people of Biafra in their own land.[26]

Adib went on to argue that if Asaba people claimed identity with Nigeria, they were only doing so out of fear, since they are not only Igbo, but indeed Biafran.

Neither of these views succeeds in capturing the complex sense of identity found in Asaba. People we encountered generally embrace the name of Anioma as a marker of their distinct identity, but only a few took Osia's position that Anioma people are not in any way Igbo. Equally, we saw little evidence of unequivocal Igbo identity. Our focus groups, in which we discussed questions of identity, often elicited contrasts and disagreement. In one group, a participant claimed "I have no links with the Igbo. I am Ahaba,

[25]   Kunirum Osia, personal e-mail to Elizabeth Bird, Sept. 30, 2013.
[26]   Ifeanyi Adib, personal online communication to Elizabeth Bird, Dec. 14, 2014.

I speak Ahaba."[27] Another participant (whose view was unique in this group) immediately disagreed: "I am proud to say I am an Igbo . . . all Igbos descend from Israel."[28] A third chimed in: "we don't have any link with the East."[29] Just as in the war itself, there are people in Asaba who identify with Biafra, but the predominant view is suspicion of the "Igbos across the river." In February 2016, the Governor of Delta State, Dr. Ifeanyi Okowa, forcefully repudiated IPOB's claims that Anioma communities belong with Biafra Republic. He noted, "We may speak the same language but we were never part of the South East. We were part of the old Midwest, we were part of Bendel, we are now Delta State and we are Deltans."[30]

In December 2015 and January 2016, Asaba social media sites lit up with discussion of the issue, following an assembly of protesters on the Niger Bridge at Asaba. Evoking the civil war suffering, the first comment in one long discussion noted, "What happened last time will be small compared to what may happen again." While some did express support for Biafra self-determination, most did not. As one commented,

> Biafra is dead and buried with Ojukwu. None of these crop of agitators witnessed that crude massacre called the civil war. They are all nothing but a bunch of myopic, ignorant, jobless and selfish miscreants.

Some wished the Biafrans well, but argued strongly against being part of their struggle, while others angrily blamed Ojukwu and his people in the East for bringing calamity on Asaba: "Our people were killed and massacred by the hands of the Ibo men who forced us into fighting that war."[31]

[27] Male, contractor, 37, focus group participant, March 14, 2014, Asaba.
[28] Male, unemployed college graduate, 37, focus group participant, March 14, 2014, Asaba. The legend that the Igbos are descended from the lost tribe of Israel is quite widespread, especially in the East.
[29] Female, caterer/beautician, 40, focus group participant, March 14, 2014.
[30] See www.ossaioviesuccess.com/2016/02/biafra-anioma-nation-not-part-of-biafra-okowa.html?utm_source=twitterfeed&utm_medium=facebook.
[31] Identities not given to protect privacy.

THE LONG AFTERLIFE OF TRAUMA

Thus although the people of Asaba certainly feel a strong sense of injustice stemming from the war, this has not translated into a desire to support any radical Biafra movement. Rather, they feel betrayed in a way that is different from Biafra itself. Not only did the town experience arguably the worst organized killing of civilians of the war, but this happened in spite of the fact that it was not part of the secession and that its people died while voicing support for a united Nigeria. Today, people still describe a feeling of marginalization; their complaints range from lack of funding for Delta State to Asaba being ignored in the 2014 centenary commemoration of the founding of the colonial entity of Nigeria, pointing to the role of Asaba as the de facto first capital. This sense of marginalization and betrayal is rooted not only in the war itself, but also in the immediate post-war policies and practices that left many Midwesterners, like their Eastern Igbo cousins, feeling disenfranchised. The national rehabilitation program did not cover areas affected by the war but outside the secessionist region, and many Midwesterners once again felt caught in the middle. As described by Daniel Olisa Iweze, the many Igbo-speaking former government employees who had fled from places like Benin City were covered by the "Winning the Peace" program created by the then-Midwest State Government:

> In the screening exercise, attention was focused on the part each person played during the Biafran occupation of the state. Those considered "the most guilty" were re-absorbed but demoted ... Most applications for re-absorption were either turned down or ignored.[32]

The Midwest, which had once seemed like a microcosm of what a diverse and united Nigeria could have been, became fractured

[32]   Daniel Olisa Iweze, "Post-Civil War Intergroup Relations: The Western Igbo and Non-Igbo Groups in the Midwest State," in Chima Koreih and Ifeanyi Ezeonu, eds., *Remembering Biafra: Narrative, History, and Memory of the Nigeria-Biafra War,* Glassboro, NJ: Goldline and Jacobs, 2010, 176.

along ethnic lines, as animosities created during the war often strengthened rather than declined:

> The Midwest State came out of the reconstruction era a highly divided people and this provided opportunity for exploitation of sectional feelings and interests which endangered ethnic harmony ... [33]

And while Asaba shares in the broader grievances of Anioma, its people also argue a more specific damage that was done to them. In a tangible sense this is obvious; the town was virtually destroyed, and its inhabitants had to rebuild after losing everything they had. A familiar expression in Asaba is *"aya buta kpum"* ("the war brought my grief"), capturing the sense that everything bad, unjust, or wrong in the community stemmed from the massacre and its aftermath. As we noted in Chapter 4, trauma was experienced at a very personal level, as people coped with the deaths of multiple beloved relatives and as children's hopes of education and advancement died with the senior men in their extended families. There is no doubt that for many families, the war precipitated a spiral of decline from which they have not recovered. One woman we interviewed, who was a teenager during the war, never received the education that had been planned and never married:

> After almost 50 years from the war we've not recovered. We are still crying for help. I was not able to finish my education because there was no one to train me ... You can look at this, my father's house ... look at the surroundings. There is nothing to talk about. People will come and say they will help – there was nothing ... No help has come to Asaba ... I wouldn't have been in my father's house ... I would have been better. I would have been better. [34]

We noted in Chapter 4 that many families lost key breadwinners and providers; influential men were often responsible not only for their

---

[33]   Ibid., 181.
[34]   Interview with Nkandelin Maduemezia, June 23, 2010, Asaba.

own children (sometimes from two or more wives), but also for the children of relatives. Rifts developed within families as people struggled to survive, as we saw with the Uraih family, whose mother was essentially abandoned by her dead husband's family. One of our focus group participants described how after the death of her grandfather, tension between his two wives led to a permanent estrangement between their children. Educational opportunities were curtailed, and some families slid into economic decline. Emeka Okelum Okonta offered a vivid picture of the long-term impacts on his family.[35] His grandfather (his father's father) was killed, along with two sons; Emeka's father and one brother survived. A wealthier uncle had taken care of this branch of the family, but worn down by the deaths of many family members and the destruction of their homes, he died "of heartache" in 1969, leaving no clear family leader. Emeka's father fled to Biafra and joined the army, as did other young men who found themselves alone. Returning from the war, he began to rebuild his life without support, his hope of education dashed by the uncle's death. He married, and obligations to take care of his family and his wife's surviving relatives forced him to take any available occupation. He found work as a driver for the Federal Ministry of Agriculture, but a lack of skills and education made him vulnerable to economic downturns and he lost his position to budget cuts in the 1980s. He briefly worked as a taxi driver, but eventually lost the car and became a motorcycle taxi (okada) driver, never finding stable employment again. Born in 1973, Emeka was a gifted student who found his prospects for higher education closed. He remembers that, to his dying day, his father repeated how "his life would have been different" but for the war. Emeka believes that his fall "from grace to grass" tore his family apart and eventually led to his father's death. He speaks for a generation that sees the disaster resonating today:

> I will never be a happy man knowing that this war, this massacre . . .
> brought penury to me . . . for instance, when I was in the Federal

---

[35]   Interview with Emeka Okelum Okonta, June 24, 2010, Asaba.

> College of Education . . . A lecturer asked me to buy his handout . . .
> Do you know how much his handout was? Forty naira [about
> twenty-five cents in today's US currency] . . . I couldn't afford it.

The lecturer berated him, saying he had repeatedly failed to buy the handouts: "I just can't forget that statement. It lives with me and it will die with me . . . and that contributed to leaving school without the certificate . . . mine is a typical example."

The trauma is also felt at a community level that is harder to define, yet very real. Kai Erikson defined "cultural trauma" as a "blow to the basic tissues of social life that damages the bonds attaching people together and impairs the prevailing sense of communality."[36] He noted that while individual trauma is sudden and shocking, cultural trauma has a more delayed and insidious effect, which is clearly apparent in Asaba. Arguably, many communities in Biafra itself suffered equal or greater loss of life, but for Asaba, the loss was very targeted, in that a large proportion of adult males died, including many of the town's most prominent and influential leaders. The importance of this was observed as early as 1969, by historian Elizabeth Isichei: "nearly all the elders . . . were killed . . . The younger generation have little knowledge of Asaba's past . . . The passage of time and a disastrous war have robbed us of their memories and perspectives forever."[37] And as time passed, the long-term impacts continued to be felt, as the kinship-based governance structure of the town was disrupted. Like many West African societies, Asaba was governed through a male age-grade structure; the senior Otu-Ihaza grade advises the *Asagba* and other chiefs, and governs issues like traditional marriage, rites of succession, and so on, and rotates out every 12 years. Many of the most senior men died or fled, meaning that when Asaba did start to get settled after the war, there was a vacuum of

---

[36]   Kai T. Erikson, *Everything in Its Path: Destruction of Community in the Buffalo Creek Flood*, New York: Simon and Schuster, 1976, 153.

[37]   Elizabeth Isichei, "Historical Change in an Ibo Polity: Asaba to 1885," *Journal of African History*, 10, 426. Elizabeth Isichei, a New Zealand–born historian, is the wife of Peter Isichei, brother (from another mother) of Celestina and Patrick Isichei.

authority and knowledge, as Elizabeth Isichei suggested. As a focus group participant remarked, "those who had been out of the country came back, and they didn't know the rules."[38] While Asaba has certainly recovered and the traditional structure is active, the legacy of this disruption has resulted in lingering disputes that still surface today.

A related challenge to the traditional structure was the impact of the war on gender roles. As we have noted, women often played a central role in keeping family and community together during the war. They made choices that went against traditional expectations, even marrying or having consensual relationships with outsiders.[39] For some, this might be seen as a positive change in this deeply patriarchal culture, but for others, such self-reliance is problematic. As one young single woman put it,

> people get different perceptions of the Asaba women, they say they are domineering, they say they are hard to keep in the homes ...
> people see us from a negative angle, they think we can't make good wives, they think we are too wise, but they are not considering the fact that situations put us through that.[40]

It seems certain that challenges to gender roles would have developed in the post-war years in any event. Nevertheless, the war once again becomes a useful lens through which to view changes, such as recent debates about the propriety of awarding women traditional titles in their own names.

Yet another perceived impact of this trauma to the traditional structure is a widespread perception that Asaba's special reputation as a seat of education and influence was damaged. One focus group participant noted that his extended family lost "12 graduates and six doctors,"[41] and others reported similar attrition. Many Asaba people

[38]   Male, 58, retired army officer, focus group participant, March 14, 2014, Asaba.
[39]   For more discussion of the war's impact on gender roles, see Egodi Uchendu, *Women and Conflict in the Nigerian Civil War*, Trenton, NJ, Africa World Press, 2007.
[40]   Female, civil servant, 29, focus group participant, March 14, 2014, Asaba.
[41]   Male, entertainment consultant, 44, focus group participant, March 14, 2014, Asaba.

believe that resentment of its tradition of education and professional success was one reason the town was targeted in the first place, and that the war destroyed that elite status. Interviewees repeatedly told us of the important people who died – the doctors, lawyers, civil servants, and chiefs, with one man noting, "The long-term effect is that we lost our rightful position in the scheme of things. In Nigeria, generally."[42] Now, in the words of a 29-year-old female civil servant, this status is diminished: "people see us as nothing because of a situation we are not responsible for."[43]

In objective terms, it is impossible to prove a direct link between the wartime massacres and many of the problems that currently afflict Asaba – and which also afflict communities across Nigeria. These include high unemployment, increase in crime, disaffected youth, challenges to traditional authority, and a crumbling infrastructure. Undoubtedly, the post-war growth of Asaba, accelerated with the 1991 designation as state capital, was the catalyst for many of these problems, and there are those in Asaba who would have preferred that the capital designation had gone to the larger city of Warri.[44] A long legacy of central corruption and failure to invest in infrastructure has affected communities across the country. Yet the perception that the war initiated a downward spiral is strong, and speaks to the symbolic meaning of the massacres today, as people speak of fundamental damage to the social fabric that stems from the war experience. Our focus group participants described Asaba people as naturally honest, open and welcoming, and yet since the war, "people are not of the same minds anymore ... everyone is suspect."[45]

Perhaps the most significant element in this narrative is the legacy of the mass rapes that traumatized women throughout the military occupation. As noted by Chiseche Salome Mibenge, concerns

---

[42] Interview with Michael E. Ogbogu, May 3, 2012, Asaba.

[43] Female, civil servant, 29, focus group participant, March 14, 2014, Asaba.

[44] Many in Asaba speculate that the choice of Asaba was affected by the fact that Maryam Babangida, influential wife of then military leader, Ibrahim Babangida, was an Asaba indigene.

[45] Male, fashion designer, 34, focus group participant, March 14, 2014.

with male honor traditionally color attitudes toward rape and are "rooted in such patriarchal considerations as fear of miscegenation ... the idea that women raped by the enemy army/nation/race will bear children that will be alienated from the targeted group."[46] Although some survivors told us that the children of raped women were not stigmatized, they were clearly not easily incorporated into the strongly patrilineal social structure. "Asaba" is a colonial corruption of the indigenous name "Ahaba," and this is a term many prefer to use when specifying their ethnic identity. To be a true Ahaba "indigene," one must be able to trace descent through the male line from Nnebisi, the town's founder, and his five sons, who each established one of the quarters of Asaba. Accordingly, anyone fathered by an outsider cannot be a true indigene and hold office in the traditional structure. A child without a recognized father has an ambiguous place in the extended family, and thus in the village and the quarter. Tradition had ways to absorb the children of unmarried mothers, such as adoption by the women's father. No doubt some children of rape experienced this, but because of the large numbers of men killed, this option was often closed. The unassimilated children of rape were known to all since they carried their mothers' names and had no inheritance rights.[47] In adjacent Edo state, Adediran Daniel Ikuomola has documented that wartime rape victims' children were often given names that identified them, such as *Okwuoeimose* (the ugly face of war), which often resulted in stigmatization throughout their lives.[48] We did not encounter evidence of such overt stigmatization in Asaba, but did come to learn that it is not uncommon for Asaba indigenes to blame the generation of children of rape for many

[46]   Chiseche Salome Mibenge, *Sex and International Tribunals: The Erasure of Gender from the War Narrative*, Philadelphia: University of Pennsylvania Press, 2013, 41–42.

[47]   This is not to suggest that all children who carry their mothers' names are the product of rape. Some may be fathered outside marriage in other circumstances; such children would not carry the same level of stigmatization.

[48]   Adediran Daniel Ikuomola, "The Nigerian Civil War of 1967 and the Stigmatisation of Children Born of Rape Victims in Edo State," in Raphaelle Branch and Fabrice Virgili, eds., *Writing the History of Rape in Wartime*, London: Palgrave McMillan, 2012, 169–183.

of the current social problems. According to Nicholas Azeh, a pastor and massacre survivor,

> They had the women and they brought forth bastards to the land ... a generation of people who are not really Asaba ... it is a very ugly social abnormality ... And the experience of these bastards is still affecting us now. It is still affecting us now today.[49]

A local history, written by a well-known town leader, developed this theme in describing the "decline in education" in Asaba, noting that the war "saw many Asaba families shattered," and pointing to the rise in single mothers of children fathered by soldiers: "In the end, a good number ended up being school dropouts. Thus, they simply attained growth without development. Today, such children have matured to adults without any visible, sustainable means of livelihood."[50] The author argued that these young men then fall into lives of crime, especially blaming them for the pervasive and fraudulent selling off of communal land that has plagued Asaba recently.

For many in Asaba, the disaffection of this generation is attributed to social and political factors, such as the violence and social breakdown caused by the war. In the words of someone who was a young boy in war-ravaged Biafra, "what makes a person a violent person is what they have grown up witnessing."[51] The subsequent stigmatization of fatherless children is also perceived as a factor in alienating them: "They are often reminded of who they are, and this makes them vicious."[52] Others, however, blame it on a kind of physical "pollution" of the genetic makeup by people who do not share real "Asaba blood."[53] Asaba people are very proud of their bloodline; indigenes are commonly described as exhibiting a blend of

[49] Interview with Nicholas Azeh, Oct. 5, 2011, Asaba.
[50] Augustine N. Ndili, *Guide to Customs, Traditions and Beliefs of Asaba People,* Asaba: His Bride Ventures, 2010, 16.
[51] Male, businessman/printer, 53, focus group participant, March 14, 2014, Asaba.
[52] Female, retired educator, 58, focus group participant, March 14, 2014, Asaba.
[53] These terms were used by many participants in our focus groups, and we also heard them often in conversation.

inherent intelligence, educational achievement, industriousness, and hospitality, which makes them stand out as distinctive from other Nigerians, including Igbos from the other side of the Niger. According to this view, all these characteristics combined to make pre-war Asaba a center of excellence that produced educators, business leaders and civil servants.

In keeping with the patrilineal principle of indigeneity, the child of an Ahaba mother and non-Ahaba father is not eligible to fully participate in the traditional leadership structure. Such individuals are not stigmatized – they become indigenes of their father's community, while retaining a relationship with their mother's natal village. Indeed, the community is proud of the prominence of some Asaba women who married outsiders, such as Maryam Babangida, wife of Military Head of State Ibrahim Badamasi Babangida (1985–1993), who is credited with developing the role of First Lady in Nigeria.

However, the children of rape or other illicit unions are inherently problematic, because they have no visible father, in Asaba or elsewhere. We heard them described as "mixed breed" or "bastards."[54] Asaba historically had a strong disdain for soldiers and women who consorted with them, dating back for decades before the war. According to Egodi Uchendu,

> To fling the word *soldier* at any woman in the town was equivalent to accusing her of licentiousness or adultery, an indictment that would automatically label her as defiled and in need of ritual purification.[55]

The troops who occupied Asaba were a combination of Westerners, non-Igbo Midwesterners and Northerners, the latter drawn largely

---

[54]   Again, these terms were used by participants in our focus groups, as well as in general conversation.

[55]   Uchendu, *Women and Conflict*, 2007, 61–62 (italics in original).

from Hausa-speaking populations, and pollution by a soldier of this origin was especially shaming.

Because of the patrilineal structure, the identity of these "mixed-blood" people is common knowledge: "I grew up in the village and I know how Asaba people behave, and who have Asaba blood."[56] While "an Asaba man is slow to violence,"[57] these people are described as volatile and confrontational, as displaying "lazy attitudes toward work," and as defiant of traditional community structures.[58] For many, this is seen as a biological issue: "A person of Asaba blood would not take an Asaba person's life ... [but] the blood of Nnebisi does not run in their veins."[59] Their presence in Asaba is held responsible for the erosion of "most of our highly esteemed culture."[60] This narrative is encapsulated by Emeka Okelum Okonta:

> We are highly educated people, we are highly intelligent people. We don't steal ... After the war you now see children, you now begin to see them steal, to see things that our forefathers never do. You now see youth come out unintelligent ... Who when they go to school, fail. This is not a trait of our people ... Our people are a race who are advanced ... How come we have children who can't express themselves and who resort to vices and crime? Some of these [were] children of those who the federal troops either raped, or those of our women who they enticed to have sex with, they now imported blood— traits—that are foreign. Most of the boys who are creating havoc in town today if you check their birth—they are those born in 1968 to '70 ... Because those are the people who have this bad blood. They are not the original stock ... That is why our people will say *ahaba amago umu wa* – that means this town knows her children ... anywhere you see a child or a man who is becoming

56   Male, retired army officer, 58, focus group participant, March 14, 2014, Asaba.
57   Ibid.
58   Male, ICT manager/administrative secretary, 29, focus group participant, March 14, 2014, Asaba.
59   Female, businessperson, 26, focus group participant, March 14, 2014, Asaba.
60   Ibid.

unruly, you will know that these are product of those, we call them *gwodogwo* soldiers.[61]

Many in Asaba would reject the strictly biological understanding of bloodline, arguing for a more socio-cultural explanation for deviance. And as one focus group participant commented, blaming the outsider is always an easy explanation; he noted that it is also common to blame the Hausa minority, or people "from across the river" for rises in crime and delinquency.[62] Population growth and an influx of new people would inevitably have changed the character of the once small town, and the traditional kinship-based structure would have faced stress. While in the 1930s, an estimated 90 percent of Asaba's population could trace direct descent from Nnebisi, the proportion must be much lower today. Nevertheless, the importance of wartime "pollution" of Ahaba bloodline can be heard regularly in conversation, or in the discussion on Asaba online forums. For instance, in discussing the impact of a flood in Asaba in October 2012, a contributor on such a forum wrote the following:

> Illegitimate half Sons and daughters gotten from Loose Asaba Women and Rape Victims in the Asaba Genocide have turned Scavengers, selling Asaba Land indiscriminately to any criminal who can give them money for illicit and worthless life style of women, drugs and alcohol.

Later that year, during a discussion about the prevalence of kidnapping, another contributor commented: "those killed or captured should undergo DNA testing to ascertain if they are real Asaba indigenes!!"[63] We see in this narrative the way that even after decades, the trauma of the war and the massacre retains its power, offering potent explanations for contemporary problems.

---

[61]   Interview with Emeka Okonta Okalum, June 24, 2010, Asaba
[62]   Male, businessman/printer, 53, focus group participant, March 14, 2014, Asaba.
[63]   To protect their privacy, we do not name these online contributors.

THE QUEST FOR TRANSITIONAL JUSTICE

Thus the legacy of the war was profound, and there is a strong sense that Asaba deserves justice. This search for justice has taken several inter-related directions. As we noted in Chapter 5, once the veil of secrecy had been lifted at the Oputa Panel, and former president Gowon had apologized, a more active movement developed. A first step in this movement has been the construction of a more complete scholarly account of wartime events, followed by informed interventions in public narratives about Asaba. Another strategy is being explored by members of our advisory board, who believe that the videotaped interviews we have collected can constitute credible evidence from which a legal claim for reparations can be developed – not for individuals, but for the community. While we do not believe it appropriate for us to be active in such an initiative, we have made all our data available as needed.

As Nicola Henry has noted, formal transitional justice mechanisms, such as trials and truth commissions, have often been much less successful than anticipated, and indeed have "exposed the gap between the promise and reality of justice."[64] This has led people to seek other avenues to justice, in particular seeking some kind of official memorialization. According to Alex Hinton, while transitional justice is often associated with formal mechanisms, "more recently the term has been defined in a broader manner ... and extended to encompass a larger set of outcomes, such as advancing development and social justice."[65] Memorialization of various kinds is one of these outcomes; as Schudson noted, the impulse to commemorate grows as people are distanced from direct experience. In Asaba, this distancing is through both time, as older generations pass away, and space, as emigrants in the diaspora now seek to know

[64]   Nicola Henry, *War and Rape: Law, Memory and Justice*, London: Routledge, 2011, 9.
[65]   Alexander Laban Hinton, *Transitional Justice: Global Mechanisms and Local Realities after Genocide and Mass Violence*, New Brunswick: Rutgers University Press, 2011, 2.

and commemorate their heritage.[66] Claims made for memorials as a form of transitional justice are varied, and include "honouring and remembering the dead; facilitating understanding of past events; providing evidence of atrocities; creating official narratives; and serving the political needs of those who initiate and fund the construction of memorials."[67] In the case of Asaba, all these are pertinent. However, Janine Clark also cautioned that a further goal for transitional justice is education and reconciliation, and that memorials can be highly problematic in that regard. She argued that "memorials often display an exclusionary logic" that emphasizes the victimhood of the community, while closing avenues for reflection and consensus-building among previously warring groups. In her case study of Croatian war memorials in Vukovar, the selective memory embodied in the memorials produces a situation in which they "represent a fundamental obstacle to reconciliation."[68]

As we have noted in Chapter 5, Asaba people have consistently told us that as direct survivors decrease in number, those who died must simply be remembered. In addition, reconciliation is indeed a goal – a point that further differentiates them from Biafra secessionists. They point to the continuing ethnic tension that plagues the country, saying that the nation must accept and understand its violent past in order to face the future united. As one of our focus group members put it, "If a young man does not find out what killed his father, then what killed his father will kill him."[69] Thus in Asaba, the goal is that the nation of Nigeria accept and acknowledge the reality of what happened in Asaba, value the commemorative process, and then move forward together – not an easy prospect, of course.

---

[66]   Michael Schudson, "Lives, Laws, and Language: Commemorative versus Non-Commemorative Forms of Effective Public Memory," *The Communication Review*, 2:1, 1997, 3.

[67]   Janine N. Clark, "Reconciliation through Remembrance? War Memorials and the Victims of Vukovar," *The International Journal of Transitional Justice*, 7, 2013, 117.

[68]   Ibid., 122.

[69]   Male, fashion designer, 34, focus group participant, March 14, 2014, Asaba.

Herbert Hirsch argued that the move of positivist social scientists into post-conflict studies has been problematic, based on quantifying and defining genocide, rather than valuing the personal stories of survivors: "Scientific analysis cannot communicate the sheer human tragedy ... nor can it accomplish the goals of enhancing understanding and of prevention."[70] In addition to pointing to the need to study the impact of atrocities on communities, he advocated for the importance of compassionate academic input into the construction of memorials and reconciliation efforts. We agree, and with great care, we have continued to have a role in memorialization efforts.

Early in the collaborative process, it became apparent that different forms of memorialization would do different kinds of work in seeking a sense of justice for Asaba. The central goal for local leaders was the construction of a cenotaph, which would list the names of the dead; this idea had been discussed for some time before we came on the scene. The design and concept for the structure was an entirely Asaba decision, in which we were (appropriately) never involved. The structure, funded through private donations, was started in 2012 and is now complete – a simple concrete base, on which names of the October 7 dead are inscribed, surmounted by a cross (Figure 6.1). The monument captures the core narrative: it is located on the site of the Ogbe-Osowa massacre, and privileges those who died there rather than elsewhere. The names inscribed are almost exclusively male and tend to favor the more prominent. They were drawn from lists created at various times that are known to be incomplete, excluding many more names (as we quickly learned during our interviews). The monument is essentially a symbol of recognition and remembrance; it does not in itself attempt to tell a narrative or draw broader conclusions.

In addition, the year after we started our project, Asaba leaders initiated an annual day of remembrance on October 7, involving

[70]   Herbert Hirsch, *Genocide and the Politics of Memory*, Chapel Hill: University of North Carolina Press, 1995, 80.

FIGURE 6.1 The October 7 monument at Ogbe-Osowa, Asaba. Photo by Elizabeth Bird.

a prayer service at the Ogbe-Osowa site, followed by a procession along the original parade route on Nnebisi Road to a gathering at a church community center (Figure 6.2). We have participated in several of these events, speaking and showing our video, and have posted news and photos on the project website. In 2011, at the second event, the program included a short address by the President of the Asaba Development Union, Chief Dr. Louis Odogwu, that included a key piece of language that marks Asaba's

FIGURE 6.2 Asaba Commemoration Day Procession, 2012. Survivor
Dr. Ify Uraih is center front. Photo by Fraser Ottanelli.

unique sacrifice, noting that those killed "paid the supreme price with
their innocent blood, *that Nigeria our dear country becomes an indis-
soluble entity*" (emphasis added).

This claim, that Asabans, unlike Biafrans, died not in opposition
to Nigeria, but *for* a united Nigeria, guided us as we developed the
materials for a museum-style exhibit, titled "Most Vulnerable
Nigerians: The Legacy of the Asaba Massacre," that was made public
during the next Asaba Day in 2012. We developed this exhibit in
consultation with our advisory board, knowing that many local people
may not know the full story, and as outsiders, we would be able to help
address the complexities and ambiguities, as well as explore the possibilities for reconciliation. The exhibit was created in the form of 11
large panels printed on heavy-duty vinyl fabric, telling the story of
what happened in Asaba in words and images, with heavy reliance on
the words of witnesses. We attempted to place the arrival of the troops
into the context of the history of the civil war up to that point, moving
on to detail about the killings before Oct. 7. We offered what we

considered to be an accurate narrative about the Ogbe-Osowa parade and massacre, presented an example of a positive action by a Nigerian soldier and devoted an entire panel to the suffering of women. The final panel included a section under the heading, "They died for their country":

> When the Federal troops arrived, they were angry and full of hate, and they took out their fury on the innocent. Asaba people, kin to Biafra yet loyal to the Federation, became "the most vulnerable Nigerians," in the words of Wole Soyinka. As Nigerians they expected protection, and were rewarded with death.
>
> Such hatred sparked inhuman brutality. Yet there are also stories of humanity that offer hope for the future. Survivors tell of soldiers, sickened by the violence, who intervened to protect the innocent, even at great cost to themselves. Such stories tell us that violence is not inevitable, and that hatred can be overcome ... Today, the people of Asaba do not seek revenge. But they ask that their suffering be acknowledged. They paid the supreme price with their innocent blood, so their country could endure.

We shared the panel layouts with our advisory board and the *Asagba* before final production, primarily to ensure accuracy. At times there were disagreements; for instance, one of our practical challenges was how to select images for the panels, since at that time we knew of few existing photographs that show either the community before or during the war. Initially, we offered surrogate images, such as a photo of neighboring Onitsha, taken just before the war. This was rejected, because it showed thatched houses, and our partners believed this presented a misleading picture of the town as "backward," since most houses in Asaba had metal roofs at the time (in fact, there were also many thatched houses in Asaba). Fortunately, we eventually discovered the previously unknown set of photos taken by correspondent Bill Norris in the aftermath of the destruction, which became an invaluable resource (See Chapter 2). Other images came from artwork just produced by a local artist, depicting the October 7 massacre from

FIGURE 6.3 Detail from an outdoor mural at the home of Dr. and Mrs. E.A.C. Nwanze, depicting the Oct. 7 massacre. Created by Tony Nwalupue.

start to finish, which adorned the home of an advisory board member (Figure 6.3). We discussed whether to include references to the probable divided loyalties of some people in Asaba. In the end we agreed that this would be difficult in the concise format of the exhibit, but would be more appropriate in longer form accounts, such as articles and books, since the full context could be provided.

The exhibit was displayed in 2012, attracting hundreds of visitors, and some regional press coverage (Figure 6.4). Our hope was that the exhibit would constitute a form of public memory work as a memorial that would reach not only those in Asaba, but also in the region more generally, while maintaining a conciliatory and inclusive message. The intention was to place it on permanent display in Asaba. Unfortunately to date its reach has been limited; it remains in the *Asagba*'s palace, where it is viewed by select visitors only. In 2014, we created a smaller replica of the panels, which were

FIGURE 6.4 Community members view "The Most Vulnerable Nigerians" exhibit, Asaba, 2012. Photo by Fraser Ottanelli.

displayed at an Asaba remembrance day in London, sponsored by a diaspora group there.

THE HOPE FOR MEMORIALIZATION

Writing specifically about the Nigerian Civil War, Obiezu wrote that "remembrance is not mere indulgence in nostalgia but an opportunity to heal the memories of past injuries and to plan practical initiatives for the future."[71] As Clark noted in the case of Croatia, memorials that simply maintain the pain of loss can renew animosities and, in the case of Asaba, could serve to rekindle ethnic tensions. As Collier, Hoeffler, and Rohner reminded us, "The principal legacy of civil war is a grossly heightened risk of further civil war."[72] People

71   Emeka X. Obiezu, "Memorialization and the Politics of Memory," in Chima J. Korieh, ed., *The Nigeria-Biafra War: Genocide and the Politics of Memory*, Amherst, NY: Cambria Press, 2012, 188.

72   Paul Collier, Anke Hoeffler, and Dominic Rohner, *Beyond Greed and Grievance: Feasibility and Civil War*, Centre for the Study of African Economies, Working Paper Series 2006–10, 13.

in Asaba are acutely aware of that potential, and most wish to avoid framing the narrative as a desire for revenge. For instance, many welcome the inclusion of stories about federal soldiers who did the right thing, like Captain Matthias. Some undoubtedly came from the same ethnic groups whose "impure blood" was seen as "polluting" Asaba. Such stories present "the more realistic nature of human relationships that transcend ethnic identity and boundary" and offer Nigerians today opportunities to reflect on how judgments and choices unfold.[73] These stories are an important part of the history and may help point the way to reconciliation rather than revenge. Chuck Nduka-Eze, a lawyer who originally helped build a case at the Oputa Panel and who lost his mother at Asaba, explained that while the panel's failure was disappointing,

> it was for us the first opportunity ... to even air the matter ... But the aim was really to begin some sort of the healing process. Because if you wrong somebody, especially the type of wrong we are talking about ... and the person has an opportunity to talk about it and gives the wrongdoer the opportunity to express a view ... assuming that you show some contrition, you apologize ... then the healing process can begin.[74]

In moving forward, they hope to build productively on the memory work that has already been achieved. Although Gowon apologized to the people of Asaba in 2002, this was as a private citizen, and the community very much wants a formal government apology from the Nigerian government, ideally accompanied by compensation that would recognize the suffering from which Asaba has not fully recovered. Significantly, none of the interviewees claimed they should personally receive money. Their views echo research conducted on other post-conflict communities that suggests the most effective

---

[73]   Nneoma V. Nwogu, *Shaping Truth, Reshaping Justice: Sectarian Politics and the Nigerian Truth Commission*, New York: Lexington, 2007, 81.

[74]   Interview with Chuck Nduka-Eze, Dec. 9, 2011, Asaba.

symbolic reparations are "physical and practical ones that translate pain and loss into outcomes that benefit the community."[75]

One of the most pressing problems in contemporary Asaba is unemployment or underemployment, as a focus group participant noted, reparations could be in the form of job opportunities: "when people talk about compensation, people think about money. Money is not everything ... When a man's heart is occupied ... he feels at peace."[76] Consistently, interviewees told us that a fitting memorial should come in the form of schools, scholarships, hospitals, and economic opportunities. Several also pointed to the importance of developing a monumental site or museum, and to recognizing the national importance of Asaba's historic sites.

As our contribution, we developed a plan that meshes with these tangible priorities. Asaba has a small museum, the Mungo Park House, an 1894 colonial structure that has considerable significance as the administrative headquarters of the Royal Niger Company, and thus in effect the administrative capital of Nigeria (Figure 6.5).[77] Although owned by the Federal Government, the building is in serious disrepair, and houses the most minimal displays. However, it has the potential to become a useful cultural and economic resource for the community; its staff already run some programs for youth, such as crafts and computer training, although lack of funds are a serious problem. While other African nations, such as Ghana, have successfully developed "heritage tourism" opportunities, Nigeria has lagged far behind, often failing to appreciate the potential of its rich history and heritage. Okpoko and Okpoko have argued that "the future of tourism in Nigeria is linked to the care of

75   Julian Hopwood, "We Can't Be Sure Who Killed Us: Memory and Memorialization in Post-Conflict Northern Uganda," International Center for Transitional Justice: Justice and Reconciliation Project, 2011, 11.

76   Male, fashion designer, 34, focus group participant, March 14, 2014, Asaba.

77   The building has never been associated with the Scottish explorer Mungo Park, known for "discovering" the source of the Niger; the name became attached to the building at some undetermined time.

FIGURE 6.5 The Mungo Park House Museum, Asaba. Photo by
Elizabeth Bird

our cultural heritage," but that this will require a change of thinking
in the country.[78]

With this in mind, we developed a proposal that made a case for
restoring the building, and brought it to some influential individuals in
Nigeria, who are working to raise funds for a public/private partnership.
The goal is to create a museum of Anioma culture, along with Nigerian
academic partners and the Asaba community. It would include the
exhibit on the massacre, but would embed this in a larger story that
could foster Anioma pride and heritage, while bringing economic ben-
efits to the community, and sponsoring programs on peace-building.
Clearly this is an ambitious goal, that will take significant time, energy,
and resources to realize, but the people of Asaba have waited for almost
50 years, and many are actively working toward this outcome.

[78]   A. Ikechukwu Okpoko and Pat Uche Okpoko, *Tourism in Nigeria*, Nsukka: Afro-
Orbis Publications, 2002, 69.

CONCLUSION: THE SIGNIFICANCE OF ASABA

The twentieth century saw a seemingly endless stream of horrifying violence, demonstrating all too clearly the inhumanity of humankind. The Nigerian Civil War was only one of those extended acts of violence, and the massacres at Asaba were but one dimension of a bloody conflict in which both federal and Biafran troops committed unspeakable acts.[79] One might ask why it seems important to resurrect the history of this event, at a time when Nigeria faces a new litany of problems.

First, the story of Asaba is important because it re-evaluates a neglected dimension of the history of the Civil War, deepening our knowledge of how and why it unfolded as it did. In the decades since the war, a somewhat settled narrative has developed about the war, and (at least as far as it is ever mentioned), Asaba's role in it. As we discuss in Chapter 3, the historical narrative has generally held that there was no genocidal intent on the part of the Federal Government, a point on which we agree. An additional element in that narrative is that the killings in Asaba were "the exception and not the rule."[80] While we argue that the Asaba event was unique in its scale, there were certainly other massacres, such as those at Isheagu and Onitsha Cathedral. Yet another element found in the narrative is that the Asaba massacres may even have been provoked by the victims: "a reprisal for an attack on federal troops after a ceasefire,"[81] a point for which we have found no evidence. As we have seen, this narrative descended from the earlier successful efforts to play down the massacre, resulting in a serious lack of accurate information about what had happened. Thus an important

[79] See Arua Oko Omaka, "The Forgotten Victims: Ethnic Minorities in the Nigeria-Biafra War, 1967–1970," *Journal of Retracing Africa,* 1:1, 2014, 25–40. Omaka discusses other "forgotten" victims of the war, many of whom were ethnic minorities within Biafra.

[80] James O'Connell, "The Ending of the Nigerian Civil War: Victory, Defeat, and the Changing of Coalitions," in Roy Licklider, ed., *Stopping the Killing: How Civil Wars End,* New York: New York University Press, 1993, 194. See also Edward R. Kantowicz, *Coming Apart, Coming Together: The World in the 20th Century, Vol. 2,* New York: Eerdmans, 1999.

[81] O'Connell, "The Ending of the Nigerian Civil War," 203.

goal has been simply to "set the record straight" and establish the reality of this significant atrocity.

This leads to another element in the prevailing view about genocide and the war. This thread argues that the Biafran claims of genocide, although initially fueled by the 1966 pogroms, continued to gain traction within Biafra almost entirely because of an extremely effective propaganda machine that convinced the people that defeat would mean certain death. According to Michael Gould, "propaganda was used to promote the idea of genocide, firstly to instill it in the Biafran people, in order to strengthen their resolve,"[82] a point also made by Roy Doron, Douglas Anthony, and Brian McConnell.[83]

Indeed, Biafran "genocide" propaganda was extremely effective internally in the early stages of the war, as it later became externally when starvation took over the narrative. However, we would argue that the fear instilled in the populace was not merely the product of careful manipulation. It was also because the people of Biafra, unlike the public in the wider world, learned first hand about the brutality that had befallen their kin across the Niger – most drastically in Asaba, but also in Benin City, Isheagu, and elsewhere, mostly at the hands of the Second Division. Those who fled and carried the word to Biafra were not concerned about where the orders came from. Their stories of families decimated and towns destroyed would have provided the "proof" that made the propaganda so potent. Meanwhile, we must not forget that the Federal Military Government also maintained an effective propaganda narrative, strongly supported by the British.[84] Its narrative, portraying a magnanimous liberating force, even in the face of repeated atrocities against civilians in the areas

---

[82]   Michael Gould, *The Biafran War: The Struggle for Modern Nigeria*, New York: I.B. Tauris, 2012, 198.

[83]   Douglas Anthony, "Resourceful and Progressive Black Men: Modernity And Race in Biafra, 1967–70," *Journal of African History*, 51, 2010, 41–61; Roy Doron, "Marketing Genocide: Biafran Propaganda Strategies during the Nigerian Civil War, 1967–70," *Journal of Genocide Research*, 2014, 16:2–3, 227–246.

[84]   See Morris Davis, *Interpreters for Nigeria: The Third World and International Public Relations*, Urbana: University of Illinois Press, 1977.

retaken from Biafra, ultimately defined the story of the first part of the war.

Thus, we argue that the disappearance of Asaba in the public record had long-lasting effects on the way the story of the Civil War came to be understood historically. It does not prove a federal intent to exterminate the Igbos, but it does explain more fully why the Biafran people continued to fervently believe in that intent, long before enforced starvation entered the picture. The story of Asaba helps us understand some of the ways in which the conflict spiraled out of control, from a "police action" to an outright and brutal war. It invites a litany of "what if" questions. What if the Biafrans had not invaded the Midwest, before abandoning Asaba to its fate? What if the advancing Second Division had followed Gowon's Code of Conduct and treated civilians with respect, thus undercutting the Biafrans' fear of extermination, and encouraging them to seek a peaceful resolution before so many died? What if foreign journalists had discovered and published graphic accounts of what had happened at Asaba, telling the horrific story of the suffering of families like the Uraihs, the Isicheis, and so many more? What if the British government had then put aside its own interests in maintaining a unified, oil-rich Nigeria, and had intervened to broker peace? Instead, Asaba was devastated, its fate unknown to the outside world, while Biafra desperately fought on to the inevitable conclusion.

Second, the telling of the story offers acknowledgment, even catharsis, to those who suffered and rarely if ever spoke out. Their stories deserve to be told and their pain remembered. Whether one defines what happened in Asaba as part of a "genocide" or not, there can be no doubt it was a war crime, for which no one has ever acknowledged responsibility or been held accountable, and for which Asaba has never been compensated. At the same time, the people of Asaba are not merely victims; their story also shows how, even after losing everything, many displayed remarkable perseverance and resilience, as they painfully rebuilt their lives.

And this leads us to our final point: that Asaba's story adds to our understanding of the impact of trauma, and the persistence of memory, sometimes for years afterwards. Communities that have suffered atrocities may be in the spotlight for a short time, before attention shifts to the next victim. Asaba reminds us of the long life of the "post-conflict" period, and speaks to larger issues of trauma, recovery, and potential reconciliation that extend beyond Nigeria. As Ferrándiz wrote, describing the exhumation of the victims of General Franco's troops during the Spanish Civil War, the recovery of historical memories speaks of the "resilience of traumatic memory through years of silence and fear."[85] In Nigeria, as in Spain, Argentina, Guatemala, Rwanda, and elsewhere, such stories offer "better understanding of the long-lasting consequences of violence and repression" and the destructive legacy of silence.[86]

The Asaba massacres were sparked by the same ethnic hostility that simmers today, and as our discussion here suggests, ethnic identity in Nigeria is considerably more complex than outdated notions of "tribe" can capture. Yet the massacres were not inevitable – they resulted from the decisions of individuals, and they provide us with opportunities for moral reflection, both about the trauma of the past, and the possible consequences for the future.[87] In Nigeria today, there is a desperate need for reconciliation and cooperation among ethnic groups.[88] Strikingly, the people we have interviewed have repeatedly spoken to the pressing need to use their experience for good – to promote reconciliation, not exacerbate hostility. As one told us: "For Nigeria to be great, people have to be educated ... to understand that

---

[85]   Francisco Ferrándiz, "The Return of Civil War Ghosts: The Ethnography of Exhumations in Contemporary Spain," *Anthropology Today*, 22:3, 2006, 12.

[86]   Ibid., 12

[87]   See Karen Murphy and Tony Gallagher, "Reconstruction after Violence: How Teachers and Schools Can Deal with the Legacy of the Past," *Perspectives in Education*, 27:2, 2009, 158–168; also Jeffrey C. Alexander, "Toward a Theory of Cultural Trauma," in Jeffrey C. Alexander, Ron Eyeran, Bernhard Giesen, Neil J. Smelser, and Piotr Sztompka, eds., *Cultural Trauma and Collective Identity*, Berkeley, CA: University of California Press, 2004, 1–30.

[88]   Aka, "The Need for an Effective Policy."

you cannot resolve differences by conflict."[89] Massacre survivor Dr. Ify Uraih expressed the importance of both remembering and forgiveness. He described how by chance he once found himself in the same London doctor's waiting room as Gen. Yakubu Gowon:

> That was the first time in my life I met him. He saw me and he knew I was Nigerian, and he asked me who I was. "There is no way you can know me, but I know you." He said, "Oh, where are you from?" I told him Asaba ... And we sat there talking about the Civil War. I told him that I lost my father and two of my brothers there, and I was also a victim ... And then, he apologized to me personally ... He said to me that the act was perpetrated by Murtala Muhammed.

Dr. Uraih concluded,

> I say this with no bitterness in my heart. My wish has always been that the world should know what happened. The promise I made to myself was that ... The memory should not die. That was my promise.

Memorialization as a form of transitional justice is complex and processual, possibly taking many forms. Fifty years ago, Father Patrick Isichei received the letter describing the horrors that had befallen his home town. He despaired at the brutality that had devastated his family, and the indifference of the world to their fate. In 2011, he addressed the second Asaba Remembrance Day, listing the names of his relatives killed in October 1967, and noting how many other families had suffered similar losses. Then he articulated the theme of reconciliation that community leaders have wanted to foreground. First acknowledging the anger of Asaba, he concluded that "there can be no better way of remembering and honoring our dead on this day than to free our hearts of all bitterness and hostility."[90] A fitting memorial, he noted, was that people worked to restore

---

[89]   Interview with Francis Nwajei, June 28, 2010, Asaba.

[90]   For full text of Father Isichei's address, see www.asabamemorial.org/data/isichei-speech.pdf.

educational opportunities for their own youth, and toward better and more just governance for their country. His sister Celestina, who left Asaba behind for a new life in Britain, sadly titled her personal Asaba memoir *They Died in Vain*. We argue that the deaths in Asaba did have meaning, and that there is value in reinscribing uncomfortable histories into a nation's sanctioned memory, acknowledging the lingering legacy of injustice and contributing to meaningful reconciliation.

Sources Consulted

INTERVIEW SOURCES

The first formal interviews with witnesses and survivors were conducted in October 2009, at the Asaba Memorial Symposium at the University of South Florida, which inaugurated the project. Between 2009 and 2016, the authors made eight visits to Nigeria, as well as one visit to London, where additional interviews with survivors and former military officers were conducted. In addition, the authors conducted four focus group interviews, each with five participants. All interviews were conducted in person, with one exception, and all were recorded. During these visits the authors also had many informal conversations and interactions with people in Asaba, Lagos, and elsewhere.

AUTHORS' INTERVIEWS WITH WITNESSES AND SURVIVORS

Achuzia, Simon Uchenna (born 1960), March 14, 2014, Asaba.
Akaraiwe, Patricia (born 1939), June 28, 2010, Asaba.
Asiodu, Philip C. (born 1934), Dec. 8, 2009, Tampa.
Awolo, Esananjo (birthdate not given), June 27, 2010, Asaba.
Azeh, Nicholas (born 1950), Oct. 5, 2011, Asaba.
Chizea, Osobodoa David (born 1937), June 27, 2010, Asaba.
Chizea, Mabel (born 1952), June 27, 2010, Asaba.
Chukwumah, Msr. Emmanuel (born 1925), June 28, 2010, Asaba.
Chukwara, Emmanuel (born 1934), Dec. 16, 2009, Asaba.
Chukura, Patience (born 1939), Dec. 10, 2009, Lagos.
Egbuinwe, Michael (born 1955), May 3, 2012, Asaba.
Eneamokwu, Ken (born 1956), 28 June 2010, Asaba.
Enenmoh, Luke (born 1928), Oct. 10, 2014, London.
Esenwa, John (born 1953), Oct. 10, 2009, Tampa.
Igbeka, Catherine Nkendelim (born 1959), Oct. 10, 2014, London.
Ijeh, Frank (born 1930), Dec. 13, 2009, Asaba.
Isichei, Father Patrick (born 1937), Oct. 6, 2015, Asaba.
Isichei-Isamah, Celestina (born 1946), Oct. 10, 2014, London.

Izegbu, Victor (born 1953), April 15, 2016, Lagos.

Maduemezia, Emmanuel (born 1954), June 23, 2010, Asaba.

Maduemezia, Nkendelim (born 1955), June 23, 2010, Asaba.

Mkpayah, Christopher (born 1947), Dec. 10, 2009, Lagos.

Mordi, Assumpta (born 1963), Oct. 7, 2011, Asaba.

Monyei, Grace (born 1930), June 28, 2010, Asaba.

Nduka Eze, Chuck (born 1963), Oct. 9, 2011, Asaba.

Nwajei, Joseph (born 1951), Oct. 10, 2009, Tampa.

Nawajei, Francis (born 1937), June 28, 2010, Asaba.

Nwandu, Felicia (born 1947), June 28, 2010, Asaba.

Nwanze, Emmanuel (born 1949), Dec. 16, 2009, Benin City.

Nwanze, Esther (born 1941), Oct. 5, 2011, Asaba.

Nwanze, Victoria (born 1954), Dec. 16, 2009, Benin City; May 3, 2012,
    Asaba.

Obaze, Nwaka (born 1920), Dec. 12, 2009, Asaba.

Obielue, Patrick (born 1954), Dec. 12, 2009, Asaba.

Obi, Emmanuel (born 1953), Oct. 10, 2009, Tampa.

Obi, Feli (born 1943), Dec. 15, 2009, Asaba.

Odiachi, Emmanuel (birthdate not given), Oct. 10, 2014, London.

Odiaka, Mike (born 1935), June 27, 2010, Asaba.

Odiwe, Catherine (birthdate not given), Oct. 7, 2011, Asaba.

Ogbogu, Michael (born 1944), May 3, 2012, Asaba.

Ogosi, Felix (born 1955), Dec. 13, 2009, Asaba

Ogosi, Frank Obi (born 1942), Dec. 15, 2009, Asaba.

Ogunkeye, Gertrude (born 1952), Dec. 11, 2009, Lagos.

Ojogwu, Peter-Claver (born 1945), Dec. 14, 2009, Asaba.

Okafor, Kingsley (born 1942), Oct. 5, 2011, Asaba.

Okafor, Stanley (born 1946), Oct. 12, 2011, Ibadan.

Okocha, Pastor Chris Adigwe Daniels (birthdate not given), Oct. 10, 2015,
    Asaba.

Okocha, Emma (born 1962), Oct. 13, 2009, Tampa.

Okocha, Akunwata S.O. (Sylvester) (born 1913), Dec. 13, 2009, Asaba.

Okolie, Onyeogali (born 1960), Dec. 13, 2009, Asaba.

Okonkwo, Emeka (born 1963), June 28, 2010, Asaba.

Okonkwo, Patrick (born 1953), June 27, 2010, Asaba.

Okonjo, Peter (born 1949), Dec. 14, 2009, Asaba.

Okonta, Emeka Okalum (born 1973), June 24, 2010, Asaba.

Okwudi, Emma (born 1939), May 3, 2012, Asaba.

Onyia, Henry (born 1939), Dec. 15, 2009, Asaba.

Onochie, Felix (born 1929), June 28, 2010, Asaba.
Onukwu, Emmanuel (born 1941), Dec. 15, 2009, Asaba.
Onyemenam, Benedict (born 1936), June 28, 2010, Asaba.
Onyemenan, Josephine (born 1954), June 23, 2010, Asaba,
Onyia, Henry (born 1939), Dec. 15, 2009, Asaba.
Osaji, Martina (born 1953), Oct. 5, 2011, Asaba.
Osakwe, Igwemma (born 1944), Dec. 12, 2009, Asaba.
Oweazim, Fabian (born 1954), Oct. 10, 2009, Tampa.
Ugboko, Charles (born 1946), Dec. 12, 2009, Lagos.
Uraih, Lucy Chineze (born 1950), May 3, 2012, Asaba.
Uraih, Ify (born 1952), Oct. 9, 2009, Tampa.
Uraih, Medua Gabriel (born 1948), Dec. 13, 2009, Asaba; May 3, 2012, Asaba.
Uraih, Victor Ubaka (born 1954), May 3, 2012, Asaba.

ADDITIONAL INTERVIEWS BY AUTHORS

Achuzia, Gen. Joseph (rtd.), Biafran army, Oct. 8, 2015, Asaba.
Gowon, Gen. Yakubu, Oct. 10, 2016, Abuja.
Haruna, Gen. Ibrahim B.B. (rtd.), Nigerian army, April 11, 2016, Abuja.
Iweze, Gen. Cyril (rtd.), Nigerian army, April 13, 2016, Lagos.
Norris, Bill, retired journalist, Dec. 14, 2011 (by phone).
Nwachukwu, Gen. Ike Omar Sanda (rtd.), Oct. 11, 2016, Lagos.
Ogbebor, Col. Paul Osa (rtd.), Oct. 12, 2016, Benin City.
Onyekweli, Gen. Philip (rtd.), Nigerian and Biafran armies, April 16, 2016, Lagos.
Williams, Gen. Ishola (rtd), Nigerian army, April 14, 2016, Lagos

ARCHIVES

Several important archival collections were consulted by one or both authors:
African Collections at Michigan State University Library, East Lansing, USA.
American Friends Service Committee Archive, Philadelphia, USA.
Bodleian Library, University of Oxford, UK.
Royal Niger Company Archive at Unliver, Port Sunlight, UK.
School of Oriental and African Studies Library (SOAS), London, UK.
United Kingdom National Archive, Kew, UK.

BOOKS AND ARTICLES

Achebe, Chinua, *Home and Exile*, New York: Random House, 2000.

Aka, Philip C., "The Need for Effective Policy on Ethnic Reconciliation," in E. Ike Udogu, ed., *Nigeria in the Twenty-First Century*, Trenton, NJ: Africa World Press, 2005, 41–67.

Alexander, Jeffrey C., "Toward a Theory of Cultural Trauma," in Jeffrey C. Alexander, Ron Eyeran, Bernhard Giesen, Neil J. Smelser, and Piotr Sztompka, eds., *Cultural Trauma and Collective Identity*, Berkeley, CA: University of California Press, 2004, 1–30.

Alexander, Philip, "A Tale of Two Smiths: The Transformation of Commonwealth Policy, 1964–70," *Contemporary British History*, 20:3, 2006, 303–321.

Akinyemi, A.B., "The British Press and the Nigerian Civil War," *African Affairs*, 71:285, 1972, 408–426.

Amoba, Mohibi, "Background to the Conflict," in Joseph Okpaku, ed., *Nigeria, Dilemma of Nationhood. An African Analysis of the Biafran Conflict*, Westport, CT: Greenwood, 1972, 14–75.

Anthony, Douglas, *Poison and Medicine: Ethnicity, Power and Violence in a Nigerian City, 1966–1986*, Oxford: James Currey, 2003.

Anthony, Douglas, "'Resourceful and Progressive Blackmen,': Modernity And Race in Biafra, 1967–70," *Journal of African History*, 51, 2010, 41–61.

Asiegbu, Johnson U.J., *Nigeria and Its British Invaders, 1851–1920: A Thematic Documentary History*, New York/Lagos: Nok Publishers, 1984.

Assmann, Jan, "Collective Memory and Cultural Identity," *New German Critique*, 65, 1995, 125–133.

Azikiwe, Ifeoha, *Asagba Prof. Joseph Chike Edozien: His Thoughts, Words, Vision*, Bloomington, IN: Authorhouse, 2015.

Baker, Pauline, "Lurching toward Unity," *The Wilson Quarterly*, 4, 1980, 70–80.

Bartrop, Paul, "The Relationship between War and Genocide in the Twentieth Century: A Consideration," *Journal of Genocide Research*, 4, 2002, 519–532.

Bird, S. Elizabeth, "Seeking the Audience for News: Response, News Talk, and Everyday Practices," in Virginia Nightingale, ed., *Handbook of Audience Studies*, New York: Blackwell, 2011, 489–508.

Blank, Gary, "Britain, Biafra and the Balance of Payments: The Formation of London's 'One Nigeria' Policy," *Revue Francais de Civilisation Britannique*, 2013, 18:2, 66–86.

Campbell, David, "Cultural Governance and Pictorial Resistance: Reflections on the Imaging of War," *Review of International Studies*, 29, 2003, 57–73.

Cookman, Claude, "Gilles Caron's Coverage of the Crisis in Biafra," *Visual Communication Quarterly*, 15, 2008, 226–242.

Church Missionary Society, "Letter from Diocese of Benin," *CMS Historical Record*, 1968, 1.

Clark, Janine N., "Reconciliation through Remembrance? War Memorials and the Victims of Vukovar," *The International Journal of Transitional Justice*, 7, 2013, 116–135.

Cole, Elizabeth A., and Judy Barsalou, "Unite or Divide: The Challenges of Teaching History in Societies Emerging from Violent Conflict," *United States Institute of Peace, Special Report* 163, June 2006.

Collier, Paul, Anke Hoeffler, and Dominic Rohner, *Beyond Greed and Grievance: Feasibilityand Civil War*, Centre for the Study of African Economies, Working Paper Series 2006–2010.

Collis, Robert, *Nigeria in Conflict*, London: Secker and Warburg, 1970.

Cronje, Suzanne, *The World and Nigeria: The Diplomatic History of the Biafran War 1967–1970*, London: Sidgwick and Jackson, 1972.

Curtis, Mark, *Unpeople: Britain's Secret Human Rights Abuses*, London: Vintage, 2004.

Das, Veena, *Life and Words: Violence and the Descent into the Ordinary*, Berkeley: University of California Press, 2007.

Davies, Patrick Ediomi, "Use of Propaganda in Civil War: The Biafra Experience," doctoral thesis, Department of International Relations, London School of Economics and Political Science, June 1995.

Davis, Morris, *Interpreters for Nigeria: The Third World and International Public Relations*, Urbana: University of Illinois Press, 1977.

de Jong, Ferdinand, and Michael Rowlands, *Reclaiming Heritage: Alternative Imaginaries of Memory in West Africa*. Walnut Creek, CA: Left Coast Press, 2007.

de St. Jorre, John, *The Brothers' War: Biafra and Nigeria*, Boston: Houghton Mifflin, 1972.

Doron, Roy, "Forging a Nation while Losing a Country: Igbo Nationalism, Ethnicity and Propaganda in the Nigerian Civil War 1968–1970," Doctoral dissertation, University of Texas at Austin, August 2011.

Doron, Roy, "Marketing Genocide: Biafran Propaganda Strategies during the Nigerian Civil War, 1967–70," *Journal of Genocide Research*, 2014, 16:2–3, 227–246.

Drinot, Paulo, "Website of Memory: The War of the Pacific (1879–84) in the Global Age of YouTube," *Memory Studies*, 4:4, 2011, 371.

Ejiogu, E.C., "On Biafra: Subverting Imposed Code of Silence," *Journal of Asian and African Studies*, 48, 2013, 741–751.

Ekwelie, Sylvanus A., "The Nigeria Press under Military Rule," *International Communication Gazette*, 25, 1979, 219–232.

Erikson, Kai T., *Everything in Its Path: Destruction of Community in the Buffalo Creek Flood*, New York: Simon and Schuster, 1976.

Falola, Toyin, ed., *Igbo History and Society: The Essays of Adiele Afigbo*, Trenton, NJ: Africa World Press, 2005.

Falola, Toyin, and Matthew M. Heaton, *A History of Nigeria*, Cambridge: Cambridge University Press, 2008.

Ferrándiz, Francisco, "The Return of Civil War Ghosts: The Ethnography of Exhumations in Contemporary Spain," *Anthropology Today*, 22:3, 2006, 7–12.

Forsyth, Frederick, *The Making of an African Legend: The Biafra Story*, London: Penguin, 1969.

Forsyth, Frederick, *The Outsider: My Life in Intrigue*, London: Putnam, 2015.

Giles, Wenona, and Jennifer Hyndman, eds., *Sites of Violence: Gender and Conflict Zones*, Berkeley: University of California Press, 2004.

Gould, Michael, *The Biafran War: The Struggle for Modern Nigeria*, New York: I.B. Tauris, 2012.

Govier, Trudy, *Taking Wrongs Seriously: Acknowledgment, Reconciliation and the Politics of Sustainable Peace*, Amherst, NY: Humanity Books, 2006.

Harneit-Sievers, Axel, Jones O. Ahazuem, and Sydney Emezue, *A Social History of the Nigerian Civil War: Perspectives from Below*, Hamburg: Lit Verlag, Hamburg, 1997.

Harrison, Paul, and Robin Palmer, *News out of Africa: Biafra to Band Aid*, London: Hilary Shipman, 1986.

Hatch, John, *Nigeria: A History*, London: Secker and Warburg, 1970.

Henry, Nicola, *War and Rape: Law, Memory and Justice*, London: Routledge, 2011.

Heerten, Lasse, and A. Dirk Moses, "The Nigeria–Biafra War: Postcolonial Conflict and the Question of Genocide," *Journal of Genocide Research*, 16:2–3, 169–203.

Hetherington, Penelope, *British Paternalism and Africa, 1920–1940*, London: F. Cass, 1978.

Hinton, Alexander Laban, *Transitional Justice: Global Mechanisms and Local Realities after Genocide and Mass Violence*, New Brunswick: Rutgers University Press, 2011.

Hirsch, Herbert, *Genocide and the Politics of Memory*, Chapel Hill: University of North Carolina Press, 1995.

Hodgkin, Katharine, and Susannah Radstone, "Introduction: Rethinking Memory," *History Workshop Journal*, 59, 2005, 129–133.

Hoffman, Eva, "The Long Afterlife of Loss," in Susannah Radstone and Bill Schwarz, eds., *Memory: Histories, Theories, Debates*, New York: Fordham University Press, 2010, 406–415.

Hopwood, Julian, "We Can't Be Sure Who Killed Us: Memory and Memorialization in Post-Conflict Northern Uganda," International Center for Transitional Justice: Justice and Reconciliation Project, 2011.

Hynes, Michelle, and Barbara Lopes-Cardozo, "Observations from the CDC: Sexual Violence against Refugee Women," *Journal of Women's Health and Gender-based Medicine*, 9:8, 2000, 819–823.

Ikuomola, Adediran Daniel, "The Nigerian Civil War of 1967 and the Stigmatisation of Children Born of Rape Victims in Edo State," in Raphaelle Branch and Fabrice Virgili, eds., *Writing the History of Rape in Wartime*, London: Palgrave McMillan, 2012, 169–183.

Inal, Tuba, *Looting and Rape in Wartime: Law and Change in International Relations*, Philadelphia: University of Pennsylvania Press, 2013.

Irwin-Zarecka, Iwona, *Frames of Remembrance: The Dynamics of Collective Memory*, New York: Transaction Publishers.

Isichei, Elizabeth, "Historical Change in an Ibo Polity: Asaba to 1885," *Journal of African History*, 10, 1969, 421–438.

Isichei, Patrick A.C., "Ex-Seminarian Ignatius Bamah in Asaba (c. 1900–67)," in Elizabeth Isichei, ed., *Varieties of Christian Experience in Nigeria*, London: MacMillan, 1982, 177–188.

Iweze, Daniel Olisa, "Post-CivilWar Intergroup Relations: The Western Igbo and Non-Igbo Groups in the Midwest State," in Chima Koreih and Ifeanyi Ezeonu, eds., *Remembering Biafra: Narrative, History, and Memory of the Nigeria-Biafra War*, Glassboro, NJ: Goldline and Jacobs, 2010, 170–184.

Kantowicz, Edward R., *Coming Apart, Coming Together: The World in the 20th Century, Vol. 2*, New York: Eerdmans, 1999.

Kansteiner, Wulf, "Finding Meaning in Memory: A Methodological Critique of Collective Memory Studies," *History and Theory*, 41, 2002, 179–197.

Keil, Charles, "The Price of Nigerian Victory," *Africa Today*, 17:1, 1970, 1–3.

Kimmerle, Erin H., "Forensic Anthropology: A Human Rights Approach," in Natalie R. Langley and MariaTeresa A. Tersigni-Tarrant, eds., *Forensic Anthropology: An Introduction*, Boca Raton, FL: CRC Press, 2012, 424–438.

Kirk-Greene, Anthony H.M., *Crisis and Conflict in Nigeria: A Documentary Sourcebook, 1966–1970 (2 Vols.)*, London: Oxford University Press.

Korieh, Chima J., ed., *The Nigeria-Biafra War: Genocide and the Politics of Memory*, Amherst, NY: Cambria Press, 2012.

Lugard, Frederick J.D., *The Dual Mandate in British Tropical Africa*, London: William Blackwood, 1922.

Mibenge, Chiseche Salome, *Sex and International Tribunals: The Erasure of Gender from the War Narrative*, Philadelphia: University of Pennsylvania Press, 2013.

Minow, Martha M., *Between Vengeance and Forgiveness: Facing History after Genocide and Mass Violence*, Boston: Beacon Press, 1998.

Mishra, Jyotsna, *Women and Human Rights*, New Delhi: Kalpaz, 2000.

Momoh, H.B., *The Nigerian Civil War, 1967–1970: History and Reminiscences*, Ibadan: Sam Bookman Publishers, 2000.

Murphy, Karen and Tony Gallagher, "Reconstruction after Violence: How Teachers and Schools Can Deal with the Legacy of the Past," *Perspectives in Education*, 27:2, 2009, 158–168.

Ndili, Augustine N., *Guide to the Customs, Traditions and Beliefs of Asaba People*, Asaba: His Bride Publications, 2010.

Niven, Rex, *The War of Nigerian Unity*, Towata, NJ: Rowman and Littlefield, 1970.

Nora, Pierre, "Between Memory and History: Les Lieux de Mémoire," *Representations*, 26, 1989, 7–24.

Norris, Bill, "Media Ethics at the Sharp End," in David Berry, ed. *Ethics and Media Culture: Practices and Representations*, Oxford: Focal Press, 2000, 325–338.

Nwogu, Nneoma V., *Shaping Truth, Reshaping Justice: Sectarian Politics and the Nigerian Truth Commission*, New York: Lexington, 2007.

Obiezu, Emeka X., "Memorialization and the Politics of Memory," in Chima J. Korieh, ed., *The Nigeria-Biafra War: Genocide and the Politics of Memory*, Amherst, NY: Cambria Press, 2012, 187–208.

O'Connell, James, "The Ending of the Nigerian Civil War: Victory, Defeat, and the Changing of Coalitions," in Roy Licklider, ed., *Stopping the Killing: How Civil Wars End*, New York: New York University Press, 1993, 189–203.

Odoemene, Akachi, "Remember to Forget: The Nigeria-Biafra War, History, and the Politics of Memory," in Chima J. Korieh, ed., *The Nigeria-Biafra War: Genocide and the Politics of Memory*, Amherst NY: Cambria Press, 2012, 163–186.

Ohadike, Don. C., *Anioma: A Social History of the Western Igbo People*, Athens: Ohio University Press, 1994.

Okafor, Stanley I., "The Nigerian Army and the 'Liberation' of Asaba: A Personal Narrative," in E. Eghosa, E. Osaghae, R. Onwudiwe, and R. Suberu, eds.,

The Nigerian Civil War and Its Aftermath, Ibadan, Nigeria: John Archers, 2002, 293–299.

Okocha, Akunwata S.O., *The Making of Asaba: A Compendium of over Sixty-Five Years of Patient Research within and without Africa*, Rupee-Com Publishers, Asaba, 2013.

Okocha, Emma, *Blood on the Niger*, New York: Triatlantic Books (2nd Ed.), 1994.

Okonkwo and Okolie, *Isheagu and the Nigerian Civil War, 1966–1970*, printed in Lagos, no date.

Okonta, Ike, "Biafra of the Mind: MASSOB and the Mobilization of History," *Journal of Genocide Research*, 16:2–3, 2014, 355–378.

Okpaku, Joseph, *Nigeria: Dilemma of Nationhood*, Westport, CT: Greenwood, 1972.

Okpoko, A. Ikechukwu and Pat Uche Okpoko, *Tourism in Nigeria*, Nsukka: Afro-Orbis Publications, 2002.

Omaka, Arua Oko, "The Forgotten Victims: Ethnic Minorities in the Nigeria-Biafra War, 1967–1970," *Journal of Retracing Africa*, 1:1, 2014, 25–40.

Omoigui, Nowamagbe A., "Benin and the Midwest Referendum of 1963," online at: http://www.waado.org/nigerdelta/ethnichistories/egharevbalectures/Fifth-Omo igui.htm

Omoigui, Nowamagbe A., "The Midwest Invasion of 1967: Lessons for Today's Geopolitics," online at: http://www.dawodu.net/midwest.htm

Orobator, Stanley E., "The Biafran Crisis and the Midwest," *African Affairs*, 86:344, 1987, 367–383.

Osia, Kunirum, "Anioma People Of The Delta," http://www.anioma.org/

O'Sullivan, Kevin, "Humanitarian Encounters: Biafra, NGOs and Imaginings of the Third World in Britain and Ireland, 1967–70," *Journal of Genocide Research*, 16:2–3, 2014, 299–315.

Owen, Olly, "The New Biafrans: Historical Imagination and Structural Conflict in Nigeria's Separatist Revival," paper presented March 8, 2016, in Changing Character of War series, Pembroke College, University of Oxford, accessible at: http://www.ccw.ox.ac.uk/news/2016/4/11/the-new-biafrans-discussing-discontent.

Oyinbo, John, *Nigeria: Crisis and Beyond*, London: Charles Knight, 1971.

Paxton, Robert O., *Vichy France: Old Guard and New Order, 1940–1944*, New York: Knopf, 1972.

Pentzold, Christian, "Fixing the Floating Gap: The Online Encyclopaedia Wikipedia as a Global Memory Place," *Memory Studies*, 2:2, 2009, 255–272.

Perham, Margery, "Reflections on the Nigerian Civil War," *International Affairs*, 46, 1970, 231–46.

Peters, Jimi, *The Nigerian Military and the State*, New York: Tauris Academic Studies, 1997.

Phillips, Kendall R., and G. Mitchell Reyes, eds., *Global Memoryscapes: Contesting Remembrance in a Transnational Age*. Tuscaloosa, University of Alabama Press, 2011.

Portelli, Alessandro Portelli, "What Makes Oral History Different?" in Robert Perks and Alistair Thomson, eds., *The Oral History Reader*, London: Routledge, 2016 (1979), 48–58.

Radstone, Susannah, "Reconceiving Binaries: The Limits of Memory," *History Workshop Journal*, 59, 2005, 135–150.

Ross, Fiona C., "On Having Voice and Being Heard: Some After-Effects of Testifying before the South African Truth and Reconciliation Commission," *Anthropological Theory*, 3:3, 2003, 325–341.

Schudson, Michael, "Lives, Laws, and Language: Commemorative versus Non-Commemorative Forms of Effective Public Memory," *The Communication Review*, 2:1, 1997, 3–17.

Simola, Raisa, "Time and Identity: The Legacy of Biafra to the Igbo in Diaspora," *Nordic Journal of African Studies*, 9:1, 2000, 98–117.

Smith, Daniel J., "Burials and Belonging in Nigeria: Rural-Urban Relations and Social Inequality in a Contemporary African Ritual," *American Anthropologist*, 106, 2004, 569–579.

Daniel J. Smith, "Legacies of Biafra: Marriage, 'Home People' and Reproduction among the Igbo of Nigeria," *Africa: Journal of the International African Institute*, 75:1, 2005, 30–45.

Smith, Karen E., "The UK and 'Genocide' in Biafra," *Journal of Genocide Research*, 6:2–3, 2014, 247–262.

Stremlau, John J., *The International Politics of the Nigerian Civil War, 1967–1970*, Princeton: Princeton University Press, 1977.

Till, Karen E., "Memory studies," *History Workshop Journal*, 62, 2006, 325–341.

Thomson, Alistair, "Four Paradigm Transformations in Oral History," *Oral History Review*, 34:1, 2007, 49–70.

Trouillot, Michel-Rolph, *Silencing the Past: Power and the Production of History*, New York: Beacon Press, 1995, 26.

Uche, Chibuike, "Oil, British Interests and the Nigerian Civil War," *Journal of African History*, 49, 2008, 111–135.

Uchendu, Egodi, *Women and Conflict in the Nigerian Civil War*. Trenton, NJ: Africa World Press, 2007.

Uchendu, Egodi, "The Growth of Anioma Cities," in Toyin Falola and Steven J. Salm, eds., *Nigerian Cities*, Trenton NJ: Africa World Press, 2004, 153–182.

Uchendu, Victor Chikezie, "Ezi na ulo: The Extended Family in Igbo Civilization," *Dialectical Anthropology*, 31:1–3, 2007, 167–219.

Ukiwo, Ukoha, "Violence, Identity Mobilization and the Reimagining of Biafra," *Africa Development*, 34:1, 2009, 9–30.

Vaux, H., "Intelligence Report on the Asaba Clan, Asaba Division," File No. 30927, Class Mark CSO 2614, Nigerian National Archive, Ibadan.

Young, John W., *The Labour Governments 1964–1970, Vol. 2, International Policy*, Manchester: Manchester University Press, 2004.

Yusuf, Hakeem O., "Travails of Truth: Achieving Justice for Victims of Impunity in Nigeria," *The International Journal of Transitional Justice*, 1, 2007.

Zandberg, Eyal, "The Right to Tell the (Right) Story: Journalism, Authority and Memory," *Media Culture Society*, 32:1, 2010, 5–24.

Zelizer, Barbie, *Covering the Body: The Kennedy Assassination, the Media, and the Shaping of Collective Memory*, Chicago: University of Chicago Press, 1992.

Zelizer, Barbie, "Why Memory's Work on Journalism does not Reflect Journalism's Work on Memory," *Memory Studies*, 1:1, 2008, 79–87.

PUBLISHED CIVIL WAR MEMOIRS

Achebe, Chinua, *There Was a Country: A Personal History of Biafra*. New York: Penguin, 2012.

Achuzia, Joe O.G., *Requiem Biafra*, Asaba: Alcel Concerns, 2002 (2nd ed.).

Akpan, Ntieyong U. *The Struggle for Secession 1966–1970: A Personal Account of the Nigerian Civil War*, London: Cass, 1972.

Alabi-Isama, Godwin, *The Tragedy of Victory: On the Spot Account of the Nigeria-Biafra War in the Atlantic Theatre*, Ibadan: Spectrum Books, 2013.

Alli, M. Chris, *The Federal Republic of Nigerian Army: The Siege of a Nation*, Lagos, Nigeria: Malthouse Press, 2000

Idahosa, Patrick E., *Truth and Tragedy: A Fighting Man's Memoir of the Nigerian Civil War*, Ibadan: Heinemann Educational Books (Nigeria), 1989.

Isichei-Isamah, Celestina, *They Died in Vain*, London: CreateSpace Independent Publishing Platform, 2011.

Obasanjo, Olusegun, *My Command: An Account of the Nigerian Civil War, 1967–1970*, London: Heinemann, 1980.

Oyewole, Fola, *Reluctant Rebel*, London: Rex Collings, 1975.

Soyinka, Wole, *The Man Died: Prison Notes*. London: Rex Collings, 1972.

Uwechue, Raph, *Reflections on the Nigerian Civil War*, New York: Africana Publishing Corporation, 1971.

Uzokwe, Alfred Obiora, *Surviving in Biafra: The Story of the Nigerian Civil War*, New York: Writers Advantage, 2003.

NEWSPAPER AND PERIODICAL SOURCES

Abasiekong, Dan, "How to Bring the Ibos Back into Our Fold," *Daily Sketch* (Nigeria), Oct. 7, 1967, 5.

Azuh, Kingsley, "Nduka Eze: A Life Dedicated to Selfless Public Service," *ThisDay*, Oct. 2, 2016: http://www.thisdaylive.com/index.php/2016/10/02/nduka-eze-a -life-dedicated-to-selfless-public-service/.

Bamgbose, Sina, "Ojukwu Captured?" *Daily Sketch*, Oct. 13, 1967, 1 and back page.

Barnes, John, "Nigeria: A Time for Slaughter," *Newsweek*, July 31, 1967, 38–39.

Commonwealth Staff, "Inquiry Urged into Nigerian 'Atrocities,'" *The Guardian*, Nov. 8, 1967, 5.

Daily Sketch (Nigeria), "The March on Asaba Bridge," Oct. 9, 1967, 1.

Daily Sketch, Oct. 6, Untitled, 1.

Daily Sketch, "Ojukwu's World of Fantasy," Oct. 11, 1967, 1.

Daily Sketch, "Rebel Army Mutiny," Oct. 12, 1967, 1.

Daily Sketch (Nigeria), "Asaba and Ika People Accept New Identity," July 24, 1967, 3.

Daily Sketch, "The Ibos Miscalculated in Seceding – Says American Newspaper," Oct. 6, 1967, 3.

Daily Sketch, "Ibos Were Victims of Ojukwu Propaganda, Says UK Paper," Oct. 7, 1967, 2.

Daily Sketch, "Ibo Blindness Killed Peace Moves: Italian Paper," Oct.13, 1967, 7.

Daily Sketch, "Now No More Ika Ibo – By Order," Oct. 27, 1967, 8.

Friendly, Alfred Jr. "City Shows Scars of the Nigerian War," *New York Times*, Sept. 26, 1967, 1; 3.

Friendly, Alfred Jr. "Battle Continues for Nigerian City," *New York Times*, 1967, Oct. 13: 1.

Garrison, Lloyd, "300 Ibo Tribesmen Killed by Troops and Nigerian Mob," *New York Times*, Oct. 2, 1966, 1;17.

Garrison, Lloyd, "Nigeria Totters on the Brink," *New York Times*, Oct. 9, 1966, E3.

Garrison, Lloyd, "Biafran War Refugees Describe How Nigerians Killed Villagers," *Toronto Globe and Mail* (*New York Times* News Service), July 21, 1967, 8.

Garrison, Lloyd, "Biafrans Accept Risk of Defeat," *The Times* (from *New York Times*), Aug. 3, 1968, 3.

"Griot," "Roundabout, the View from the Bridge, Asaba," *West Africa*, Oct. 21, 1967, no. 2629, 1355.

Guardian (London), "Compromise – or Ruin for Both in Nigeria," Nov. 10, 1967, 10.

Legum, Colin, "How 700 Ibos Were Killed by Mistake," *The Observer*, Jan. 21, 1968, 21.

Mounter, Julian, "No Evidence of Genocide in Nigeria," *The Times*, July 21, 1969, 5.

Newsweek, "Nigeria: Setting Sun," Oct. 9, 1967, 41–42.

Norris, William, "War across the Niger," *The Times*, Oct. 24, 1967, 14.

Norris, William, "Biafrans' Ordeal by Air Attack," *The Times*, April 25, 1968, 8.

Nwobu, Lawrence Chinedu Nwobu, "Remembering Murtala Muhammed: The Butcher of Asaba," Feb. 19, 2009, online at http://www.nigeriavillagesquare .com/forum/articles-comments/29729-remembering-murtala-muhammed-butc her-asaba-2.html.

Nwosu, Philip, "I'm Pro-Biafra – Soyinka," *The Sun* (Nigeria), July 15, 2016, http://sunnewsonline.com/im-pro-biafra-soyinka/.

Obioha, McLord, "Why FGN Used Hunger against Ibos: Interview with Anthony Enahoro," *The Nigerian and Africa*, March 1998, 9–10; 13.

O'Brien, Conor Cruise, "A Condemned People," *The New York Review of Books*, Dec. 21, 1967, 14–21.

Ogwuda, Austin, "Gowon Faults Setting Up of Oputa Panel," *Vanguard News*, Dec. 09, 2002, available online at: https://groups.yahoo.com/neo/groups/Naija-news/conversations/topics/2517.

Ojeifo, Sufuyan, and Lemmy Ughegbe, "No Regrets for the Asaba Massacre of Igbo – Haruna," *The Vanguard*, Oct. 10, 2001, http://www.nigeriamasterweb.com/ nmwpg1HarunaIgboMassacre.html

Osifo, Iredia, "Five Rebel Spies Held in Asaba," *Daily Times* (Nigeria), Nov. 17, 1967, 1.

Schwarz, Walter, "Why Nigeria's War Splits Hawks and Doves in Whitehall," *The Observer*, Aug, 27, 1967, 4.

Shepherd, Jack, "Memo from Nigeria: Old Headaches for our New President," *Look*, 26, Nov. 1968, 74.

The Times, "Execution of Nigerian Officer Filmed," Sept. 4, 1968, 1.

Time, "Drums of Defeat," 90:14, Oct. 6, 1967, 70.

Uzodinma, Emmanuel, "You Have Made Nnamdi Kanu a Hero, Igbo Youth Movement Tells Buhari," *Daily Post*, July 12, 2016, http://dailypost.ng/2016/07 /12/you-have-made-nnamdi-kanu-a-hero-igbo-youth-movement-tells-buhari/.

Vanguard, "Confusion, as MASSOB Disowns Radio Biafra Boss, Nnamdi Kanu," *The Vanguard*, Oct.19, 2015, http://www.vanguardngr.com/2015/ 10/confusion-as-massob-disowns-radio-biafra-boss-nnamdi-kanu/.

Wolfers, Michael, "Nigerian Troops Close in on Ibo Heartland," *The Times*, Aug. 30, 1968, 3.

Wolfers, Michael, "Nigeria Observers Find no Evidence of Genocide," *The Times*, Oct. 4, 1968, 8.

Zeitlin, Arnold (Associated Press), "8,000 Ibo Tribesmen to Lack Food," *Gettysburg Times*, Dec. 10, 1968, 12.

Index

Abacha, Sani, 183
Abagana, ambush at, 115, 116, 140
Abasiekong, Dan, 84
Abudu, reported violence by Biafrans, 16
Aburi summit meeting, 10
Achebe, Chinua, 169, 180
Achuzia, Joseph, 26, 32, 58
Achuzia, Simon Uchenna, 109
Action Group (AG), 7
Ade, Sunny, 172
Adebayo, Robert Adeyinka, 93
Adib, Ifeanyi, 188
Adichie, Chimamanda Ngozi, 181
Agbor, 13, 28, 101, 144
Agbor, reported violence by Biafrans, 16
Aguiyi-Ironsi, Johnson, 8, 9
Ahaba identity, 25, 188, 196, 197, 198, 200
Aisida, Francis, 17, 58
Akaraiwe, Joseph, 129
Akaraiwe, Patricia, 129, 140
Akintola, Samuel, 7, 8
Akpan, N.U., 67, 110
Akundele, Benjamin, 114, 115
akwa ocha attire, 41, 162
Alabi-Isama, Godwin, 13
Alli, Chris, 81, 82, 146
American Friends Service Council
    (Quakers), 138
Amnesty International, 185
Anglican Girls Grammar School (AGGS),
    Asaba, 23
Aniocha district, 186
Anioma, 18, 20, 26, 155, 186, 188, 189,
    191, 211
    identity movement, 186
Anthony, Douglas, 213
Argentina, 215
Asaba
    and arrival of Biafran troops, 27
    and British knowledge of massacre, 112
    and life under occupation, 116–118
    and reported violence by Biafran
        troops, 13, 16

and tradition of education, 24
complex ethnic identity of, 25–27,
    188–189
destruction of Niger Bridge at, 32–35
effects of massacre on kinship structure,
    122–124, 193–194
federal troops killing civilians, 37–41
federal troops occupy, 35–37
history as de facto capital of Nigeria, 23
indigeneity. See Ahaba identity
kindness of some Federal soldiers, 55–56
massacre of Oct. 7, 42–51
monument to massacre victims, 203
plans to welcome federal troops, 41–42
refugee camp at, 116, 117, 132, 133,
    141, 143
relief operations in, 86, 94, 133, 138, 139,
    140, 141, 147
Second Operation, 129, 130, 135, 137,
    138, 141, 163
significance of massacre, 212–217
social structure in, 22
St. Joseph's Catholic Church, 44, 133,
    149
support for united Nigeria, 30
Asaba Development Union, 204
Asagba of Asaba, xiv, 21, 30, 41, 133, 146, 159,
    193, 206, 207, 221
Asagba-in-Council, Asaba, 41
Asika, Anthony Ukpabi, 94, 95, 105
    on Asaba massacre, 94
Asiodu, Philip, xiii, 26, 92, 95
    as spokesperson for Federal
        Government, 86
    on government response to Asaba
        massacre, 93–94
    role in Federal Government, 73
Asiodu, Sydney, 86, 93
Assmann, Jan, 150–151
Auchi, 129
Awolowo, Obafemi, 7
Azeh, Nicholas, 55, 197
Azikiwe, Nnamdi (Zik), 4, 8

Babangida, Ibrahim, 198
Babangida, Ibrahim Badamasi, 146, 183
Babangida, Maryam. *See* Okogwu, Maryam
Backhouse, Jane, 24, 118
Balewa, Abubakar Tafawa, 8
Banjo, Victor, 12, 15
Barmah, Brother Ignatius, 49
Barsalou, Judy, 160
Bell, Gawain, 102
Bello, Sir Ahmadu (Sardauna of Sokoto), 8
Benin City, 6
    actions against Igbo in, 18, 29
    Biafran troops reach, 14
    federal troops retake, 17, 28
Benin, "Republic of," 15, 17
Biafra
    bight of, 180
    declaration of "police action" against, 11
    in final stages of war, 145
    invasion of Midwest, 12–14
    Memory and Political Resurgence,
        180–185
    movement toward secession, 10
    occupation of Midwest, 16
    predictions of defeat, 60
    propaganda efforts, 145
    response to Asaba massacre,
        107–110, 112
    retreat across Niger Bridge, 19
    secession of, 11
    starvation in, 62, 142
Black Scorpion. *See* Akundele, Benjamin
Blank, Gary, 67
Blood on the Niger. See Okocha, Emmanuel
    (Emma)
Boji-Boji, reported violence by Biafrans, 16
Boko Haram, 184
Bonny
    bight of. *See* Biafra, Bight of
    island of, 12, 114
Brierly, T.G., 102
British arms sales to FMG, 69, 72,
        106, 116
    attempts to conceal, 106
    attempts to defend, 143
British Broadcasting Corporation,
        BBC, 88, 89
British Government, 65, 66, 68, 69, 92
    and indirect rule, 3, 4, 5
    and Murtala Muhammed, 100–101

and oil. *See* oil as factor in Civil War
arms sales to FMG. *See* British arms sales
    to FMG
control of press, 87–90
revokes charter of Royal Niger
    Company, 3
Buhari, Mohammadu, 185
Burness, H.M., 101, 102, 103

Cable Point, Asaba, 81, 90, 92, 117
Calabar, 114
    killings of civilians in, 103, 115
Caritas, 138
Caron, Gilles, 142
Catholic Relief Services, 138
Christian Council of Nigeria, 103
Chukura, Christian, 30, 40, 123
Chukura, Edwin (Eddie), 30, 40, 123, 150
Chukura, Patience, 26, 55, 150
Chukwara, Dennis, 40, 123
Chukwara, Emmanuel, 30, 31, 40, 123
Chukwara, Mgbeke, 31
Chukwara, Samson, 40, 123
Chukwumah, Eunice, 32
Church Missionary Society, 23, 101
Clark, Janine, 202
CMS. *See* Church Missionary Society
Code of Conduct, federal army, 30, 64, 82,
        95, 214
Cole, Elizabeth A., 160
Commonwealth Office, UK, 67, 72
Conlon, Father Hugh, 133, 140
Corriere della Sera, Italy, 86
Cronje, Suzanne, 143

Daily Sketch, Nigeria, 82, 85
Daily Times, Nigeria, 84, 85, 86
Davies, Patrick (Paddy), 145
De St. Jorre, John, 19, 88, 104
Delta State, 179, 186, 189, 190
Division 101, Biafran Army, 12
Doron, Roy, 213
Drinot, Paulo, 168

Eastern Region, 5, 8, 10, 11, 12, 105
Edewor, Juliana, xiii
Edozien, Prof. Joseph Chike, Asagba of Asaba,
        xiv, 159
Egbuiwe, Anthony, 133
Ejoor, David, 12, 16

Enahoro, Anthony, 116
Enenmoh, Luke, 42, 56, 118, 121, 136
Enugu, 11, 12, 26, 67, 115
    capture by federal troops, 60, 71, 72, 109
Erikson, Kai, 193

Federal Military Government (FMG), 62, 64,
        66, 67, 68, 69, 71, 72, 83, 84, 88, 90,
        92, 95, 99, 107, 108, 142, 143, 155
    and British support, 96, 111
    and control of press, 84–86
    and knowledge of Asaba massacre, 93, 95
    and propaganda efforts, 144
Federal soldiers as "upstanders," 55–57
Ferrándiz, Francisco, 215
First Infantry Division, Federal Army, 11, 60,
        71, 114, 115
Forsyth, Frederick, 88
    on media control, 89
    pro-Biafa stance, 89
Friendly, Alfred Jr., 19, 64, 91

Genocidal intent evidence for and against,
        112–113
Genocide, 80
    Asaba reinforces Biafran claims of, 105
    Biafran claims and propaganda, 213
    Biafran claims of, 109, 115, 213
    Biafran fears of, 107
    problems defining, 203
Gould, Michael, 111, 213
Gowon, Yakubu, 9, 10, 26, 56, 67, 70, 71, 72,
        84, 94, 96, 98, 103, 104, 108, 116, 141,
        144, 216
    "No victor, no vanquished," 152,
        180, 181
    apology to Asaba, 95, 155, 201, 209
    becomes head of FMG, 9
    concerns about civilian casualties, 64, 98
    concerns on military discipline, 75
    conflict with Murtala Muhammed, 15,
        32, 64, 69, 70, 96, 100, 171
    creates 12 new states, 10
    denounces "propaganda," 96
    international support for, 86
    knowledge of Asaba massacre, 95, 155
    Operational Code of Conduct, 30, 64, 82,
        85, 88, 214
    pressure to remove Murtala Muhammed,
        107, 116

rationale for maintaining Nigerian
        unity, 64
    removed in 1976 coup, 171
    seeking international support, 64
Guardian, UK, 86, 101
Guatemala, 215
Gwam family, Asaba, 107
gwodogwo, 54, 200

Half of a Yellow Sun. See Adichie,
        Chimamanda Ngozi
Hansen, Christian, 133
Harneit-Sievers, Axel, 114, 180
Haruna, Ibrahim B., 141
    and Oputa Panel, 80
    and training of Federal Second Division,
        14, 19
    denies Asaba massacre, 80
Henry, Nicola, 201
Hinton, Alexander Laban, 201
Hirsch, Herbert, 203
Hodgkin, Katharine, 150
Hoeffler, Anke, 208
Hoffman, Eva, 158
HRVIC, Human Rights Violations
        Investigations Commission. See
        Oputa Panel
Hunt, David, 70, 72, 89
    concern over civilian casualties, 68
    on importance of oil, 65–66
    urging support of FMG, 67

Ibadan, 27, 48
Ibusa, 107, 135, 136, 146, 186
Ibusa, reported violence by Biafrans, 16
Idah, 70, 115
Idahosa, Patrick, 58, 78
    role in Asaba massacre, 55, 79
    role in Isheagu massacre, 137
Igbeka, Catherine, 130, 133
Igbeka, Martin, 130
Igbeka, Patricia, 130
Igbodo, 107
Ijeh, Frank, 49, 56
Ika district, 186
Ikuomola, Adediran Daniel, 196
Ilorin, 171
Inal, Tuba, 118
Indigenous People of Biafra (IPOB),
        184, 189

International media coverage
    inadequacies of, 87, 156
    of famine in Biafra, 142
    racism in, 104
International Observer team, 143
Irwin-Zarecka, Iwona, 158
Isamah, Peter, xvi, 60
Isichei, Celestina, xiii, xvi, 1, 21, 27, 28, 43,
        44, 60, 74, 147, 177
    letter written after massacre, xvi, 93, 97
Isichei, Elizabeth, 124, 193
Isichei, Emmanuel (Emma), xvi, 43, 51, 75, 97
Isichei, Father Patrick, xiii, xvi, 43, 97,
        105, 216
Isichei, Francis Okafor, 41, 75
Isichei, Leo, 177
Isichei, Osi, xvi, 43, 44, 46, 51, 73, 75, 97
Iweze, Cyril, 143
Iweze, Daniel Olisa, 190
Izegbu, B.R.O., 74, 75
Izegbu, Beatrice, 74
Izegbu, Victor, xiii, 74, 75

Joint Consultative Assembly of Biafra, 109
Jonathan, Goodluck, 185

Kaduna, 25, 73, 130
Kano, 25, 125, 129
    actions against Igbo in, 9
Kanu, Nnamdi, 184
Keazor, Emeka (Ed), xiv, 94
Kimmons, Carol, 23, 24
Kirikiri Prison, Lagos, 14, 93
Kissinger, Henry, 172
Konwea, Frederick, 42

Leapman, Michael, 67
Legum, Colin, 90, 105
Lugard, Frederick, 3

Macaulay, Herbert, 4
Markpress, 142
Matthews, Richard J.H., 99
Matthias, Capt., 56, 57, 60, 146, 170, 209
    attempts to save woman from
        abduction, 121
    identified as Matthias Ogbude, 56
    in Ibusa, 136
    influence on other soldiers, 57
    preventing violence in Asaba, 56

saving civilians from harm, 77
McConnell, Brian, 213
McCullin, Don, 142
McDermid, Angus, 88
Memory, 215, 216, 217
    "communicative" and "cultural"
        memory, 150–151
    absence of war in Nigerian collective
        memory, 180
    and academic collaboration, 166
    burden of, 185
    by families of Asaba victims, 157–60
    collective, 158, 176
    collective memory of Asaba massacre,
        xvi, 73, 161–163, 179
    constructed nature of, 163
    constructive use of, 158
    contested nature of, 167
    dangers of, xvii, 152
    formation on social media, 156–158
    new formations of, 181
    of Biafra, 180
    of Nigerian Civil War, 62, 176
    of trauma, 215
    process of, xvii, 156, 171
Memory work, 156, 158, 165, 166,
        176, 209
    academic engagement in, 165, 167, 168
    and new media, 178
    defined, 158
    public exhibit as, 207
Memoryscape, 164, 165
    and social media, 166, 176, 178
    definition of, 164
Mibenge, Chiseche Salome, 195
Midwest Region, 12, 16, 19, 24, 25, 29, 41, 71,
        74, 75, 76, 77, 86, 94, 96, 101, 108,
        114, 129, 140, 142, 186
    "liberation" of, 95
    and influence by Britain, 65
    and trade ties to Biafra, 12
    around Asaba, 16
    Benin City as capital of, 14
    Biafran occupation of, 28
    Dennis Osadebay as premier, 24
    ethnic conflicts emerging, 15
    events ignored by foreign press, 63
    government of, 74
    invasion by Biafra, 12, 63, 67, 70, 84, 92,
        98, 109

Midwest Region (cont.)
    multi-ethnic nature of, 12, 25
    neutrality of, 12
    recapture by Federal forces, 114
    targeting of civil servants, 38
    violence against Igbo in, 19, 64, 92, 144
Midwest State, 190, 191
Military coup July 1966, 9
Military coup, January 1966, 7, 8, 64, 73
Minow, Martha, 148
Mkpayah, Christopher, 31, 44
Mordi, Assumpta, 122
Mordi, Benedict, 122
Mordi, Daniel, 122
Mordi, Emmanuel, xiv, 119
Mordi, Gabriel, 122
Mordi, Okechukwu, 51
Mordi, Rose Eziunor. *See* Nduka-Eze, Rose
Movement for the Actualization of the
    Sovereign State of Biafra
    (MASSOB, 184
Movement for the Emancipation of the Niger
    Delta (MEND), 184
Movement for the Survival of the Ogoni
    People (MOSOP), 183
Muhammed, Murtala, 9, 16, 20, 64, 100, 114,
    116, 157, 171
    advice from soothsayers, 35, 58
    and "Nigerianism," 172
    and massacre of civilians in Onitsha, 112
    as "war lord," 100
    as folk hero, 171
    assassinated, 171
    concerns about leadership, 59, 97,
        100–101, 115
    conflicts with Gowon, 70
    criticisms by fellow-officers, 70
    crosses Niger River at Idah, 115
    defeat at Abagana, 115
    defies orders at Niger Bridge, 35
    described as "Butcher of Asaba," 157
    discussed on social media, 174–176
    executes soldier for looting, 144
    faces discipline problems in Second
        Division, 69
    failed attempts to cross Niger River,
        57–60
    goal to take Onitsha, 32, 33
    lack of progress toward Onitsha, 61
    named as perpetrator by Gowon, 216

    pressure to remove him, 107
    radio address in Benin City, 18, 28
    removed from command of Second
        Division, 116
    responsibility for Asaba massacre, 75,
        82, 171
    retakes Benin City, 17
    takes command of Second Division, 15
    topples Gowon in 1976 coup, 171
Mungo Park House Museum, xiii, 210

National Council of Nigerians and
    Cameroons (NCNC), 7
Ndayawo, Maj., 35
Ndokwa district, 186
Nduka Eze, nationalist politician, 51
Nduka-Eze, Chuck, xiii, 51, 150
    role at Oputa Panel, 159, 209
Nduka-Eze, Rose, 150
Newsweek, 87
Newsweek, US, 60
Nicholson, Michael, 144
Niger Bridge, 32, 33, 72, 85
    Biafrans cross back to Onitsha, 19
    Biafrans cross over into Midwest, 12
    destruction of, 35
Nigeria Nostalgia Project, xiv, 170, 174
Nigerian Village Square (website), 157
Njoteah, Ezeoba, 32
Nnebisi Road, Asaba, 37, 44, 46, 77, 204
Nnebisi, founder of Asaba, 21, 196, 199, 200
Norris, Bill, 90
    in Asaba, 90
    on press control, 88, 89
    photos taken in Asaba, 206
Northern People's Congress (NPC), 4, 7
Northern Region, 5, 8
Nsukka
    capture by federal forces, 114
    federal troops advance on, 87
Nwachukwu, Ike Omar Sanda
    on Asaba massacre, 80
    opinion of Murtala Muhammed, 32
    reaches Asaba, 32
Nwajei, George, 38
Nwajei, Joseph, 27, 28, 38, 48, 52
Nwandu, Felicia, 124
Nwanze, E.A.C., xiii, 29
Nwanze, Esther, 49
Nwanze, Victoria, xiii, 121

Nwobu, Lawrence Chinedu, 157
Nwogu, Nneoma, 155
Nwosa, Renny, xiii
Nzeogwu, Patrick Chukwuma, 7, 73

O'Brien, Conor Cruise, 62, 104
Obasanjo, Olusegun, 154
    and Asaba massacre, 78
    establishes Oputa Panel, 154
Obaze, Nwaka, 77
Obelue, Patrick, 49, 133
Obi, Emmanuel, 32
Obi, Felix, 50
Observer, UK, 88, 95, 103, 105
Odiachi, Emmanuel, 28
Odoemene, Akachi, 181
Odogwu, Louis, 204
Ogbebor, Paul Osa, 15, 35, 36, 46, 54, 59, 77,
    81, 82
    and training of Federal Second
        Division, 14
Ogbeke market, Asaba, 46
Ogbemudia, Samuel, 18
Ogbe-Osowa Village, Asaba, 46, 51, 56, 75, 79,
    122, 155, 161, 163, 206
    bodies remain after massacre, 51
    monument to massacre victims, 203
    site of massacre commemoration, 204
Ogbogonogo market, Asaba, 46
Ogbogu, Michael, 57
ogbunigwe, Biafran missile, 115
Ogosi, Felix, 135
Ogosi, Frank Obi, 36
Ogundipe, B.O., 99, 100
    denies Asaba allegations, 99
Ogunkeye, Gertrude, 26, 30, 35, 53
Ogwashi-Ukwu, 60, 107, 135, 147
Ohadike, Don C., 186
Ohanaeze Ndi Igbo, 186
Ohanaeze Petition, 154
Oil
    and Niger Delta, 183
    as key factor in Civil War, 11, 65–68, 72,
        101, 214
Ojukwu, Chukwuemeka Odumegwu, 9, 10,
    11, 26, 66, 74, 84, 85, 86, 88, 89, 98,
    105, 107, 109, 112, 141, 144, 157, 189
    and justifications for secession, 11
    as Governor of Eastern Region, 8
    declares independence of Biafra, 11

Okafor, Benedict, 53
Okafor, Joseph Anene, xiv
Okafor, Nwadu, 108
Okafor, Stanley, 37, 53, 78, 155
Okafor-John, Dorothy, 146
Okene, 70
Okocha, Akunwata S.O. (Sylvester), 38, 52,
    93, 153
Okocha, Benedict, 38
Okocha, Emmanuel (Emma), xiii, 125, 153,
    154, 159, 161
Okogwu, Leo, 39, 48, 146
Okogwu, Maryam (Babangida), 146
Okonkwo, Emeka, 50
Okonkwo, Patrick, 39, 133
Okonta, Emeka Okelum, 192, 199
Okonta, Ike, 183
Okowa, Ifeanyi, 189
Okpanam, 73
Okpanam road, Asaba, 39, 54
Okpoko, A. Ikechukwu, 210
Okpoko, Pat Uche, 210
Okwuarue, Chief, 41
Okwudiafor, Francis Dike, 54
Omeje, Chika, xiv
Omezi, Onianwa, 77
Omo, Richie, xiv
Omu of Asaba, Mgboshie Okolie, 41, 146
Onitsha, 12, 17, 21, 30, 32, 71, 85, 91, 97, 100,
    109, 115, 117, 129, 141, 173, 206
    attempts by federal forces to take,
        57–60, 61
    Biafrans cross back into, 19
    capture by federal forces, 115
    explosives detonated on Niger Bridge, 32
    killing of protesters at, 185
    massacre of civilians in, 105, 111, 112,
        138, 212
Onochie, Emmanuel, 131
Onochie, Felix, 131
Onyekeli, Philip, 16, 108
Onyeneman, Josephine, 119
Onyetenu, Umejei, Asagba of Asaba, 30
Oputa Panel, 80, 154, 155, 156, 159, 160, 172,
    183, 201, 209
Oral history as method, 162–164, 165, 177
Ore, 14, 71
Organisation for the Advancement of
    Africans, UK, 101
Organization of African Unity, 143

Osadebay, Dennis, 24, 74, 186, 188
Osaji, Martina, xiii, 125
Osakwe, Igwemma, 117
Oshimili district, 186
Osia, John Kunirum, 135, 136, 140, 186, 188
Osula, Andrew, 101
Oweazim, Fabian, 39, 42
Owen, Olly, 185
Oyewole, Fola, 16

Paris Match, France, 142
Parker, James, British High Commission,
    Enugu, 67
Parker, John, ITN journalist, 88
Paxton, Robert O., 160
Peace Corps, 23, 140
Pentzold, Christian, 166, 176
Peoples Movement for the Liberation of
    Angola, 172
Perham, Margery, 99, 101, 102, 103, 107
    receives Isichei letter on Asaba, 97
    travels to Nigeria, 144
    writes letter to Times on Asaba
        massacre, 98
Pogroms against Igbo 1966, 9, 11, 13, 16, 21,
    31, 62, 98, 104, 109, 110, 126, 145, 213
Port Harcourt, 66
Portelli, Alessandro, 161, 163, 164

Radio Biafra, 105, 184
Radstone, Susannah, 150
Rape
    and forcible "marriage," 119
    as crime of war, 118
    by Biafran soldiers, 16
    by federal soldiers, 60, 75, 99, 109, 119
    children of, 196, 198
    long-term effect of, 120
    social attitudes toward, 120, 121, 196
    strategies to avoid, 121
Reconciliation, xvii, 86, 175, 209, 215, 217
    academic contributions to, 203, 205
    and Oputa Panel, 154
    and reconstruction, 85
    as consequence of apology, 155
    challenges in contemporary Nigeria, 215
    Gowon's pledge for, 84
    in annual Asaba commemorations, 216
    in post-conflict situations, 180, 215
    memorials as obstacles to, 202

Reconciliation, Reconstruction, and
    Reintegration, 182
Red Cross, 49, 86, 93, 117
Rohner, Dominic, 208
Ross, Fiona C., 165
Royal Niger Company, 2, 23, 210, 220
Rusk, Dean, 87
Rwanda, 215

Sapele
    Biafran advance to, 13
    killings of Igbo, 19, 102
    looting by Biafran troops, 16
Saro-Wiwa, Ken, 183
Scanlon, David, 133
Second Infantry Division, Federal Army, 14,
    35, 60, 71, 78, 81, 82, 96, 140, 171, 214
    discipline problems in, 69, 70, 80, 111
    Eighth Brigade, 35, 59, 78, 81
    formation of, 14–15
    Haruna replaces Mohammed as
        commander 1968, 80
    killings of civilians by, 213
    recruitment in Midwest, 19
    retakes Benin City, 17
    Sixth Brigade, 58, 80, 96, 133
Sharwood Smith, Bryan, 98
Shuwa, Mohammed, 11, 60, 71, 72
    takes Enugu, 114
Siollun, Max, xiv
Smith, Arnold, 111
South African Truth and Reconciliation
    Committee, 165
Soyinka, Wole, 20, 155, 181, 206
    imprisoned, 84
Spain, 215
Spanish Civil War, 215
St. Patrick's College, Asaba, 23, 28, 32, 35, 36,
    42, 43, 108
    as refugee camp, 117, 132

Taiwo, Ibrahim, 76, 77, 78
    death of, 171
    role in Asaba massacre, 77
Tebbitt, Donald, 112
There was a Country. See Achebe, Chinua
Third Marine Commando Division, Federal
    Army, 12
ThisDay, Nigeria, 166
Thomas, George, 66, 67

Till, Karen E., 165
Time Magazine, US, 60
Transitional Justice, 201
    and Oputa Panel, 154
    and reconciliation, 202
    efforts in Asaba, 160
    mechanisms of, 179, 201
    memorials as, 202, 216
Trauma, 180, 188, 194, 215
    and community, 179, 190, 193, 200
    and community of Asaba, 148, 193–194
    and individuals, 191
    and rape, 195
    in post-conflict situation, 215
Trouillot, Michel-Rolph, 152

U Thant, 110
UN Committee on Human Rights, 109
Uchendu, Egodi, 18, 20, 51, 78, 128, 137, 146,
    155, 198
Uchendu, Victor, 123
Ugboko, Charles, 54, 55, 79, 122
Ugbomanta quarter, Asaba, 21, 46
Ugoh, Michael, 39, 48
Ukiwo, Ukowa, 182
Umenede, 46
Umuagu quarter, Asaba, 21
Umuaji quarter, Asaba, 21
Umuezei quarter, Asaba, 21
Umuonaje quarter, Asaba, 21
UNICEF, 139
United Nations, 109, 143, 154
University of Ibadan, 29
Uraih, Emmanuel (Emma), 47
Uraih, Ify, xiv, 47, 48, 76, 125, 126, 148, 155, 216

Uraih, Medua, 36, 37, 47, 48, 126, 127
Uraih, Paul, 47
Uraih, Robert, 56, 125
Uraih, Veronica, 126, 127, 128
Uraih, Victoria. *See* Nwanze, Victoria
Usman, Baba, 79
Usman, Lt., 76, 77
Uwazurike, Ralph, 184
Uzokwe, Alfred Obiora, 107

Vaux, H. colonial administrator,
    Asaba, 23

Warri, 131, 195
    Biafran advance to, 13
    killings of Igbo, 19, 102
    looting by Biafran troops, 16
West Africa Magazine, UK, 92
Western Region, 5, 6, 7, 8, 93
Whiteman, Kaye, 92
Wicinski, Roman, 141
Wikipedia, 166
Williams, Ishola, 79
    on training of Federal Second Division,
        79, 83
    opinion of Murtala Muhammed, 82
Wilson, Harold, 65, 67
Wolfers, Michael, 82
www.asabamemorial.org, 166, 175
www.asabamemorial.wordpress.com,
    166
www.nairaland.com, 167

Zandberg, Eyal, 156
Zelizer, Barbie, 156